The Overweight Patient

The Overweight Patient

A Psychological Approach to Understanding and Working with Obesity

Kathy Leach

Jessica Kingsley Publishers
London and Philadelphia

First published in 2006
by Jessica Kingsley Publishers
116 Pentonville Road
London N1 9JB, UK
and
400 Market Street, Suite 400
Philadelphia, PA 19106, USA

www.jkp.com

Copyright © Kathy Leach 2006
Printed digitally since 2009

Library of Congress Cataloging in Publication Data

Leach, Kathy, 1949-
The overweight patient : a psychological approach to understanding and working with obesity
/ Kathy Leach.
p. cm.
Includes bibliographical references and index.
ISBN-13: 978-1-84310-366-0 (pbk. : alk. paper)
ISBN-10: 1-84310-366-4 (pbk. : alk. paper)   1. Obesity--Psychological aspects. 2.
Obesity--Treatment. I. Title.
RC628.L357 2006
616.3'98--dc22

2006004145

British Library Cataloguing in Publication Data
A CIP catalogue record for this book is available from the British Library

ISBN 978 1 84310 366 0

Contents

List of figures

Acknowledgements

My thanks go to Charlotte Sills, Training and Supervising Transactional Analyst, who liberally and unselfishly read and engaged with my work. To Jackie Cox the founder of TOAST (The Obesity Awareness and Solutions Trust), who generously offered to read and comment. To Heather and Helen and to my husband who, as a layperson, read every word and every rewrite, offered constructive criticism and praise and spent many bachelor hours whilst I wrote. And to all my patients from whom I have learnt so much.

Introduction

In the light of recent growing emphasis on what has become known as the 'great weight debate', I believe that it must be understood that if it were easy to lose weight then sufferers (for that is what these patients are) of obesity would lose weight rather than face the ridicule, non-acceptance and feelings of shame resulting from their size. This book offers a way of understanding the psychological aspects of the problem that prevents people from losing weight or maintaining weight loss.

As a psychotherapist, I use an approach called Transactional Analysis (TA) in my clinical work both as a diagnostic tool and as a method of working towards change in the patient. The beauty of TA is that the concepts can be understood and used on many levels, from simple application to highly complex analysis. This means that the patient can learn and use TA concepts from the earliest stages of her treatment, or later on in the process when she is ready to do so. This in turn means that she is taking responsibility for her part in her psychotherapeutic journey towards health.

In relation to this book, it means that the non-Transactional Analysts and non-psychologically trained practitioner readers involved in this field of work can understand and use the concepts at whatever level has meaning for them. I have chosen a selection of concepts to write about and I hope that I have represented them simply and appropriately for the non-Transactional Analyst, and with enough advanced thinking and complexity to interest my trained TA readers.

TA is a theory of personality that offers a paradigm to help us to understand how people communicate, interact and form repeated habitual patterns of relationship and behaviours. It offers various theoretical constructs of child development and psychopathology and a system of psychotherapy that is appropriate for the treatment of a wide range of problems, from 'here and now' problems and neuroses through to psychoses.

The basic philosophy of TA is that people are essentially OK, that everyone has the capacity to think unless severely psychotic and, perhaps most importantly, that people decide their own destinies and, like all decisions, they can be changed, substituted and updated with new information. The mode of thinking in TA encompasses self-responsibility and self-determination, which are important for obese patients as is their need to see themselves as essentially 'OK' and able to think.

Classical TA has a basis of both cognitive and behavioural therapeutic methodologies. Eric Berne, the father of TA, indicated that the initial focus of psychotherapy should be behavioural change through understanding and enlightenment in the present, using the patient's ability to think and to make new decisions on how to be in the world. He believed that if this does not provide adequate resolution it is necessary to work into the deeper levels of the psyche. His way of explaining the process was that it involves pulling the splinter out first and only finding out why it is there if it is necessary to do so. When obese people ask for psychological help, they have already been through the initial 'splinter' stage a number of times, having dieted repeatedly and either not lost weight or not maintained weight loss. The purpose of using a psychological approach is to find out why they need to maintain weight or consistently overeat. The therapeutic task is not, therefore, to focus primarily on weight loss, as weight gain or maintenance of a high weight are the symptoms of the underlying psychological process, but to find the cause of the weight problem.

Transactional Analysis offers a decisional model that is very powerful. The obese patient comes to understand that she has, at some stage in her life, made a decision to be fat. TA proposes that decisions can be changed and updated, that is, we can re-decide in the light of new information and awareness. This is one of the most useful basics of the TA approach. It acknowledges the responsibility of the patient. It upholds that the practitioner can do nothing without the cooperation and understanding of the patient and that, in the final analysis, the patient will be the one to take the initiative and make the changes.

From my work with obese patients I have found that there are two major clinical concerns, both of which are addressed in this book. They are:

1. That there are two aspects of maintaining a large body size: the need to eat excess food and the need to be fat. These are two separate, albeit related, issues. What this means is that, if the patient psychologically needs her large body size then attention focused only on her eating and feeding non-biological needs with food will be ineffective. The therapist needs to enable the patient to discover the meaning of, and reasons for, her protective body armouring. These patients will undoubtedly also be using food to feed psychological needs, but attention to both aspects is necessary for the patient to change.

2. That there are differences in the defensive structure of the patient who has been overweight for a shorter length of time or is in the lower half of the obese to morbidly obese index compared with the long-term or lifelong sufferer or morbidly obese patient. The therapeutic direction and the availability of the patient to work with cognition (thinking) and affect (feelings) will differ depending on the length of time the patient has been overweight.

Transactional Analysis advocates drawing up a 'contract' with the patient for the work she wants and needs to do. Again this is vitally important to the obese patient, as so often treatments revolve around the patient being told what to do rather than empowering the patient to learn and make decisions for herself. I outline the clinical implications of contracting in Chapter 3.

Layout and language

This book is broadly divided into two halves. Chapters 1 to 3 outline the background or the 'big picture', which provides a context for understanding and working with the clinical issues of obesity. This part of the book is useful as a means of understanding the obese client's experience in the world in order to enable a degree of issue-related empathic discourse from the first meeting. It addresses cultural persuasions that will affect the patient, gives an overview of patients' belief systems that ensure that they stay fat or misuse food and explores why some people can lose weight while others cannot. I also outline some of my own experiences in the field before I began working psychotherapeutically with this patient group, which made me realize that the non-psychological treatments commonly employed do not effectively tackle the problem.

Chapters 4 to 12 centre on clinical work and findings and offer ways of thinking about and working with obese patients and illustrate methods of working with patient histories and transcripts. I have studied obese patients over a period of over 20 years. Much of what I write about is based on my own findings and will not therefore be referenced to any other clinician except where my thinking has been influenced by another's work. I provide references and a recommended reading list.

Since I am writing for a multi-disciplinary readership I have chosen to use the word 'patient' rather than 'client' and for easy flow, I refer to the patient as 'she'. The major work I have done has been with female sufferers, and though there are some differences in the belief systems of male overweight patients, the basic diagnosis and working through will follow the same methodology whatever the gender of the patient. Finally, I use the words 'obese' and 'overweight' as interchangeable, even though the BMI (Body Mass Index) gives a different weight range for each and I make distinctions between the lower and higher brackets of obesity and morbid obesity where it is necessary to do so when considering diagnosis and treatment options.

A glossary of clinical and Transactional Analysis terms is included at the end of the book, which can be referred to should readers meet any unfamiliar terms while reading through, though I have tried, where possible, to offer explanations where technical terms first appear.

Where I have made unqualified statements about obese patients I ask the reader to understand that these may not apply to all patients and that they are meant to convey my observations of repeated patterns in a large sector of this patient group. The clinical material I have chosen reflects the most commonly reported experiences and beliefs of the patients with whom I have worked. The patients specifically featured have generously given their consent to the inclusion of their stories.

Chapter 1

Obesity and Therapy

Anorexia and bulimia are commonly seen medically, socially and psychologically as eating disorders that are representative of disorders of the self, arising from developmental deficit between early childhood and adolescence. 'Deficit' implies something missing in the response of the parent or carer to the needs of the infant or developing child. Overeating and obesity are not so commonly seen in this way, even though early deficit and sexual abuse are regularly a feature of a long-term overweight and overeating condition. In my own clinical experience I have found that maintaining overweight and overeating are survival decisions. That is to say, the patient has an unconscious belief (until brought into awareness) that she will not survive unless she overeats or remains obese.

Eating disorders as a decisional defence against such early trauma or deficit are a unique form of addictive behaviour in so far as they, all things being equal, relate to substances needed to survive physiologically. 'Decisional defence' means that the patient has at some stage made a decision that it is best for her to overeat or maintain a large body size in order for her to cope in her world. Addiction is generally clinically managed alongside abstention from the addictive substance. Clearly, unlike alcohol, and in normal circumstances, drugs, food is needed to survive and so methods of cure using complete abstention are not possible. This means that the patient struggles with the addictive substance that is both her enemy and a necessity for her ability to live and thrive. The nature of overeating as an addiction is addressed further in Chapter 3.

The potential for the misuse and misunderstanding of the primary function of food begins as life begins at birth and continues in the subsequent months when holding and bonding between caretaker (usually mother) and infant are experienced significantly at meal times. (The implications of this process is expanded on in later chapters.) The baby is born with the potential to know when she is hungry and when she has had enough. Life in most modern cultures dictates schedules and meal times such that the infant loses something of the natural sense of hunger and satiation. The adult obese patient will have lost a true sense of biological hunger and the ability to know when she has had enough. She therefore eats when she is not hungry for food and tends only to stop when she feels overfull and distended. Heightening the patient's awareness of body sensations will reconnect her with her body self and enable her to begin more accurately to understand the difference between a need for food and a need for some other kind of self-care, attention or response.

The goal of therapy

In my own work with obese people I hold in mind that I am working to find out why the patient needs to maintain a large size or to eat excessively. I do not work towards weight loss as the primary goal, I aim to treat the cause not the symptom and so I aim/encourage the patient to understand why she needs the food or the weight and what options are open to her to address these reasons. My goal is for the patient to have a choice about her weight loss and that genuine psychological and social choice comes from knowing why she has needed to overeat or be big in the world in order to cope. If the patient attends slimming groups, the surgery or diets by herself in response to such feelings as guilt or disgust, or cultural demands that say she ought to lose weight, she is not choosing from an integrated (whole and healthy) sense of self to do so. She is only adapting to external and/or her internal psychological demands.

Ultimately the patient needs to establish a sense of self-worth, self-esteem, self-love and self-validation and from this position she can decide whether she can and will lose weight or not. The psychotherapeutic goal is the autonomy and empowerment of the patient.

Choices need to be made from a 'here and now' rational self (the Adult self) who sees reasons and options, and moves to being able to act upon those options. Free choice is never made from the dictates of the negative internalized Parent (Parent ego state) – the part of self that represents parental messages that control and direct without reference to the here and now. Neither is it made from the adapting or fearful inner Child self (Child ego state) – the part that adapts or rebels in accordance with irrational belief systems laid down from early childhood. Both these parts of self are the driving forces that compel the patient to gain and maintain weight and use food to compensate for unmet needs. At the same time, within these parts of the self are the forces that jibe the patient to lose weight with negative messages of unacceptability. With such a 'psychological tug of war', the patient is unlikely to lose weight or to maintain any weight loss. Freeing herself from these forces through understanding and self-awareness is vital if she is to make a genuine and psychologically secure choice to lose weight or not.

I have worked with many overweight patients who have become more confident and self-accounting; by self-accounting, I mean that the patient is able to think and act in response to her own needs rather than in response to outdated adaptions and self-recriminations. They have shifted from being the person who is dismissed, disrespected and ignored to the person who can stand up for herself, command respect and valid attention, and who has decided that weight is no longer an issue. They have extended their lifestyles to include going to the gym, swimming, dancing and socializing and found themselves to be acceptable both to themselves and to others without losing weight. They have decided that they are OK as they are and have made a choice to stay so. Others have chosen to lose weight because it is what they want for themselves.

Provided the self-harming issues have been addressed and the patient is healthy enough, that is, not morbidly obese, which would remain self-harming, then to gain enough self-worth and self-esteem to function contentedly in the world is a significant therapeutic outcome. Self-valuing, self-esteem and self-worth are about seeing oneself as equal to any other human being who has a right to take up her place in the world; as someone who is able to account for herself, defend and promote herself and who refuses to be put down by another and as someone who can accept her shadow side and her mistakes and still feel whole. Self-esteem and self-worth are about loving oneself.

Morbidly obese patients and those in the higher brackets of obesity who need to lose weight to avoid disease and disability present a more complex problem. Though it would clearly not be recommended, they do still have the choice to remain obese. Such a choice would not be made from clear Adult thinking.

It is intriguing that whilst patients engage in their psychotherapeutic journey they often begin to change their eating and lose weight without conscious effort to do so. For the moderately or short-term obese person, this works well. Morbidly obese patients take longer to reach this initial stage and often still need to attend a slimming group. They will, however, improve their self-awareness, self-esteem and self-confidence with which to approach the group with a functioning, discerning Adult self that knows what she wants rather than operating from a dependent and compliant Child self who is dependent on another, the group leader, to control and monitor her. This is important if the patient is to have a sense of her own ability to make decisions for herself and to work through her weight loss in an equal relationship. It is only under these circumstances that the patient will avoid becoming dependent on the slimming group and be able to maintain weight loss independently of it when she is ready to leave. I expand on this in Chapter 4 when considering why some people can lose and maintain weight loss and others seem unable to do so.

Attitudes toward obesity

Even in today's politically correct culture there remains a stigma around overweight people. Unless someone is either a sufferer or a compassionate worker in the field, they cannot know the misery that overweight causes people both socially and psychologically. Suggesting that people should have some self-control and lose weight is, for many people, asking the impossible. Patients often report feeling dismissed in medical spheres because of a lack of understanding of the seeming impossibility of losing weight. Patients feel the failure of not being able to lose weight, which is compounded by a cultural stance that believes that weight loss is just a matter of self-control and therefore, anyone who cannot lose weight, has none. A doctor colleague was working with another doctor who became frustrated with a patient he had been treating who was not losing weight and in his frustration would shout at her. When he told my colleague that he shouted at his patient but she still did not lose weight, her retort to his outburst was: 'It's no wonder she can't lose weight, she needs at least two cream cakes to get over seeing you!' Though his intentions were good, this doctor did not understand the psychology of obesity. Shouting at the patient compounded her feelings of inadequacy and she did what she habitually did when feeling a failure, she reached for food.

Understanding that lack of willpower or gluttony are not key issues for the majority of obese patients is important. I have seen people moved to tears when I have addressed groups of overeaters and responded empathically to their painful experiences, their questions and observations. For many, this appeared to be the first time they really felt understood, heard and respectfully acknowledged.

Prejudice

Prejudice against obesity continues to be apparent and it may be argued that it is growing in the light of media, medical and government attention on the condition. A survey carried out by TOAST (The Obesity Awareness and Solutions Trust), an active movement for obesity awareness, in 2004, showed that there was still prejudice in the work place and in the community. Stephen Morris (2004) studied the impact of obesity on employment in England and found that discrimination against overweight people is very much present. Jeffery Jupp, Employment Barrister, states that there is no law against this discrimination in the UK and as a result employers can name obesity as the reason not to take someone on as an employee and there is no restriction on commenting on an employee's weight gain (PersonnelToday.com 2005). Indeed there was no repercussion when the manager of a large leisure group explained on BBC Radio 5 why he would not employ very fat people. He described them as taking more time off work, tending to be more unhealthy, and tending to have a more slovenly slothful attitude towards the job they do. These were highly prejudiced remarks that went unchallenged.

I would not expect therapists and counsellors to hold such strongly prejudiced views. However, it is quite likely that some, if not most, will hold some less obvious prejudice. Practitioners must recognize these prejudices, for it is certain that the patient will sense them. As long as the therapist is aware of them she can deal with them keep within, or keep them out of, the therapy process. If she does not, they will linger in the dynamic between patient and therapist and interfere with the effectiveness of therapeutic process. Honesty with oneself as a practitioner working in this field may be disturbing but it is important and I advocate open discussion with colleagues and supervisors on this subject in order to achieve full awareness of even the mildest prejudiced attitude.

I am reminded of psychotherapist Irvin Yalom's experience as described in his book *Love's Executioner* (Yalom 1989). When working with an overweight woman he wrote: 'I have always been repelled by fat women. I find them disgusting' (p.87); 'When I see a fat lady eat, I move down a couple of rungs on the ladder of human understanding' (p.88); 'Poor Betty, thank God – knew none of this' (p.89). Then when ending and reflecting with the patient, Yalom explained to her that he had not worked before with overweight patients and, having now worked with her, had changed his thinking. In the course of this confession he said 'When I started [with Betty] I personally didn't feel comfortable with obese people.' She replied 'Ho! Ho! Ho!' 'Didn't feel comfortable, that's putting it mildly. Do you know for the first six months you hardly ever looked at me?' (p.115). She also pointed out that he had never touched her even though he had touched and held other group members. His prejudiced feelings were there in the room throughout the therapy with Betty and she was aware of them.

When working with one of my groups early in my career, I was using some self-disclosure as illustration and talked about looking at a photo of myself as a fat child. I grimaced and said 'Disgusting'. Immediately a group member picked up my comment and highlighted my prejudice. She saw it as evidence of what I really thought about obesity. On examination of my response I realized that I had not completed the work I needed to do in relation to my own Child-self. Whereas I felt I could be empathic towards my obese patients and their inner world, I needed to resolve this relationship with myself before I would be completely unprejudiced. It meant that I was still holding prejudice about the condition of being obese if not about the person with the condition of obesity. This was somewhat nonsensical since the condition could not be separated entirely from the person who suffered it and the consequence of my unresolved prejudice served to detract from the patient's sense of me as an accepting and trustworthy therapist.

As these illustrations show, the patient is highly sensitive to negative responses to her size, in fact I would go as far as to say she expects it. Hence she will detect even the most remote allusion to unacceptability. She will test out even after it would seem that the working alliance, therapeutic relationship and trust have been established. Any whiff of prejudice will disrupt the working alliance, and though this may be resolved and in the resolution give the patient a reparative experience, it may well wound deep enough to maintain an impasse in the relationship for some lengthy period or even result in premature termination.

The importance of discussing these prejudices in supervision must be emphasized. It is difficult to be really clear without open discussion and honesty. If they are not attended to they remain without active scrutiny and evaluation. If a practitioner is fully aware of her prejudices and has declared them in discussion with colleagues she can harness them or use them appropriately with the patient. In this way she may avoid the dynamic that arose between Yalom and Betty and my patient and I.

Differing degrees of the problem

It is important to be aware that there are different degrees of the problem of overweight, not just in terms of the amount of extra weight people carry but in terms of the depth of the psychological issues that prevent them from losing weight or maintaining the weight loss. There are significant differences between the short-term and long-term sufferer, the reactive overeater, that is, the person who eats in response to life events, and the continuous overeater. There are also different degrees of 'defences' needed in response to differing depths of perceived historical trauma and negative experiences of the patient. My observations have been that the more obese the patient the more likely it is that she has experienced life situations, usually in infancy and childhood, that have been more seriously disturbing to her than those who carry less weight. Her fantasies about the dangers of losing weight will be more bizarre and her need to hold on to her defences will be stronger. These patients believe that something unmanageable will happen if they lose weight. Likewise there are different degrees of impulsive and compulsive eating that will reflect the levels of psychological disturbance felt by the patient.

Anyone displaying panic or fear at the thought of losing weight will be someone who has a deeply subconscious need to keep the weight on and a belief system that implies devastating sanctions if weight is lost or weight loss maintained. These people may or may not lose weight, but if they do, they will surely put the weight back on until they have resolved the underlying issues. Invariably they put on a little more each time. It is as if the psyche is ensuring it will be a harder task to lose weight next time.

A patient who had been sexually abused and who, we discovered, experienced her body size as being her defence system showed me a pattern of her weight gain and losses. Figure 1.1 below illustrates her pattern of weight loss and subsequent increased gain. This is a common pattern amongst obese patients in the higher obesity and morbidly obese brackets.

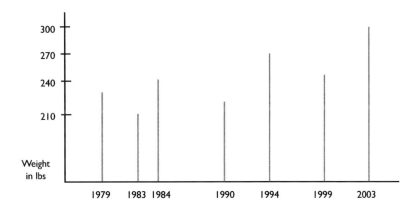

Figure 1.1 Graph showing increased weight gain after significant weight loss, a common pattern in long-term sufferers of obesity

Determining who is overweight

The question of who is overweight, whether it matters and who decides is interesting. So far, I have assumed a common understanding of obesity and overweight. However, what one person sees as being overweight may not be the same as another, or more particularly, what one person sees or experiences as being an overweight problem may not be a problem at all to someone else. This does have clinical implications that will be addressed, but first let us consider the medically recognized standards.

The Body Mass Index (BMI), which basically states that one's weight in kilos divided by height in metres squared should fall between 20 and 24.9 in order to be a healthy weight, is the current standard in medical spheres. Twenty-five to 30 is overweight, 30 to 40 is obese and 40+ is very or morbidly obese. A BMI of up to 40 can mean the patient is 84 lbs (38 kilos) overweight and those termed morbidly obese are in the next bracket.

The morbidly obese patient is immediately recognizable as being so because of her large size. People in the lower range of obesity or overweight category may not see themselves as overweight or not think that it matters. If someone does not have a problem with being overweight, they will not be in therapy or will not present in therapy with this as an issue. However, there may be patients who do present in therapy who either are very obese and do not present with this as an issue and those who present with an issue of overweight when they do not appear to be outside the recommended BMI.

In face to face contact with the patient each practitioner will be making his or her own judgements. These will be swayed by his or her cultural frame of reference, social influences and collective understanding of what constitutes overweight or obesity, together with the significance of such conclusions.

Where a dilemma may occur for therapists is in the question of whether the patient who is not overweight and wants to be thinner or the patient who is morbidly obese and does not offer this as a focus for therapy, are self-harming. And if they conclude that the patient is self-harming what do they do about it? The questions this raises are: in what circumstances is it psychotherapeutically valid to open discussion on an issue that is apparent and yet not being named by the patient? Under what circumstances would it be appropriate to work with someone who is self-harming without addressing this behaviour? Is it appropriate to ask the patient her weight?

I believe it is advisable for practitioners to know what is generally perceived as obese by health authorities that have researched the condition of both health and ill-health relating to weight. How that information is used to inform the work and choice of interventions with patients will depend on other factors, particularly the clinician's field of psychotherapy or counselling. My guiding considerations are the therapeutic value of any intervention and the desire for congruence (genuineness) and transparency whenever possible, bearing in mind that if a dilemma exists for the therapist, it is likely to be picked up by the patient in the therapeutic process.

Is complete cure possible?

I am not certain that it is ever possible for the long-term sufferer to be completely cured of the need to turn to food when under stress. She will however, manage the process better and will be able to accept and tolerate the times when she reverts to using food again because she will have the tools to analyse and understand her own behaviour. She will be able to look for the reason why she is misusing food again and to integrate her experience. She will understand that if she is adversely using food there is something she needs to attend to. She will not panic and feel that a relapse into eating means failure and she will not give up, feeling that such transgressions are ruinous. This is more likely to be a brief relapse phase rather than a reversion to the previous hopeless and helpless behavioural pattern. She will be able to think about her need to eat at this time rather than surrendering to compulsion. If the patient understands that her eating and weight gain are indications that something needs to be addressed in her life, food and size become a useful indicator rather than the enemy.

When food and fat are seen as the enemy, the patient will always experience the exhausting battle. Understanding lapses as indicators of needs that are not being met reduces the sense of struggle and allows energy to be directed towards managing the 'lapses' in a framework of self-love and self-care, which is what maintaining a reasonable weight is about.

Chapter 2

Cultural and Parent Influences on Decisions Regarding Weight

Eating is at the centre of our being. It is both interesting and significant to think about the norms, values and folklore around both food and size in order to fully understand the problem in terms of the struggle of the patient and the environmental issues surrounding that struggle. A significant piece of work with the patient will be to understand how her family and cultural influences have been interpreted and internalized and how she is limited, persuaded and ruled by them. From these influences she will have internalized the most persuasive elements that will then seem to become her own beliefs. For example, she will no longer need to hear or be told what to do, or how to behave, by people who have controlled her in the past, she will have her own internal mental representation of them, and will be governed by the voices these take up in her head.

'Messages' of how to be in the world are passed down from the widest global sources, including existential realities, historical mores and collective experiences, through cultures, families and significantly, parents. I take time here to refer to some of these influences to stimulate thought and provide a backdrop for understanding the patient in context. My thinking has been influenced by Berne (1963), Drego (1983) and Hargaden and Sills (2002), each of whom has written about the properties of the cultural 'Parent', its persuasion and the implications of being bound by cultural introjects.

Below in Figure 2.1 is a chart mapping the influences that affect the patient's decisions regarding weight.

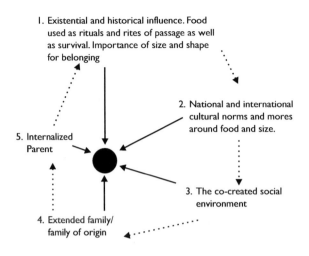

5. Internalized Parent

1. Existential and historical influence. Food used as rituals and rites of passage as well as survival. Importance of size and shape for belonging

2. National and international cultural norms and mores around food and size.

3. The co-created social environment

4. Extended family/ family of origin

Key
● The patient
→ Influences on patient beliefs and behaviours
··▸ Infuences on each cultural Parent on the next, culminating in the patient's internalized Parent

Figure 2.1 Historical, cultural, interpersonal and intrapsychic influences

In Figure 2.1 are the sources of cultural scripting with arrows of ever-decreasing length to indicate the power they have over the patient at the centre. The shortest and nearest are the most immediately influential. (1) and (2) represent cultural influences. The co-created social environment, that is, the environment that is created by the psychological, emotional and social needs of any group of people (3) and family (parents, extended family, siblings) (4) may have different meaning in different cultures and stages of development. It may be that the ethnic mores are most powerful and if they are they will be transmitted and reinforced by the actual parent figures in the patient's life. The decisions that the patient makes and has made in response to these influences are logged within the internal, self-regulating Parent self of the patient (5). Each of the five influences are explored below.

Existential and historical influences

We need food in order to survive. The existential reality is that we cannot do without food. Food is all around us, ready at hand. In wealthy countries we are rarely far from somewhere that sells food. Food has always been and still is, at the centre of rituals and rites of passage, social gatherings and shared quality time whether within the family or with friends. It promotes a way of life. Many television programmes today are based on food, whether cooking it or sharing it. The most fundamental reason to eat is to have energy to work and play. Everything beyond this is about lifestyle. That is the truth, and it is helpful at times to come back to this basic premise with patients who overeat, especially when moving from understanding of the psychological issues to acting upon that understanding towards behavioural change. In fact I would advocate empathically weaving this reality into the consciousness of the patient when she is ready to hear it and when it is psychotherapeutically valid.

The purpose in thinking about the fact that food is both central to our being and to our socialization is not to suggest that people will automatically eat above their needs but to highlight the fact that food is, and always has been, more than fuel for our bodies and that it is the centre of cultural rituals. It is not just about eating but about what sharing food represents in this wider context. Partaking in cultural rituals is a way of belonging and belonging is third in the hierarchy of human needs identified by Maslow (1987). He suggested that there are needs that must be adequately met before less existential conditions can be fulfilled. Thus he put the most basic need as biological, that is, food and shelter, followed by safety and then belonging. He proposed that self-esteem, mastery and independence can only follow when these basic requirements are adequately satisfied. I address the issue of belonging in a number of ways because the lack of a sense of belonging, or a sense of conditional belonging (e.g. 'You can only belong if you are fat' or 'You can only belong if you are not fat') is a key issue for obese patients.

Size and shape

In affluent and technological societies there are cultural demands about size and shape. This is not a new phenomenon. The ancient Greeks and Romans valued lean and muscular men, not just because they were obviously fitter on the battlefield but intelligence and wisdom were equated with the slimmer body. Apparently, Plato who was fat, was only accepted as a senator by the leading body-focused Greeks because of his mental genius. They saw the combination of fat and brain as rare. This belief is still maintained to some degree today. Fat people are still equated with stupidity, slovenliness and laziness. They are seen as unintelligent and lacking in self-control. These attitudes mirror the inner process of the patients, many of whom think of themselves as stupid, unimportant and 'bad' inside.

In other cultures, overweight is seen as a demonstration of affluence, or a sign of fertility, desirability or sexuality. Meals are provided in huge quantities to demonstrate the status of the provider or to honour the standing of the recipient. There are many ways in which food and size are seen as indicative of a person's position or worth in different cultures and it is necessary to be aware of the diversity and not to apply western norms to non-western cultures. What is interesting is how much acceptance and unacceptability is based on food and size historically in so many disparate ethnicities.

It seems that the demand to belong by conformity to a certain size has long been within the global culture. I include these thoughts to emphasize the fact that the pain caused by overweight has a dimension beyond many other psychological or social problems that may be presented. Fat people are notice-able by virtue of their size; they cannot in that sense hide their issue. By this 'displaying' of the problem they will attract negative attitudes that are common in a rejecting society. The fact that size and shape have so repeatedly been at the centre of acceptance historically means that there is a collective sub-consciousness about the right to belong. There is an endemic judgemental attitude towards size and shape that has been laid down over centuries.

I find it curious that a conclusion is often reached that people turn to food, seemingly just because it is there. Surely the considerations missing are the quality of relationship and social and emotional interactivity that suffer in a highly technological culture. Considering the consequences of industrializa-tion, Emile Durkheim (1984; 2002) as long ago as 1893, noted the increasing numbers of suicides that he related to increased levels of alienation and anomie. As the cultural norms changed, inter-social expectations became unclear, confused and even absent. In the post-industrial, complex societies, people are no longer tied to one another and social bonds are impersonal. Where value is placed on production, wealth and possessions, there is opened up a possibility of a corresponding devaluation of one's own life and of one's self. This must be a consideration in the reasons why people reach for food to fill the void left by the disintegration of communal purpose and specific role identity, or to structure time that would otherwise have been filled with goal-orientated or interpersonal and mutually dependent activity. This alien-ation from work, social order and family plays a part in heightening the psychological hungers described in Chapters 4 to 12.

It is not sufficient to imply that if food is made available, people will eat it until they are obese. Not everyone does. Our advanced 24/7 society detracts from the quality of relationships and the sense of satisfying purpose accompanied by high levels of stress. The alienation and anomie described by Durkheim operates as truly today as it did post-industrialization. A further existential reality, then, is the need for love, social contact, communication and belonging, which are natural to the human condition. Absence or depletion of adequate response to these needs will lead to a desire to meet them in other ways; the overweight patient has used and continues to use food for this purpose.

National and ethnic cultures

It is important to hold in awareness the attitudes towards food and size in a patient's culture of origin if they differ from her present cultural setting. And indeed, for the therapist to understand the norms of that original culture whether the patient experiences conflicting values or not. If the patient is struggling with the incompatibility of the demands of the culture of origin and her present cultural setting, it needs to be understood and acknowledged. Work towards some level of integration that is satisfactory to the patient and does not alienate is indicated. Because there are strong underlying premises with regard to food and meals in any culture, it is easy to work with a patient from the therapist's own frame of reference in this respect rather than that of the patient.

Case study: experiencing conflicting values and traditions

A patient, presenting with obesity and depression, had married into an ethnically different family. She experienced their family and social interactivity as always being centred on food. The food, she said, was high in calories and it was important to provide large amounts to indicate the strength of love and welcome extended. Her own culture and family norms did not demand that she provide food for visitors and she was allowed to refuse food. The camaraderie and importance associated with food in her husband's family was alien to her and she felt both overwhelmed and overfed. She was unable to withdraw but felt suffocated when yielding to this alien demand. She felt angry and resentful, scared and vulnerable. This caused her to withdraw and soothe herself in the lonely hours of the day with foods she associated with self-comfort such as chocolate, crisps, cakes and biscuits. She felt she did not belong, which in turn caused her to re-experience the struggle to belong and be accepted in her family of origin. Although mealtimes were clearly not the only struggle for her, they became the focus of her discontent.

Food rituals preserve racial traditions and unity. Some third and fourth generation immigrant families continue to eat the diets of their ethnic origins and meal times will follow similar cultural patterns. Some still speak their ancestral native language at the table to preserve their identity and belonging.

Conflicts also arise with regard to size. A patient's West Indian culture accepted a rotund female shape as desirable. Even though she was born in England, she still felt the influence of this cultural scripting. Her struggle was not only with her desire to be rotund when she related to her culture of origin and slimmer when she related to her British culture, but also with her dilemma with respect to which culture she felt the most allegiance. These are issues that the patient will need to resolve, because while they perpetuate, the patient is clearly unable to decide on her therapeutic goal or work towards it.

In western culture, obesity and overeating are seen as lifestyles rather than biological or psychological problems. Evidence shows that health professionals reflect the bias of the culture, not least by the lack of resources available in the National Health system for dealing with obese patients. Patients report their perception that doctors have little time for them and will 'blame' any ailment, about which they seek advice, on their weight. However, one GP explained to me that doctors harbour feelings of impatience and rejection of these patients because they feel defeated; defeated because they have no answer and even a sense that with some patients the problem seems insurmountable.

It is only possible to write briefly here about the ethnic and cultural persuasions that may affect the patient's ability to reach her goal. As with the subsequent considerations, this book's intention is to raise awareness of the need to think about the patient in context and understand the less obvious struggles that might be present in relation to her eating and size and her journey towards her desired goal.

The socially co-created environment

Socially co-created environment means the roles set up between the participants in the patient's social setting that are dependent on the patient remaining obese or eating more than she would like or want to. This aspect is discussed further in chapters on the Child ego state, psychological hungers and games.

As in all human groups, roles are ascribed to different members, most of whom will naturally fall into the assigned roles because of the interlocking nature of relationships and fulfilment of relational needs. Others will take on a role because the group looks to them to do so, even though it may not be their normal stance. When any member steps out of the accredited role the group equilibrium is disturbed and the lure for all is to get back to the comfort of the former group cohesion. For the obese patient, whose fear is often of rejection, the possibility of that rejection becomes real if some part of the group cohesion is seen to be dependent on her being fat, or indeed, eating the same indulgent foods as everyone else.

As so often with the alcohol drinking group who persuade the abstainer to drink, without which inclusion seems impossible, so with the overeater. The alcohol abstainer is seen as dull and boring, the dieter likewise. The message is 'You can't fully belong round here unless you subscribe to the group norm'.

If the group depends on the patient being fat and she loses weight she is possibly going to face choosing between her slimmer self and belonging to the group. When patients have resolved enough psychological issues to feel confident and robust they will choose to leave the group and maintain a good sense of their worth. Patients who have not reached this point are more likely to put weight back on in order to maintain their position in the group. Group demands and rituals (see psychological hungers) can be very compelling and add to the complexity of the therapeutic journey.

The extended family/family of origin

Whereas all the above existential, historical, social and cultural influences form part of the internalized Parent self (Parent ego state) in the patient and need to be held in awareness and investigated with the patient as necessary and appropriate, the last two 'influences' form a vital source of intervention with the patient if we are to understand the blocks to the patient achieving her agreed goal.

For patients who present with shorter-term weight issues and less weight to lose, working with these family introjects may be all that is needed to effect significant change. For others they will be part of the ongoing programme of psychotherapy or counselling and will be used at different stages in the treatment flow, according to the needs of each individual patient. This will be demonstrated in the chapter on the Parent ego state.

Family sayings and attitudes towards food and size reveal both the direct verbal and the indirect psychological messages given to the child. The child will internalize both the verbal messages and the psychological messages together with her reaction to, and her experience of, them. This combination will determine the behaviour she will choose. There is huge significance, therefore, in enabling the patient to recall the sayings about food and eating, and in the way mealtimes were conducted and to understand how these are affecting the patient's choice or need to eat in the here and now. Likewise, the family sayings about size reveal what decisions the patient has made in using size as a defensive structure. In Chapter 5 is a questionnaire that focuses on gleaning this information and may be used directly with the patient as a diagnostic tool or may be used as a 'mental template' of therapeutic intervention for the practitioner.

The internalized Parent

The final influence is the patient's own internalized Parent self. This is not the messages transmitted from others outside the self but what the patient has taken into her own psyche, the verbal and non-verbal, the social and the psychological content and the patient's interpretation of the messages she received. This final influence is the one that the patient used and uses to control her own behaviour to fit into her world in the best way she knew, and still knows. It can be seen as the repository of all those influences above, both the positive and negative, whether in their original form or with some modification and the patient's personal perception of them.

This is the part of the self that so far has been called the Parent self. It is what Transactional Analysts call the 'Parent ego state' and is described more fully in Chapter 7. The Parent ego state develops in response to the patient's historical experiences from childhood. Those experiences will have been fashioned by each of the influences outlined above. The global and existential realities affect ethnicity and culture as well as the individual; ethnicity and culture affect the family norms and belief systems and these in turn socialize the child. The task of the practitioner is to understand with the patient how these influences negatively affect her ability to gain self-esteem and self-worth and how they might block her move towards weight loss.

Chapter 3

Clinical Considerations in Working with the Overweight Patient

This chapter comprises an overview of the experiences and psychological beliefs of the overweight patient. They are expanded upon in Chapters 4 to 12, which outline methods of diagnosing and working with these issues.

Sexual intrusion

Sexual abuse or abuse of sexuality or the right of passage into adulthood is less common in the life history of obese people than in anorexics. It is still however, in my experience, significantly present. Many obese people I have worked with have a fear that if they lose weight they will become sexually promiscuous and thus 'ruin' their marriage or relationship. Many believe that men will line up to have sex with them and that they will have no power or control over these would-be perpetrators.

Non-survival

Some patients believe that if they lose weight they will disappear or shrivel and die, or if they do not, then some significant others, who depend on them to be fat, will not thrive. This is a deeply disturbing and self-limiting belief.

The obese body as container of the bad self

It is common for the overweight person to be in touch with her 'bad self'. She believes that she is bad deep down and can substantiate that belief by recalling events in her life where she has felt that people have treated her as if they have seen this unworthy part of her. As will be seen in later chapters, the events to which the patient refers as supporting evidence have occurred for very different reasons and are not related to what the patient has decided is her bad self. The protective aspect of this fantasy is that the fat keeps the bad self from being seen. It keeps others at a distance and of course, this, in some respects, is physically true. The anorexic appears to withdraw her body self from the world whereas the obese person pushes out her body boundaries. This extension of the body boundaries has a number of functions: to hide the bad self; to protect the vulnerable self; to keep the world at bay; to support the heaviness of being overburdened with problems and demands from others, and occasionally is a bid to be seen and take a place in the world. This latter function often accompanies the sense that if the patient loses weight she will disappear, or 'be nothing'.

Obese patients are anxious about being touched because the fat layers may repulse and the reality often is that others are repulsed. They believe themselves to be too big to be held and, again, the reality is that others do find it difficult to hold them because of their extended size.

When a patient believes that fat hides the bad self, she is likely to believe that if she loses weight this bad self will be apparent to others. There is, however, little comfort in being fat since the patient who comes into therapy also believes that she is bad because she is fat. Patients who believe that people think they are 'bad' because they are fat have produced a recognizable reason for being thought of as worthless, which is more comfortable than believing that people sense that they are intrinsically bad. It is less destructive to believe that others dislike them because they are fat than because they are worthless to their very core.

Those that suffer with obesity as a psychological defence will often shield themselves socially by being available to others, pleasing them as much as they can and rarely saying 'no' to demands and requests made of them. They have little sense of themselves as worthwhile unless validated by being servile to others. They will create situations where others are dependent on them and so they can feel wanted and liked. Mostly, this is a pattern learnt in childhood.

An issue of belonging

Many patients have a sense of not belonging, though desperately wanting to belong. Their weight and eating may be a method of belonging in their family or social group, whilst it is a deterrent to belonging in the wider culture – for example, the patient whose social group or family needs her to be the 'fat happy clown'.

A sense of belonging is a prerequisite for building self-esteem and self-worth and moving towards self-actualization, that is, attainment of life goals. Patients have indicated having had a sense that they needed to avoid belonging, having internalized such an injunction indirectly from the environment, from their mother or the primary carer or some significant other person.

Psychological needs

The overeater, who may or may not be morbidly obese, is undoubtedly responding to psychological needs rather than the needs of the healthy functioning body. There has been much written about the need to overeat and the major reasons highlighted tend to be boredom, replacing love and holding down feelings. There are, however, other hungers that are psychological hungers, which patients try, unsuccessfully, to feed with food. Chapter 10 is dedicated to looking at what Transactional Analysts consider to be the existential hungers that need satisfying in order to maintain a healthy mind, and thereby, a healthy body.

Once links between emotion, deprivation and food have been laid down, a repeated and reinforced behavioural pattern of stimulus–response will become established. It is a link that may or may not be fully overcome in the course of therapy but it can certainly be adequately and satisfactorily modified such that any reversion to this behavioural pattern in response to certain stressors can be integrated into the patient's experience, tolerated and managed. Thus the patient will be able to manage the period of 'relapse' without self-denigration or at least will know that she can regain appropriate mastery when the time is right. She will have a real sense of that self-mastery for which she has the potential but which she lost at some developmental point.

Deprivation and scarcity

For both the obese patient and the overeater, feelings of scarcity and deprivation are rife. When changing behaviour, that is losing weight or changing eating lifestyle and rituals, the patient is likely to hit the fear of deprivation again. In other words, if she is feeding herself in response to a psychological feeling of deprivation, it follows that if she stops feeding herself she will experience the sense of deprivation even more strongly. This will force her to eat again, and quite possibly to eat even larger volumes of food as she responds to a heightened sensation of there being an unfulfilled need. The deprivation the patient feels in the face of a controlled dietary regime is only about there not being enough food in so far as the food is feeding psychological hungers. Without food the patient is left psychologically starving.

Scarcity is about there not being enough. It is different from deprivation in that the patient feels that there is not an adequate supply of what she craves. What she craves needs to be identified through the therapeutic process and again this will relate to one or more of the psychological hungers being unmet. When the patient is overeating she is meeting this scarcity with an abundance of food.

When some patients decide to diet, they will eat even more fattening foods in the same way as, historically, people feasted before winter shortage and enforced fasting. The patient has a sense of there going to be a scarcity of food and will 'stock up' before embarking on the regime she sees as restrictive.

The sense of scarcity is a major reason for overeating. It is as if the patient always believes that there will be some time at which she is forced to stop eating or supplies will not be available. The origin of this belief would normally lie within the early infant experience of the patient. If she psychologically believes there is a shortage, she will eat compulsively, as if there is no tomorrow. Teaching the patient to put distance between her impulse to eat and her action of eating will enable her to understand that (1) the food will still be there in five, ten or 30 minutes' time, or even tomorrow; (2) it is possible not to eat immediately in response to this psychologically perceived shortage; (3) this need is indeed psychological and not reality.

Overeating as an addiction

The addictive nature of the behaviour of overeating and needing to be obese was referred to in Chapter 1. This section describes what constitutes addictive behaviours and how overeating corresponds to that description.

An addiction involves a pathological and dependent relationship on someone, something, an event, circumstance or substance that has mood-altering properties and short- or long-term life-changing consequences. The dependent relationship may entail over-indulgence or abstinence. The overeater is indulgent in the substance, which is food, in contrast to the anorexic who fulfils the abstinence polarity of addiction. Eating is certainly a mood-altering experience. It is pacifying, exciting and pleasurable and in some circumstances patients have reported a euphoric state when eating. Patients will also detach whilst eating, such that they feel tranced by the experience. Though the food is rarely tasted, the process of eating can transform the patient into an almost transcendental state. The aftermath is usually painful, recriminatory, guilt-ridden and the patient feels disgusted and angry with herself.

Other addictive conditions are the preoccupation with food or abstinence from it, the need to use, misuse or avoid food in isolation and secrecy, a specific feeling of numbing and the self-harming condition of obesity. There may be an accompanying inability to fulfil commitments and for some obese and particularly morbidly obese patients there is certainly a reduced ability to partake in some social activities. Throughout this book there are descriptions of patients' behaviour that are indicative of the obsessive and addictive conditions of overeating and obesity.

The addictive nature of the problem alerts us to the fact that the cessation of the use of one addictive substance may lead to a replacement by another. That is to say that if the patient does change her eating habits to a more 'normal' intake without intrapsychic shift, she may well replace this addictive substance for another. The awakening or exaggeration of sexual energy in self or other, feared by patients if they should lose weight and become slim, may be an indication of a possible and certainly feared addictive substitute, that is, sex. Sex is also one of the psychological hungers. It is often misinterpreted as love.

Because the addictive substance is food and food is necessary for survival, abstention methods used with other addictions are not possible with obese patients. This, together with the ready availability of food in affluent cultures, renders food addiction more complex than other forms of addiction.

The nature–nurture debate and self-responsibility

A major question that is asked repeatedly is how much of the problem of overweight is a physiological condition passed through genes and how much is it a psychological or social problem that can be redressed? If 'fat runs in the family', for instance mother and father and grandmother were all overweight, does this mean that the patient has to accept that this is his or her lot? Are there cells that determine size and is the patient fighting a losing battle if she has cells that make her fat? There is some level of consensus on the idea that a predisposition to put on weight may be inherited. There seems as yet to be no consensus on the influence of genetics and fat-making cells (see Jade 1999).

It is possible that fat parents teach their children how to be fat, directly or indirectly by their words or by modelling fatness and of course, by feeding their children foods in quantities that will ensure weight gain. It is also true that psychological messages regarding size and food are transmitted from parent to child in both open and more subtle, out-of-awareness ways. These form the basis for the efficacy of working with obese patients psycho-therapeutically. I believe the psychological or ulterior messages endemic in the patient's relationships form the most significant component of her need and choice to be obese.

Because I believe that we have the choice to be as we are, or to change, I take the view that patients must accept responsibility for their behaviour and both their conscious and unconscious decision to be big in the world. Although therapeutic work entails investigating parental influences, such investigation must not be seen as laying responsibility at the feet of the parents or significant others. When the patient accepts responsibility for her decisions and choices made in or out of awareness, she can work with the therapist to find out why she would uphold decisions that cause her suffering and emo-tional, as well as physical, pain. Unless the patient accepts this responsibility, the relationship with the therapist must be rendered unequal to the extent that she is likely to see the therapist as being the expert and the authority on whom to depend for cure. As in all psychotherapeutic relationships, there has to be mutual commitment to work. If the patient sees herself as being fat because it is in the genes and therefore predetermined, there is no room for movement and counselling or therapy on the issue of overweight is contraindicated.

When arriving in therapy, the patient does not have a fully integrated sense of having a choice: a choice to lose weight or not and a choice of when it is appropriate for her to do it. She knows in the here and now that she should lose weight but feels overwhelmed by the prospect and the time it will take, which is confirmed by the times she has attempted to lose and maintain weight loss before coming into therapy. She feels compelled by external forces and controlled by internal impulses.

If patient and therapist understand that, in the absence of there being an organic or medical reason for overweight, being obese is a choice, the possibility of making a different choice arises. If the patient is locked into a belief that nature has made her fat, she may not appear in therapy, but if she does, she is likely to believe that the therapist has a 'magic wand' that will do the work for her.

The function of the slimming club and diet sheet

It is fact that people develop and maintain a sense of themselves through others' response to them, that is, in relationship. This applies from birth and continues through life. It can be a subtle and supportive dynamic. However, it becomes pathological when this is the only way a person can have a sense of their own OK-ness and this is generally the case with overeaters and obese people. They have little sense of themselves as good enough. Overeaters look for a parent figure who can change their lives and they do this from a needy and dependent child position.

The typical slimming club provides just such an external controlling parent, one who can tell the participants what to do and how and when to do it. The group provides the sense of a positive support system and membership is dependent on there being a struggle with weight and eating.

More recently, slimming groups have provided food regimes that allow for far more choice and self-monitoring than was previously the case. However, the aim is not specifically to educate and hand over self-awareness and self-direction to the patient. The slimmer is not taught to be in tune with her own body sensations or to be more attuned to the physiological experience of food intake, hunger and repleteness. Clearly the regime of most slimming clubs or groups does not involve any significant level of psychotherapeutic direction that would enable this type of patient empowerment. This means that unless a group member has a truly integrated sense of self when joining the group, and can ascertain for herself what she takes from the group without a need to become dependent, she is likely to have to remain in the group for an extensive period of her life in order to maintain her weight loss.

Most slimming clubs would accept that participants may need to remain members virtually for life in order to maintain weight loss as a high percentage of their membership regain the weight on leaving the club. It is essentially a dependent relationship. There is also a level of interdependence in so far as the clubs get their money, their products are bought by their membership and they get satisfying results and their members lose weight whilst in attendance and perhaps gain some self-esteem through that weight loss. They have the comfort of being with others who are experiencing the same struggle and pain and can understand. When the symbiosis (interdependence) is relinquished by a patient leaving the group, she is likely to regain the weight. Symbiosis means co-existing for mutual benefit and the patient loses the benefits the group offers when she leaves.

It is clear that many people lose weight and feel good whilst attending slimming clubs. They give their own power for self-mastery to the leader and the group process and feel that they gain support and camaraderie, and of course, understanding, as the homogeny of the group is the shared problem of obesity. If someone feels the need to attend a slimming group, I believe a healthy position is to attend from an Adult thinking position with a sense of equality in the relationship between group leader and patient rather than a Parent–Child dynamic where the leader is seen as the person in charge. The patient may then be able to take what is important to her from the group, decide for herself when to leave or take a break and test out what she has learnt about herself and her eating. This is possible, if the patient does indeed learn, but she can only learn if she applies her Adult, thinking self to the problem. Psychotherapy and counselling can prepare someone to see the slimming group as an additional aid to her journey in weight loss rather than the authority in the process.

The patient needs to be constantly aware of the pull towards dependency, for this will be magnetic to (1) her feelings of isolation and need to belong; (2) her need for confirmation of her OK-ness from others as well as recognition of herself and the type of person she is, through other people's response to her, which is supplied by the group leader and the group; (3) her need for identity (in her own mind, her identity is 'the fat person' but in the group 'the fat person who is slimming'); and (4) her masochistic stance whereby she relinquishes self-initiative in favour of the control of the powerful other that resides both in the group and, specifically, in the group leader.

As previously noted, I prefer my patients not to be undergoing a slimming regime whilst, at least initially, they are in therapy with me. The activity makes it difficult for the patient to work with the understanding of the reasons for their eating and need to be big. However, I will work with morbidly obese patients whilst they follow a prescribed eating regime, if their health is endangered or they need to lose weight before they are admitted for non-weight-related surgery.

The diet sheet and the slimming club or medical practice weigh-ins and guidance may be seen as 'external parents'. The task of psychotherapy may be seen as increasing the patient's sense of her internal moderator, to become in tune with the body self and natural body rhythms and to move away from the limitations of success and failure; as enabling the patient to be intrigued by the learning about herself rather than judgmental; as aiming for awareness, spontaneity, and intimacy, which are the essence of the autonomy that will enable the patient to make the right choices for herself. In the long term she needs to eat healthily and appropriately for weight loss and stability and she needs to learn to do this her own way. She needs to be able to monitor her intake in terms of 'enough'. That is, enough to live and enough to enjoy the social aspects of sharing food. She needs to eat as naturally as possible. If she learns about healthy eating, she will have more chance of being able to eat out with friends and to allow herself a dosage of those compelling extras that seem like treats.

For some patients it will take years of intensive work and self-focus to get to a point of renouncing the fat script where excessive food and a large size are no longer needed for existence and survival. This dedication is rarely accessible (or perhaps affordable). However, when the patient reaches a satisfactory level of self-knowing, self-esteem and self-worth she will manage her weight and eating to a satisfactory and satisfying point and ride the relapses. She will have a sense of self-mastery and will need neither the slimming club group leader nor the therapist.

Exercise, relaxation and meditation

Undoubtedly exercise is important in the journey towards a healthy body and does aid weight loss. However, given that many obese people feel too ashamed to join in any public exercise arena and too demoralized to do any sort of workout at home, emphasis on exercise is not useful in initial stages of treatment. Patients need to see that exercise is about self-care. When a patient is ready to exercise publicly when she has been unable to do so previously, there has been a significant psychological shift. Attending for exercise in whatever way is not necessarily a goal for psychotherapy, although it could be an agreed goal as a behavioural outcome if that is what the patient wants. The patient may choose this form of self-care when internal psychological restraints have been overcome. When a patient does this with a sense of achievement, it may be seen as the behavioural indicator of such a release.

Relaxation and guided meditation give the patient the experience of calm that is generally absent in their lives. When relaxed, the patient tends to feel the potential to be in control, to be who she wants to be and to access her potency. She removes herself from the agitation that both consciously and subconsciously typifies her experience. Through tightening and releasing sets of muscles throughout the body, (neuro-muscular relaxation) the patient can increase awareness of the body self, which is essential in determining a personal eating regime geared to natural sensations of hunger and repleteness. Such methods also enable the patient to re-associate with the previously dissociated (or disconnected) body self.

The body self

The extent of body dissociation experienced by many overweight patients is intriguing. It is not only evidenced by a lack of knowledge about when they have had enough to eat or are genuinely in need of food (biologically hungry) but by a lack of physical sensation in other areas. They will be out of touch with some levels of body pain and discomfort. Some dissociate their body selves by never looking at it in the mirror. Others will not even look at their faces. They will not come face to face with themselves.

Some patients do not relate to certain parts of their body. At times this can involve dissociation from the whole body self, or parts such as the waist, stomach and hips and thighs. It is also common for the obese patient to dissociate from her arms, usually in association with other parts of her body. The major link is the inability to self-soothe using the arms and hands. There is often an inability to offer the arms to others either both physically and metaphorically to reach out to others or to feel that others would not want to be hugged and held by an obese person. This can, in turn, entail the fantasy that others would not want to have the close proximity to the obese body that hugging and holding implies.

Becoming aware of the body self is vital if patients are to have a full and integrated sense of self. The mind and body work in unison, the body holds pathology and memory. With the advance of neuroscience, we cannot ignore the part the body and brain play together in our attempts to cope with the world. Evidence has shown that talking therapies change neuropathways in the brain (Cozolino 2002). Body work therapies have been shown to release patients from their script-bound selves (Staunton 2002). Attention needs to be paid to the patient's whole experience of herself and this involves both the physical and the psychological selves.

Attention to the body is an essential part of the therapeutic treatment direction in working with overeating and obesity. The body is being used in a specific way just as overeating, bingeing or abstaining from food are recognized as bids to resolve emptiness, fear and lovelessness and to have some sense of control in a chaotic and frightening world. In Chapter 12, the development of the body self alongside the psychological self is specifically addressed and I explain how I see this as being important information for the clinician to hold in awareness when treating obese patients.

Eating and body size as distinct issues

I wish to reiterate that there is a difference in the psychotherapy offered to the patient who overeats because of the psychological need for food and that offered to the patient whose large size is a major defence and even a survival issue. It is clear that people need to overeat in order to be fat, hence the fact that there are two separate issues, one the need for food and the other the need to be fat, can be missed. The practitioner and patient need to determine which of these behaviours is at the core of the problem. The chapters that follow attend to both these aspects.

Chapter 4

Losing Weight, Maintaining Loss and Regaining Weight

My early work with overweight patients began in 1979 when I trained to teach classes of women healthy eating, weight control, exercise, relaxation, stress management and life-style. Questions that intrigued me when working with the groups of women who came to these classes were: 'Why do some members lose weight, why do some maintain loss, why do others regain weight and why do some not lose at all?' Later on, when I retrained as a psychotherapist, I began to see patterns in the different ways the members presented in class and their weight management. I also began to understand the more subtle psychological aspects of what the group format and focus provided for its members.

The approach I used in these classes was centred on the whole-person, that is, exercise, weight loss, stress management, lifestyle, relaxation, fun and emphasis on working together, and was significantly successful for many of the class members in terms of weight loss. A by-product was increased confidence and self-esteem for most members whether they lost weight or not. I concluded that the experience of belonging to a group that was fun, physically demanding and mentally stimulating through discussion and instruction on lifestyle nutrition and healthy eating, would meet varied cognitive, affective and psychological needs. I took an interest in my group members as far as the class format allowed me to. I advised and weighed and always held the hope that was needed for them to reach a goal of weight loss when they might feel discouraged.

I was aware that many of them would have used me as a parent figure and would lose weight to please me but I was not then a psychotherapist and did not have the skills to be discerning with regard to the implications of this transferential relationship. (Transference, where patients transfer attitudes, beliefs etc. that belong to someone else onto another person, is explained more fully in Chapter 11.) The possible sabotage of this relational dynamic became apparent when they left the group. Some would put the weight back on. At a basic level it can be seen that once someone left the group I was no longer available as a parent figure, not only monitoring, encouraging and believing in the class members but having fun with them too. I observed that those who were less dependent on me, and who did not need to bid for a closer relationship with me, lost weight and maintained the weight loss. Those who wanted more from me were more likely to be the ones that regained weight on leaving the class or would register with a new group and find a new 'parent' in the next group leader.

This suggested to me a difference in the needs of each member, not just at a physical level but psychologically too and that those who had more Adult ego state energy available to them were significantly less dependent on me and the group. They could get what they wanted and internalize their learning and their experience without the interference of either their unhelpful internal Critical Parent or debilitating archaic Child beliefs. There were also those in the group who did not present with an integrated sense of self and struggled to relate except in the few moments when they would be with me in a smaller space in the room whilst weighing and neither did some of these make new relationships within the group. A significant percentage of these members did not lose weight.

When I began working as a Transactional Analyst I wanted to focus on the aspects I had noted from this group work experience, which, with the improved understanding of the human psyche, lead me to look for the distribution of energy in all the ego states of my patients. As I did this, there emerged a correlation between the heightened energy in the Child and Parent ego states and the extent of the patient's struggles to lose weight over a period of time. In addition, there seemed to be a clear connection between the amount of weight gained, and in many cases, the length of time the patient had suffered with the problem of obesity, and the traumatic, painful and discomforting experiences of infancy and early childhood. I hypothesized that the deficit experience lodged in the Child ego state caused the patient to find solace in food and in some instances, protection in an obese body. A powerful and negatively controlling internal Parent ensured low energy in the self-accounting part of the Adult and the natural awareness and needs of the Child ego states. Since sustained weight loss needs to be self-regulated in an environment of self-love and self-worth, it would be difficult for many of these patients to achieve such loss and maintain it.

Belonging in a group and the impact of leaving

I have often observed a commonly held injunction (self-regulated strategy) of 'don't belong' in the Child belief system of the overweight person (often validated by the attitude of our culture). I concluded that part of the deficit re-experienced by leaving the group is that loss of a sense of belonging. It is also possible that the twinning transference (we are all the same here), present in the experience of group members with obesity, provided a supportive mechanism of comfort thus meeting a psychological hunger for recognition and the human need to have a place in a recognizable structure for some level of social bonding. When this was ended, these needs were no longer met in this way and the patient looked to food once again.

It was clear that some members of the group related to me as the good and helpful parent figure who not only taught, encouraged and advised, but who listened, heard and played with them. On leaving the group they would lose this positive parenting. I believe that the influence of the positive parent-figure and the corresponding internalization of that figure into the patient's Parent ego state or internal Parent self is the key to the success of slimming clubs and externally moderated regimes. If the parent figure is empathic, understands the issue and is not shaming, a dependency is set up between leader and member, unless the power of regulation and agency is handed back to the patient.

I discovered some ex-members of my group had internalized me in their own Parent ego state, such that they would say to themselves: 'What would Kathy say now' and would find the answer within themselves. I would see this as a transference cure (Berne 1975, 1994), which is workable in some circumstances. Transference cure is when a patient replaces her own negative Parent messages and introjects with the positive messages of the practitioner. It implies some degree of idealization. Provided separation from me was healthy, the incomplete individuation process was acceptable. It did not, however, completely empower the group member to think for herself or trust herself to continue her self-care without reference to me on given occasions.

These people did not yearn to come back to the group because they had moved on enough not to need the group or me – they did not need the group to fulfil a need to belong. Neither did they have a punitive and self-deprecating, if not self-harming, structure. They did not have to be fat in order to survive or eat excess food in order to feed psychological hungers.

Through retrospective observation of these multi-task groups I formed some basic conclusions about the reasons for the weight loss, maintain and gain process on which to develop my work as a psychotherapist. These were:

1. That some obese patients need a place to belong where they are accepted and can relate to others with similar needs. Group members exercising, discussing, experiencing and playing together provided a place to belong, which for some enabled weight loss and maintenance of the loss whilst remaining a member of the group. These members, however, would be likely to regain weight on leaving the group or during summer recess. This is an important factor in considering a patient's need to stay in a slimming group in order to maintain weight loss and how she may learn to fulfil her need to belong in other ways than those centred around her weight and weight loss and remaining in the group for life.

2. The Parent to Child relationship set up by the group leader and group member can lead to a dependency in the relationship, which will mean that the patient loses weight to please the group leader, not primarily for herself and that without the continuation of that relationship the patient cannot maintain weight loss. This Parent–Child dynamic might also be set up within the psychotherapeutic relationship such that the patient sees the therapist as a parent figure and at times the therapist might be lured into playing this role.

3. That if the patient internalizes the group leader, on leaving the group she may be able to recall the words of the leader, which she then uses to self-regulate, that is to say, she will hear the words or advice from the leader in her head and will 'obey' them. This may constitute a satisfactory outcome, that is to say, she will hear the words or advice the leader in her head and will 'obey' them. This is also a possible consequence of the relationship between therapist and patient and, though the patient may have

internalized a more positive and supportive parent figure, it must be recognized that this is only a part-cure and does not result in the empowerment and autonomy of the patient.

4. That there is a difference in the energy levels in each ego state between those who can lose and maintain weight loss and those who either do not lose or lose and regain the weight. In the latter cases, there is little constant Adult energy available to gain or maintain the autonomy the patient needs in order to manage her own weight in accordance with her wishes. Therapeutically this means that focus on building the patient's Adult ego state energy is important. This will be achieved through updating the Parent ego state such that the patient is no longer responding to outdated messages, and through understanding the fears and needs of the Child ego state. Therapeutic interventions by which these shifts can be achieved are described in ensuing chapters.

5. Some members were unable to lose weight at all, suggesting deeper psychological issues.

6. All ego states need to be used positively in the process of weight loss and maintenance. Overall weight loss will only be maintained when the patient has enough Adult energy to consistently make appropriate choices and to manage relapses without self-recrimination. Positive Parent regulation and self-nurturing are as important as Free Child fun and awareness of body sensations that indicate the difference between psychological and biological hungers.

If a patient fears losing weight she cannot maintain weight loss

If a patient is dependent on her weight for survival then losing weight challenges her ability to survive. Without attention to this belief, she cannot risk losing weight, for if she does so, she senses that she cannot exist. Clearly for patients holding this level of fear, a diet regime is not sufficient in resolving the problem. This is a point at which some practitioners become frustrated and feel defeated. Television programmes based on 'fat clubs' and following a group of people under strict surveillance and an austere plan for weight loss miss entirely the psychological aspects of the problem. I have seen some group members on TV disintegrate under fire from the leaders when they do not lose weight and some display extreme panic. They are treated as failures and of weak character. What actually happens is that as they are forced into situations where they are expected to lose weight they are thrown back on their psychological and archaic fears and do not have the ability to lose weight under such a regime.

Therapeutic considerations when size is the issue

If a patient has a need for a large body size for her protection, the problem is likely to be associated with early development. Thus she is far less able to lose weight or maintain any weight loss than those who experience a more recent onset of obesity. These people also tend to be in the larger weight band of 'morbidly obese' on the BMI. They are likely to have struggled and suffered with their weight over a long period and may have a sense of it being forever. They may also have experienced losing some weight from time to time and regaining the weight they have lost and more. This is a common pattern for long-term victims.

Those who are in the obese (rather than the morbidly obese) bracket of the BMI and who present in therapy may also have struggled with their weight problem for a long time. My observation of these patients is that they are less likely to be using their size for survival but are more likely to have injunctions against being important, being successful, being themselves or being sexual. They often need to play the fat clown, the pleaser and the provider and they feel unattractive and are less likely to make themselves available for sexual relationships whether with a spouse or other. Thus they fulfil their script or life plan by being fat. For these people, learning through the therapeutic people method and process that they can be successful, sexual, important and their true selves will be an important goal. They need to gain self-esteem and value themselves.

My focus in therapy agreed with the patient is not primarily weight loss for the reasons stated previously. However, many patients begin to lose weight within weeks of working psychotherapeutically. This weight loss is not due to dieting or restricting eating but patients report that they do not have the urges to eat in the way they normally have. In many cases of obese patients, this initial weight loss is sustained. Morbidly obese patients and those who unconsciously depend on their size for survival are less likely to make these initial shifts.

Weight gain during therapy

Depending on the nature of the underlying issues to be resolved, some patients may gain weight before being ready to lose more. When a patient is faced with major script change, the archaic defence structures become heightened until the patient feels safe enough psychologically to make the change. This is not a regressive stage and does not normally entail many pounds and does not occur in all cases. Diagnostically it will demonstrate the reaching of a critical stage in the patient's development towards health.

There are clear differences between those who can lose weight and maintain it and those who cannot. Those who can lose weight and maintain weight loss have a more integrated sense of self, demonstrated through a higher level of energy in their Adult ego state and little or no need to seek someone to act as an external control centre or monitor of their own OK-ness. They do not have to attend a group in order to have a sense of belonging though they may enjoy the camaraderie such a group might offer. These women would be unlikely to enter into therapy because of their integrated sense of self and their apparent self-agency, that is, their lack of need to refer to others to monitor their OK-ness and actions.

In contrast, patients who do not lose weight or lose and then regain the weight present a more fragmented sense of self and a neediness for care and control from someone who represents their external control centre and moderator of their OK-ness. They will have less Adult energy available to use the information and experiences in the group. They demonstrate less age-appropriate Child energy and at times, excruciatingly punitive Parent energy. These patients are more likely to present in therapy.

It may sound simplistic to say that those in the highest weight band are those who will experience most difficulty in losing weight. They have more to lose and the task seems daunting and insurmountable. However, the fact is that highly obese and morbidly obese patients who are troubled by their size and eating patterns, also generally demonstrate a deeper level of deficit and disintegration. The body has become the store of their real or perceived trauma. It is the repository of both the memory of traumatic or painful experience and of the ill-attuned caregiver and the repository of the anger against those experiences and caregiver. Their anger is turned inward and they experience self-loathing, which the patient then justifies by her size, which she experiences as repulsive. She believes others also see her in this way and this belief will have been verified by comments made, and name calling, by others. At the same time, unconsciously, the body may be established as the protector. It becomes the defensive armouring that will keep others away and will hide the 'bad' self. It will guard against inappropriate sexuality and, in more extreme cases, will provide the means for survival of self or even another.

Patients who have struggled with their weight for a long time will generally be either very obese or morbidly obese or have deep-seated psychological issues relating to early development, or both. Patients experiencing shorter-term weight problems present different therapeutic consideration.

The shorter-term problem is likely to involve reactive behaviour. That is to say that the patient tends to gain weight during stressful periods of her life, such as bereavement, relationship issues or breakdown, divorce, children leaving home, problems at work, and so forth. For these patients, the psychotherapeutic work is likely to be more cognitive and behavioural, such as making links between the recent stress or trauma and the eating behaviour and discovering satisfying alternatives to self-soothing. If overeating is a repeated pattern in such circumstances, then the patient may need or want to explore why she uses food when overstressed. Interventions will be aimed at the Adult ego state more significantly than the other ego states. The patient can be gradually introduced to the concepts of TA, which gives them the tools to monitor and understand their own actions and experiences in terms of their thoughts, feelings and behaviour patterns independently of the practitioner. This in turn promotes and maintains self-agency. It is important that the patient gets to understand the relationship between thoughts, feelings and behaviours and to be able to put distance between impulse (the urge to eat) and action (the action of eating) in order to allow time for thinking and assessing. This then provides the patient with the choice of whether to eat the food now, later or not at all, which, impulsive eating per se, clearly does not. The use of this intervention with long-term sufferers is a more complex process as will be seen in the ensuing chapters.

The need for food and ability to lose weight

So far, this chapter has concentrated on the extent of the patient's need to maintain a large body size as an indicator of whether she can lose weight and maintain that loss. It is also apparent that there are differing levels of need for food to feed psychological hungers and that whether the patient can lose and maintain weight loss will also be commensurate with the depth of her psychological needs. The more dependent on food the patient is, the less likely she is to lose or maintain weight loss. It is therefore important to ascertain what psychological hungers the patient is attempting to feed and how she can get these needs met appropriately. In my experience, a patient who needs a large body size also tries to assuage psychological hungers with food. However, the patient who uses food in this way may do so without being dependent on her large size as a defence structure.

The patient's ability to lose weight and maintain weight loss is dependent on many factors. If a patient has repeatedly tried diets, slimming clubs, pills, potions and dietary aids and does not maintain a weight loss, it can be concluded that there are psychological reasons behind her struggle. Throughout the following chapters some of these psychological reasons are examined and psychotherapeutic focus and methods offered as a way of attending to the patient's intrapsychic process.

Chapter 5

Inquiry and Diagnosis

Investigation in the early stages of therapy needs to determine whether the patient has a short-term or long-term history of overweight. This can of course be established by straight questions and an invitation to the patient to describe her history of weight gain and losses. It is important to ascertain whether the problem is reactive or persistent and in either case when she remembers her weight becoming an issue. The following questions can be used to glean this information:

1. *How long has the patient had a weight problem?*

   This is to ascertain whether it is a short- or long-term problem. If the problem is short-term, the next question would be whether there was a significant event or change in the patient's life at the point of onset.

2. *Is there any organic reason for being overweight?*

   This is to confirm that there is not a medical reason for the excess weight. With long-term sufferers I recommend that they check with their GP. If there is a medical reason for the patient's weight, the psychotherapeutic journey would be towards integration and management of the fact and would clearly not be focused on understanding the causes of her need to eat or be fat.

3. *At what age was the onset of the problem?*

   This is to allow for later investigation of any significant events, trauma or experience that may indicate deficit in a specific domain of development.

4.   *What is the history of the patient's weight gain and loss?*

This is to ascertain the pattern of dieting, weight loss and weight gain; to understand what interventions the patient has already tried; to learn whether the patient has increased her weight after each dieting phase.

5.   *How does the patient present her eating regime?*

If there is no medical reason for obesity, the patient is overeating. A brief investigation into her own understanding of her eating will indicate whether the patient is in denial or discounting (unconsciously ignoring) the extent of her food intake. Some patients will be transparent about their consumption, others will claim they do not eat very much. In the early stages of therapy, confronting denial or the patient's ability to (unconsciously disregard) aspects of her eating behaviour, discount needs to be non-shaming, supportive and congruent.

6.   *Is the patient willing to agree to a goal of understanding why she uses food?*

I work on the premise that unless the patient understands why she eats she will not break the pattern. Therapy is about enabling the patient to make a decision to lose weight when she is ready to do so. The patient needs to agree to work on understanding the psychological reasons for her weight rather than a goal of weight loss.

7.   *How might the patient sabotage herself?*

The patient is asked to recognize the repeated patterns she uses in order to ensure that she does not get what she wants. If she is able to recognize how she disrupts her progress she can enter into negotiation with the therapist about what part they each play in dealing with the sabotage if and when it interrupts the therapy. Patients seem to be able to recognize their ways of sabotaging themselves in life, for example, getting disillusioned and giving up, leaving, feeling that one transgression means all is lost.

These questions provide a basis for getting to know the patient and how she sees her weight and food consumption. From these basic questions the practitioner will begin to understand whether the patient has a short- or long-term

problem of obesity and the depth of the problem. I recommend these questions for anyone working with patients in this field. Depending on the qualifi-
cations and expertise of the practitioner concerned, these questions will
enable the planning of an appropriate treatment direction with the patient.
Treatment may include referral to other practitioners or clinicians.

These questions lead to an understanding of whether the patient has a
short- or long-term problem. The implications of working with patients in
either of these initial diagnostic categories are outlined below.

Working with patients with short- and long-term problems of obesity and overeating

In my experience, there are significant differences in the presentation of patients
depending on whether they have suffered their condition for a shorter period or
long term and thereby differences in the clinical considerations and treatment
direction. The following is a summary of these differences:

1. *Shorter-term obesity or reactive overeating and weight gain*

    - Weight has been gained over a shorter period of time.

    - The weight gained is not extreme and if this a recurrent
      problem, the weight rarely goes beyond a recognized limit for
      the patient.

    - The weight gain is likely to be reactive, that is, in response to
      a life change or event, or identifiable stressors.

    - Food and weight will not be survival issues.

    - There is likely to be a temporarily reduced sense of self-worth
      and self-esteem, as either or both, cause and effect of the
      weight gain.

    - The patient is likely to report a pattern of overeating in
      stressful situations, generally with prolonged periods of her
      'normal' eating regime.

    - Being the obese person is not likely to be her identity.

    - The patient is not likely to need long-term psychotherapy or
      counselling based on self-psychology.

    - The patient is likely to have more uncontaminated Adult
      energy available and is unlikely to cathect, that is, experience,

the force of a 'scared Child' when discussing how it would be to lose weight. This means that a cognitive style approach with goals of behavioural change may be appropriate and sufficient whether in psychotherapy and counselling or in other related practice.

- The patient will readily see her ability to change obstructive Parent messages and replace them with her own permissions (positive messages).

- Investigating what food means to the patient will be the centre of the therapeutic work. Maintaining a large body size is not usually found to be the pivotal issue.

- Invitations to put distance between impulse and action can be assessed from the patient's Adult, and finding strategies to support evaluating whether she needs to eat this food now, later or not at all will be more easily accessible.

- It is not normally necessary to work with debilitating extremes of, or life-threatening, injunctions.

2.   *Considerations for therapy for long-term or lifelong overeaters and obese patients*

- If the problem of weight and overeating has been long-term or lifelong the issues for resolution are more complex than for the shorter-term problem.

- It is likely that scarcity, lovability and survival issues are at the core of the need to eat and be fat.

- Severe levels of injunctions will be present, particularly those that give rise to self-harming and self-neglect.

- Consider the possible presence of a 'Don't Exist' injunction. Escape hatch closure, that is, the patient's agreement not to harm self or others should be discussed with the patient with the understanding that overeating and obesity constitute harmful behaviours that the patient cannot relinquish. Checking suicidal thoughts or attempts to commit suicide must be carried out early in therapy.

- Early life experience and birth story are likely to be informative and necessary lines of enquiry if the patient has a sense of her weight and eating being lifelong issues.

- Losing weight or images of herself as slim are likely to cause a panic reaction in the patient if weight and/or eating are survival issues.

- Evidence shows a significant incidence of sexual abuse, abuse of sexuality or experience of inappropriate attention to sexual matters, invasion in sexual development and inappropriate or insufficient consideration to the period of passage into adulthood at puberty.

- The patient is likely to be discounting the body self, demonstrated by avoidance of using mirrors to see the body and face.

- She is likely to discount body sensation and to have lost the sensation of true hunger and repleteness.

- The sensation of being overfull will be how the patient knows she has had enough, or too much, to eat. It also enables her to experience her existence.

- Shame is a major issue.

- Psychotherapy focused on the patient's sense of self is indicated.

- Cognitive behavioural therapies are less likely to be successful in initial work with the patient if she fears weight loss.

- Cognitive and behavioural approaches may be appropriate in the final stages of the therapeutic journey, and would be less likely to be effective until survival issues have been resolved.

- Encouraging weight loss is contraindicated except where the patient is dangerously overweight, in which case the therapist may need to negotiate working alongside those in the medical team who weigh and administer dietary regimes. The patient's reactions to weight loss would then be analyzed together in therapy.

- Working with the Child ego state is essential.

- Body work therapies are successful in reclaiming the body self and enabling the patient to be attuned to her own body sensations.

- Self-esteem and self-worth are goals of therapy.

- The therapist needs to be particularly aware of, and work with, her own prejudices.
- The therapeutic journey is likely to be long-term.

The patient's use of food and eating behaviour

In addition to knowing the history of the patient's problem it is important to know how the patient thinks about eating and food in the here and now and her actual eating behaviour. In order to find this out, the following questions may be asked:

- *When does the patient eat?* This will determine whether the patient is reacting to biological hunger or to some other stimulus such as anxiety, loneliness, anger or depression and so forth. Asking this question establishes the significance of the food that is eaten at times other than when the patient might consider normal meal times. Ask *when* the patient eats to be aware of repeated patterns and to investigate associations the patient makes between the situation or types of situations and her impulse to eat.

- *How does the patient eat?* Does she eat in secrecy, when no one is around? Does she eat quickly? Does she stuff her mouth with food as if there is no time to lose or as if there may not be food available later? These questions need to be asked in such a way as to allow the patient to trace her own patterns and it is important not to lead her.

- *Where does the patient eat?* What would be the significance of the places where she chooses to eat, for example, the sitting room, the bedroom, the car, standing or walking around?

- *What does the patient eat?* Do not be judgmental about the foods she chooses. This question is helpful in establishing the significance of those foods for the patient.

When asking when and how and where and what she eats, be alert to her verbal and non-verbal responses in order to build a picture of the patient's eating habits; the meaning of which can be made later in the treatment programme. Be alert to her body language, her tones, gestures and look for incongruities.

Though these questions appear simple and straightforward they can lead to the revelation of the patient's unconscious processes that result in the over-eating. Below, I outline why these questions need to be asked and offer examples of their use in two patient case studies.

The patient case study that follows shows how a patient's story evolved from investigation of *when* she recognized herself to be binge-eating. From the simple question of 'When?', the patient was able to make links with events and relationships in her past that she was unconsciously replaying, and that led her to repeat past eating behaviours. This process enabled a clearer focus for establishing what therapeutic work needed to be done.

Case study: linking past relationships with current eating patterns

Jill sometimes binge-ate at lunch time, leaving her office to buy large amounts of food and eating it somewhere away from other people. She also ate excessively before and after seeing her father. She reported that sometimes, she felt that her husband 'drove' her to eat. It became apparent that there was a link between the three people around whom she felt the compulsion to eat: her father, her female manager and her husband. She was psychologically transfer-ring the traits of her father on to her manager and her husband and was able to do this because each of them displayed some character-istics that reminded her of him. Her father had always been very dominant and controlling. He had not allowed her to be herself ('Don't Be You') and was dismissive of her when she did something that he did not like or agree with. At times he would sulk and passively act out his anger by withdrawing moodily and at other times he would become outwardly angry with her, which involved shouting, banning her to her bedroom, humiliating her in front of her friends or by making her cancel arrangements she had made with them. Though in other spheres, Jill had 'grown up' and was her own master, she continued in the relationship of Adapted Child (con-forming and adapting to the demands of others) to Controlling Parent with her father who in turn persisted with his controlling behaviour, being cool and dismissive if she did not acquiesce with how he wanted her to behave.

Jill cast her manager in the role of father at work. The primary stages were that the manager was, by virtue of her senior position, the parent figure. At times, she used phrases that reminded Jill of her father and occasionally was too busy to be available to her, which Jill

experienced as her father's dismissive actions. In addition, Jill identified a certain look that her manager unwittingly displayed that was
reminiscent of her father. In all these situations Jill was rubber-
banded back into her childhood experience, feeling the sadness,
frustration, shame and at times fear that she associated with her
father's anger, withdrawal and humiliation.

When she was young, her mother would give her food when Jill
was upset. She would sneak food into the bedroom for her when she
had been banished by her father. Jill had learnt from an early age, that
food could be used as recompense and later, she would stock up on
chocolate and cakes and hide them in her bedroom so that she
had her own supply. She would secrete the wrappers behind the
wardrobe or drawers.

When Jill married, she chose a husband who would shout and
then leave the house if he was angry, thus demonstrating both the
anger, of which Jill was archaically scared, and her father's dismissive
behaviour, that is, leaving the house. Her part in this was, in fact, also
to withdraw as she had learnt to do from her father. Her husband
found her way of dealing with conflict irritating, which escalated his
withdrawal behaviour to leaving the house, banging the door as he
went. Eventually, even his minor show of anger could trigger Jill into a
regressed state and she would compulsively reach for sweet and
stodgy conciliatory foods akin to those her mother had used.

The task in therapy was for Jill to understand how her present
behaviour linked to her historical experiences and for us to define
and name the transferential phenomena. In doing this, Jill and I identified her need to resolve the relationship with her father and to end
the unhealthy symbiosis with him in favour of an age-appropriate
attachment. In naming and dissolving the transference with her
manager and husband, Jill began to see them as the people they are
and to tolerate their behaviour traits without being unduly affected
by their anger or withdrawal. In fact, as therapy progressed towards
this end, her husband modified his reactions and outbursts of anger
in response to her calmer and more contented presence.

As Jill began to understand the decisions she had made from
childhood and to investigate the Parent messages lodged in her
Parent ego state, she began significantly to reduce her binge-eating.
As therapy continued, she was able to partake in two-chair, and
multiple chair work (described in Chapter 9) in order to free herself
from both the parental control to which she was still adapting and
from her limiting internal dialogue. She found strategies to deal with
lingering archaic 'rules'.

In the final stage of therapy, the stage at which therapy offers the support and buffer whilst the patient orientates herself to her new learning and new way of being, Jill showed a marked shift in her impulse to eat and lost significant weight. Her relationship with her husband changed, which she felt was due to her move away from discounting him, herself and the situations that made him angry. She realized that she had never been available to manage his anger or discuss the cause of it because of her withdrawal into her Child state. In her work, she learnt to check out with herself whether her manager was angry with, or dismissive of, her. In her Adult ego state, she was able to ask for what she needed and negotiate availability for discussion with her boss. When Jill exercised her new sense of agency and autonomy, food was not required.

Asking *where* is helpful to ascertain whether the patient eats the extra food in the presence of others or alone and secretly, and whether there is a particular place in the house where she eats. Or there may be some other significant place outside the house where the patient binges or 'sneaks' food to. It may be that she shares food with others who also want to eat without scrutiny or criticism. As with the question of *when*, whatever the patient's story there will be implications with regard to her decisions about herself, others and the world. The following case study offers an instructive example of a situation in which asking *where* the patient eats is central to establishing the motivations of her overeating.

Case study: from where to why

Having been a fat child, Sal (280 lbs) would eat extra food when there was no one in the room with her. She would generally sneakily finish food left in a serving dish or eat from the dish in the kitchen whilst clearing the table. She would eat the food quickly in large mouthfuls, and almost swallow without chewing. At the table she often ate very little, feigning lack of need or lack of hunger and thereby supposedly demonstrating being in control of herself and her eating. Eating in public was hard for Sal. She felt self-conscious, as if she should not eat. She associated this with her childhood when she was overweight and her father would watch her eat as if he resented her size. She recalled people making comments about fat people eating in the street, or always seeming to be eating. She concluded that 'If you're fat you shouldn't eat'. And so much of her eating was done clandestinely. She bought stores of biscuits, cakes and chocolate to take home and, although she said she did not hide them away as such, she would place them in containers or behind other items that would render them less visible. She would then eat them, as she described it: 'gradually', resealing the packaging if she could. This way she could pretend to herself that she was not eating to excess until the time came when the food had all gone. She would then be faced with the reality of her behaviour and feel disgusted, guilty and resentful.

Sal always carried food with her when she went out. She would pack food 'in case'. When she was asked 'In case of what?' she could see the absurdity since she was never very far from a food supply. However, her 'in case' was a fear of being without food, as if famine was round the corner. In fact, she always kept a stocked-up supply of chocolate and sweets in the car 'in case' she should be unable to pack her snacks before leaving home. For Sal, this supply issue felt very young, as if she was experiencing something from her infancy, and, as she said, 'sometimes it feels like a matter of life or death'.

Sal believed that others would see her as someone who gained weight easily even though she did not eat very much. She had been able to deny the amounts she ate to such an extent that she underwent numerous tests to ascertain whether she had a medical condition that caused her obesity. Tests showed no reason for her persistent overweight.

Sal had been fat since a child and had developed an early poor relationship with food. Her description of where she ate revealed a need for a constant supply and a desperate compulsion to take in food, often without chewing or tasting before swallowing. When she talked about her need to take a food supply with her when going out in the car, she was able to see the absurdity momentarily, but then displayed agitation at the thought that she may be persuaded to abandon what she was clearly experiencing as a necessary safety measure. At this moment she was unable to find words but was clearly contacting emotion and sensation. In investigating where Sal ate, she and I moved into understanding why she needed to eat in these places.

Asking how highlighted the level of pathological disturbance that the patient tried to soothe and protect against. Both Jill and Sal's psychological needs may have been revealed by asking the question 'How?'. The fact that Sal 'stuffed' food down her throat without chewing revealed the intensity of her agitation and fear. It was not the luscious taste of the food that provided a comforting sensation for her. Jill, however, could describe the sensation of eating her foods. At times she ate with a determination and resolution to finish the large amounts she supplied for herself and would 'lock into' eating non-stop for half an hour or more. She had to eat away from others to ensure she was not disturbed in her quest. Jill could describe her eating and her sensations with comparative ease; Sal displayed fearful discomfort and lost her verbal skills.

Asking *what* the patient eats prompts for links between certain foods and related historical experiences by listening to the patient's account of her normal dietary regime. Some patients will deny they eat the large amounts that would be expected given their size. I would consider carefully the therapeutic value of challenging the patient on her reported food and quantity intake early in treatment. Challenging might be shaming and shame is better faced when a therapeutic alliance and trust are well established. When a large body size forms the core of the defensive armouring it sometimes appears that the patient is actually eating less than one would expect, given her size. However, it must be acknowledged that to produce excessive layers of fat the patient needs to eat large amounts of food unless there is a medical reason for weight gain. Only a small percentage of morbidly obese and higher range obese patients binge-eat in the normal sense of this behaviour.

What the patient eats in terms of the use of food to recreate positive archaic sensation and feelings is also important. The power of smells, tastes and sight of food to stimulate physical and emotional memory is considerable as is particularly well demonstrated in Nigel Slater's book *Toast* (2003). He recalls his life graphically alongside the foods he associates with each new era.

As is evident in the example above, tracking answers to simple questions can lead to the discovery of core areas that can form the basis of treatment planning. The questions reveal key aspects of the patient's life script, beliefs about herself, others and the world and some understanding as to how she might play out her script. From the answers it is possible to generate a TA and developmental diagnosis that can summarize the patient's dependence on food or large body size. Understanding when, where, what and how a patient eats will lead us to the central investigation as to why she needs the food, which is the purpose of the psychotherapy.

The full diagnostic questionnaire

Below I have reproduced a full diagnostic questionnaire which I and many of my colleagues and trainees have found to be a most powerful therapeutic tool. It is important to read the guidelines for its use before including it in a treatment programme. An explanation of each focal area follows the questionnaire.

How to administer the questionnaire

I advocate always using the questionnaire with the patient in an agreed session and would discourage giving it to the patient to complete at home or elsewhere. I have come to this conclusion because of the potency of the questions in exposing core issues: the therapy room provides the containment appropriate for the patient to experience possible overwhelming emotion and pain. The containment exists within the therapist's empathic inquiry and response, his/her attunement, potency to maintain psychological holding (that is, the patient feels held and contained by the potency, competence and understanding of the therapist) and ability to remain in his/her active and observing Adult with the ability to choose between the ego states she wishes to use in response to the patient's needs at any time. The patient needs to sense the protection this containment provides if she should regress or experience consuming fear, anger or sadness.

Except with those questions that need the patient to recall actual events, such as family sayings, and details of diets, the patient should be encouraged to respond quickly rather than deliberating and thinking. The words that occur first in the patient's mind are usually more reliable than when they have been monitored by an intrusive Parent message or an assessing, rational Adult. It is not the rational decisions that limit the patient's ability to lose weight.

The most powerful question is the final one in each section: 'Which of these questions had most impact on you?' This connects the patient with a core issue raised by one of the previous questions. You may wish to use some of the questions from any of the sections for the purpose of gathering information whilst forming the working alliance and therapeutic relationship. In this case you would not ask the final question of each section. The full questionnaire, including the final question, may then be employed at an appropriate stage of treatment.

The questionnaire may be worked with in sections: Historical synopsis and childhood experience; Current synopsis; Diet cycle; Body size, each section forming another stage of treatment direction. It may also be used in its entirety, asking the 'impact' question at the end of each section and as a final question in respect of the whole questionnaire.

It is valuable for the therapist to write down the answers as the patient responds to each question. It is possible to write and remain connected with the patient. It is vital to stay in attuned and empathic contact. At any point, continuing the questions might be contraindicated in favour of pursuing a specific reaction from the patient should a question raise uncomfortable affect (emotion or feeling).

The questionnaire may be used repeatedly, as, at different stages of treatment, the patient will contact discrete new themes from her script. That is to say, in response to her increasing capacity to face her fears and vulnerabilities as her psychotherapeutic journey progresses, she will become conscious of new and deeper influences from her past life and relationships that will not have previously been available to her. Hence, the questions will produce new themes each time they are asked.

Whilst asking the questions, it is pertinent to be aware of inconsistencies in the patient's words, tones, gestures and body language. A particular example might be that of 'gallows' laughter when she is speaking of something disturbingly painful whilst smiling or laughing. It is also important to observe when the patient's affect changes significantly in response to a particular question and to note whether this is the same question she chooses as the one that has had most impact. It would not be unusual for the patient to choose a question that seems to have had less impact to avoid facing a disturbing level of pain or trauma. The therapeutic path is, of course, to follow the route the patient chooses whilst holding the observed significant question in awareness.

Those questions that are followed by *why* need to be asked as two questions, with time to answer the first before asking the second. The focus of treatment at any time is on the question the patient discloses as the most impactful. This may vary each time the questionnaire is used.

Questionnaire

Section I Historical synopsis and childhood experiences

1. What were meal times like for you?
2. Where did you most commonly eat as a child?
3. Who would eat with you?
4. What sort of food were you given?
5. What did you like to eat most? Why?
6. What were you not allowed to eat? Why?
7. Where were you not allowed to eat? Why?
8. Was withdrawal of food used as a punishment?
9. Was food used as a reward?
10. Did all the family eat the same food?
11. What were common sayings in your family about food and eating?
12. *Which of these questions had most impact on you? Why?*

Section II Current synopsis

1. What do you feel before you eat a meal?
2. What do you feel when you eat a meal?
3. What do you eat that you feel you shouldn't?
4. When do you eat that you feel you shouldn't?
5. Where do you eat when you feel you shouldn't?
6. How do you eat when you feel you shouldn't?
7. What is your sensation immediately before you reach for extra food?
8. What do you feel after you have eaten extra food?
9. How important is food to you? Why?
10. What do you relate to most when you feel negative about eating and food? Why?
11. Whom do you relate to most when you feel negative about food?
12. What behaviours from your family experience are you still using for yourself or your own family now? Why?

13. What sayings from your childhood are you still using for yourself and your family now? Why?

14. *Which of these questions had most impact on you? Why?*

Section III Diet cycle

1. What types of diet have you used? What happened?
2. What has made you stop dieting?
3. How do you feel when you are dieting?
4. What do you feel when you are not dieting?
5. What do you feel if you stop the diet?
6. What would you like to have or to do most in relation to food and eating?
7. What happens if you close your eyes and take a few moments to think about dieting?
8. *Which of these questions has been most significant for you?*

Section IV Body size

1. What were the sayings about bodies and body size in your family?
2. What was said about fat people generally?
3. Who was fat in your family?
4. Who was slim in your family?

If there were both fat and slim people in the family:

5. What was said about the fat people/person in your family?
6. What was said about the slim people/person?
7. Who were you like? What was he or she like? How are you like her/him?
8. What sayings do you repeat to yourself or to your family and friends about size now? Why?
9. If you close your eyes, relax and *take some time* to think about being thin or thinner, what happens in your body?
10. *Which question had most impact on you?*

Final Question: *Which question overall has had the most impact on you?*

Explanation of the questions

Related to each question there is likely to be a discernable Parent introject, a Child adaptation and an accompanying phenomenological experience. (The phenomenological experience is the internal experience and sensation that is felt in response to an event or relationship. The body sensation, particularly of ease or unease, is a reliable source of information in the therapeutic process.)

Section I Historical synopsis and childhood experiences. The first set of questions are to ascertain what meal times were like and what the family attitudes were towards food and eating and their use of food for social control. In the ensuing process of enquiry, the therapist gets to understand the interpretations the patient has made with regard to the rituals, sayings, the provision of food and the organization of mealtimes, or lack of them, within the family of origin.

Section II Current synopsis. These questions indicate to the patient those behaviours she may have brought into her adulthood from her past and which she now has a choice of changing. The questions that refer to feelings and sensations open a pathway to ascertain the patient's relationship with food and the triggers that cause impulsive or compulsive eating.

A particularly central question in this section is what sensation the patient experiences immediately before reaching for extra food (Q7). The patient is normally clear about this sensation. The most commonly reported experience is that of agitation and panic. When this is investigated it will lead to the disclosure of the psychological hunger the patient is attempting to satisfy with food.

Section III Diet cycle. It would be unusual for an obese patient to enter therapy without having embarked on a number of slimming diets and regimes. This section is to discover something of the patient's experiences of those regimes and to identify her own understanding of why she abandoned them. Her feelings about dieting and stopping dieting will indicate her internal dialogue, for instance, how she might chastise herself or feel shame.

The questions are also designed to discover the meaning of the diet–non-diet cycle. For example, two possible dietary cycles are 1. that the patient goes on a diet in response to external Parental persuasion. This persuasion might emanate from actual parental figures who tell her she should lose weight, or whom she perceives as wanting her to lose weight. Or it might be that the general cultural attitude towards obesity compels her to start a slimming regime. At the point at which her Child experiences deprivation, the patient rebels and abandons the diet in favour of bingeing or eating excess. The unconscious fear induces the patient to return to her defensive eating pattern or fatty armouring. This indicates a dependence on obesity as an early decisional defence mechanism. 2. The patient may embark on a slimming regime for reasons such as those outlined above but find a loss of her identity accompanies the weight loss. Obesity can become the patient's recognizable identity, without which she fears emptiness.

Section IV Body size. These questions seem to be the most emotive. Question 9 is salient. If the patient has developed a strategy for survival that involves her being fat, she will experience fear. When the patient is ready to reply, it is crucial to listen to her reply and then check out her body physiology. That is, the sensations she is experiencing within her body self. I make this suggestion because, cognitively, the patient would want to be thin. She would be aware of this without closing her eyes. However, her body sensation is more reliable as a measure of her congruence with the welcome of weight loss. In larger obese women and morbidly obese patients, I have observed a tendency towards sensations of panic and fear, sometimes accompanied by disturbance in breathing, dryness in the mouth and tearfulness. For these patients, attention to resolution of her dependence on body size must be the psychotherapeutic goal before any lasting change in eating can be achieved.

Though I have drawn attention to certain questions for explanation of their significance, the actual crucial question in each section and with any repeated use of the questionnaire, will be the one the patient names as the most impactful for her. This will be the agreed therapeutic focus.

The questionnaire with the answers can be referred to at any time in the treatment programme. Each question highlighted by the patient as the most impactful will lead the therapy to core issues for resolution.

Two contrasting series of answers to these questions show the difference in the level of availability and denial of two patients in the morbidly obese weight bracket. The first (A) was less defended (more open and less fearful of facing her demons such that she did not need to withhold information) in the social interaction, the second (B) well defended (both unconsciously and consciously resisting commitment to the process) against thinking about her history and facing the possibility of change.

Section I Historical synopsis and childhood experiences

1. What were meal times like for you?

   A. Non-existent.

   B. Alright.
      Big meals.

2. Where did you most commonly eat as a child?

   A. In front of TV.
      Father ate his in arm chair
      or on a tray in bed.

   B. At the table in kitchen or
      dining room.

3. Who would eat with you?

   A. Mum.

   B. Mother mainly, Father
      worked.

4. What sort of food were you given?

   A. Whatever I wanted.
      I could have crisps and
      chocolate for breakfast if I
      wanted.

   B. Meat and two veg.
      I was never denied
      anything.

5. What did you like to eat most? (why was not relevant)

   A. Chips and chocolate.

   B. Shepherd's pie.
      Veg, pies.

6. What were you not allowed to eat?

   A. Nothing. Except cream –
      when couldn't afford it.

   B. Nothing.

7. Where were you not allowed to eat?

   A. Nowhere.
      I could eat where I
      wanted.

   B. Bedroom, lounge.

8. Was withdrawal of food used as a punishment?

   A. Never.

   B. No.

9. Was food used as a reward?

   A. Yes.

   B. No.

10. Did all the family eat the same food?

    A. No. Dad had to have his within five minutes of getting home. He had to have chips and egg or meat and two veg. Me and Mum ate separately.

    B. Yes.

11. What were common sayings in your family about food and eating?

    A. What do you fancy? Clear your plate.

    B. I was called greedy if I got stomach ache.*

12. *Which of these questions impacted you most? Why?*

    A. Eating what I wanted and where we ate.

    B. None. Can't remember.

*Later Patient B remembered that she was always told to clear her plate.

Section II Current synopsis

1. What do you feel before you eat a meal?

    A. Excited long before. From when I plan it I get more and more excited. Then I really focus on the preparation.

    B. Hungry. Sometimes it's just habit, it's mealtime.

2. What do you feel when you eat a meal?

    A. Lots of positive things. Laughter...happy. Guilt after though – I eat two cream cakes and they're lovely and then I tell myself off.

    B. Enjoyment then when I eat too much – I think 'How stupid'.

3. What do you eat that you feel you shouldn't?

    A. Fish and chips. Butter, big cooked breakfast.

    B. Chocolate, crisps.

4. When do you eat when you feel you shouldn't?

   A. I feel guilty snacking.   B. Evenings are danger times.

5. Where do you eat when you feel you shouldn't?

   A. In car; at desk at work.   B. Living room.
                                          When not at table.

6. How do you eat when you feel you shouldn't?

   A. Quickly, rushed – I stuff   B. No different.
      my mouth.

7. What is your sensation immediately before you reach for extra food?

   A. I feel I am filling up my   B. There is an urgency.
      hunger.   I've got to have it.
      I eat as if there is no
      tomorrow.
      At work if I feel bushed or
      pissed off I eat chocolate.

8. What do you feel after you have eaten extra food?

   A. I can be full and feel I   B. Guilty.
      need more now.
      As if it will not feel as
      good tomorrow.
      I feel a degree of guilt.

9. How important is food to you? Why?

   A. Very.   B. Very, I enjoy it.
      It's the excitement.

10. What do you relate to most when you feel negative about eating and
    food? Why?

    A. I feel fat and ugly.   B. It makes me fatter.
       I will never be slim.
       Annoyed.

11. Whom do you relate to most when you feel negative about food?

   A. My husband.
      We split up once because
      he said he didn't love me
      any more because of
      my fat.
      He was embarrassed to be
      seen out with me.

   B. No one, just myself.

12. What behaviours and sayings from your family experience are you
    still using for yourself or your own family now? Why?

   A. I'll cook you something
      nice it will make you
      feel better.
      I am negative with myself
      when I overeat.

   B. None.
      I never call anyone greedy.
      I fight against thinking
      I'm greedy.

13. *Which of these questions has impacted you most. Why?*

   A. (11) I think of when I was
      being bullied at school.

   B. The sayings (12) and
      the fact that I can't think
      of any.

Section III Diet cycle

1. What types of diet have you used?

   A. Calorie counting; (300
      cals per day)
      Cambridge diet;
      WeightWatchers;
      Rosemary Connolly,
      a few weeks; Slimming
      World twice.

   B. Everything.

   What happened?

   A. Lost three stone when I
      was 20 years old.
      Put more on each time.
      Lost 1½ stone
      maximum since.

   B. Lost and gained more
      each time.
      Gave up.

2. What has made you stop dieting?

   A. Couldn't stick to it.
       Give up.
       Don't succeed.

   B. Got bored.
       One diet made me ill.
       Not quick enough.

3. How do you feel when you are dieting?

   A. Positive, then bored.

   B. Resentful.
       Other people can eat what
       they want.
       I get fed up.
       Bored.

4. What do you feel when you are not dieting?

   A. Happy.
       I can choose my food.
       I feel guilty when I sit
       with others who are slim.
       I don't worry if I am the
       only one eating.

   B. Fat, I suppose.

5. What do you feel if you stop the diet?

   A. Happy and failed.
       I ask myself 'why have I
       failed?'

   B. Relief.

6. What would you like to have or to do most in relation to food and
   eating?

   A. Enjoy foods that are good
       for me.

   B. Cut down the amount
       I eat.

7. What happens if you close your eyes and take a few moments to
   think about dieting?

   A. I see a happy, thin me.
       I feel excitement in
       my chest.
       It's a bit exciting and a
       bit scary.

   B. I feel a churning in my
       stomach.
       Nervous.
       I feel rebellious.
       I don't want to do it.

8. *Which of these questions has been most significant to you?*

   A. The last one.

   B. I can't remember.

Section IV Body size

1. What were the sayings about bodies and body size in your family?

    A. Skinny people were seen as being very negative.

    B. Everyone was plump. Dad was large. Mum was always dieting.

2. What was said about fat people generally?

    A. Nothing negative.

    B. Nothing.

3. Who was fat in your family?

    A. Mum and Dad were big.

    B. Everybody.

4. Who was slim in your family?

    A. No one.

    B. Grandma and Brother.

5. What was said about the fat people/person in your family?

    A. My brother called me fat.

    B. Nothing.

6. What was said about the slim people/person in your family?

    A. N/A.

    B. People were called skinny, as if skinny is not good.

7. Who were you like? What was he or she like? How are you like him or her?

    A. Dad had a temper. I am like him with my temper. I like the same foods as Mum and cooking nice things. I please people by cooking them things.

    B. Father. I am outgoing, friendly, open to people.

8. What sayings do you repeat to yourself, your family and friends about size now? Why?

    A. I make excuses for my weight, lots of excuses.

    B. We still clear the plate (*she related this then to some money issue from the past*).

Inquiry and Diagnosis

Investigation in the early stages of therapy needs to determine whether the patient has a short-term or long-term history of overweight. This can of course be established by straight questions and an invitation to the patient to describe her history of weight gain and losses. It is important to ascertain whether the problem is reactive or persistent and in either case when she remembers her weight becoming an issue. The following questions can be used to glean this information:

1. *How long has the patient had a weight problem?*

   This is to ascertain whether it is a short- or long-term problem. If the problem is short-term, the next question would be whether there was a significant event or change in the patient's life at the point of onset.

2. *Is there any organic reason for being overweight?*

   This is to confirm that there is not a medical reason for the excess weight. With long-term sufferers I recommend that they check with their GP. If there is a medical reason for the patient's weight, the psychotherapeutic journey would be towards integration and management of the fact and would clearly not be focused on understanding the causes of her need to eat or be fat.

3. *At what age was the onset of the problem?*

   This is to allow for later investigation of any significant events, trauma or experience that may indicate deficit in a specific domain of development.

Chapter 6

Ego States

Eric Berne described an ego state as a 'system of feelings which motivates a related set of behaviour patterns' (1964, p.49). There are three basic types of ego states: Parent, Child and Adult. They develop in response to our environment from birth and as we grow. Clarkson (1992) describes ego states as 'chunks of psychic time – complete and discrete units of psychological reality'. I relate to this definition as it indicates that at any given time we are responding to the environment within our own perception and reasoned or unreasoned assessment of what is going on.

The most basic representation of the ego states in the field of Transactional Analysis is as three stacked circles, as shown in Figure 6.1. Each circle symbolizes one of the three ego states and together represent the whole person. Each state 'contains' thoughts, feelings and behaviours that have been controlled or influenced by other people and life experiences. As will be explained in more detail in the chapters that follow, the ego states operate interdependently, so they are always represented as three circles, even when one or more of the states are more dominant.

Each and every moment of our lives we are reacting to other people and situations both consciously and unconsciously, voluntarily and involuntarily. There is both the reality of the activity or happening of the moment and the way it is perceived and understood by the participants. How the event is perceived will depend on what has been experienced before, how what has happened before has been understood and what decisions have been made about one's self and others in one's world in response to those events. For each event there will be some information received that will confirm, add to or deny what has already been understood. This will be 'logged' in the ego states. Ego states are seen as developing over a period of time. For instance, the Adult

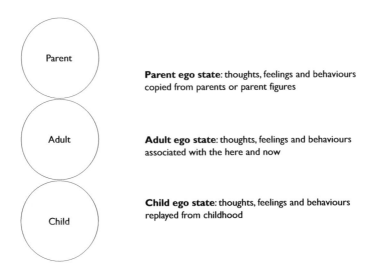

Figure 6.1 The basic ego state model

is not available to the early infant except in terms of a primitive and intuitive form, and the Parent only within the young infant's capacity to judge and self-regulate through its interpretation of how to please the carers on whom it depends. Therefore, early experiences in life are perceived through primitive filters and 'stored' in primitive ego states. Later, when the child begins to symbolize and conceptualize the Adult ego state begins to form.

Ego states are like banks of experience. They pay out and receive in accordance with what is in them until such time as something significantly different happens and what is then available to 'deposit' will change the account. I use ego state analysis both to find what is in the patient's 'account' and to understand how it is paid out. In other words, lodged in the ego state are the experiences, beliefs and conclusions about how to be in the world gleaned from life events (intrapsychic analysis) together with how the patient behaves or interacts with others from those ego states (interpersonal analysis). It was through Berne's observations of people that he concluded that we each have three modes or styles of communicating: Parent, Adult and Child. Why each of us behaves in certain ways in each of these modes in the present is discovered by examining past experience.

As we have seen, use of the questionnaire in Chapter 5 can establish how the patient is behaving, thinking and feeling in the present, which relates to messages she has received and decisions she has made in the past. Practitioner and patient can work together to understand the ego states she is using in the present to regulate herself in accordance with messages and decisions from the past.

It is worth clarifying here that at times discussion about what an ego state actually is can seem to be academic and reifying. As my aim is to demonstrate how to *use* ego state analysis to understand the behaviour of the overweight patient, rather than to give a complete academic description of an ego state (attempts at which can be read elsewhere) I use shorthand phrases that may seem as though I am describing an entity rather than a constructed mode of being. This is a conscious decision to enable the non-Transactional Analyst to understand and use the theory. I have always felt that the beauty of TA is that the practitioner can share the basic tools for understanding what makes people behave as they do with the patient who wants to know.

When a patient 'rubber-bands' into the past, she does not only remember that past but re-experiences it phenomenologically. In fact, she can re-enter past encounters sensing the experience, but not remembering it, if the regression takes her back to pre-verbal infancy. Patients feel those feelings in the here and now. The fact that they do remain in the here and now whilst recalling the past in this way, demonstrates how the ego state energy related to the past influences the present and is part of it. It is not fixed in the past but is with us continuously. I treat ego states as containers of historical experience as well as the manifestations of those experiences that manipulate us consciously or unconsciously in the present.

A child will have both positive and negative experiences throughout her development. A child needs 'good enough' parenting in order to thrive. Berne saw the negative experiences as bent pennies in a pile of straight pennies, which represent good experience (1961, p.53). Provided there are enough straight pennies the pile will stand. Too many bent pennies and it will collapse. Too many bad experiences cause disorganization of the self and psychological disturbance. In working with the Child ego state both positive/happy and negative/painful experiences can be used to effect change in the patient.

From birth, the developing infant holds a sense of the primary, and subsequent, carers. In her Child ego state she will hold her experience of her mother, who initially represents her world. She will internalize this experience of the mother, together with her own non-reasoned interpretation of it. She begins to make decisions about self, others and the world in relation to her primitive understanding of events.

The Parent ego state, symbolized in Transactional Analysis literature as P2, starts to develop later than the Child ego state, which holds the primitive Parent, symbolized by P1. P1 is also known as the Magical Parent. It is the fantasized version of the intimations the child perceives as the messages delivered by the behaviour of her parents. It has both frightening and comforting components. P2 is identifiable by the fact that the words, behaviours and emotional displays, or lack of them, may be traced to actual figures in the child's life. She will speak like her mother, sit like her mother, sulk or get angry like her father, repeat sayings that will have been passed down from identifiable sources, she will reproduce opinions of others, and so on. Many of these introjected others will be supportive, useful and benign. Others will be limiting, debilitating and toxic.

The Parent ego state is dynamic, not fixed, which means that we are constantly available for change of attitudes and beliefs; we are able to change our response to new information and understanding. I call this "updating". At the same time, we still respond to messages we have not yet updated or checked out in the present; this I call the archaic Parent. The patient will therefore function from her Parent ego state either in an archaic manner, or in updated mode. The Parent is constantly developing both from significant other people and cultures around her and from figures she may create.

New positive information can be incorporated into the Parent ego state at any age. What and who is internalized will be determined by the Child ego state. The Child self needs to be convinced that the parent figure (or culture) from whom new information will be assimilated is dependable, trustworthy and, in most cases, more potent than the original parent.

Whilst the parent is giving verbal and non-verbal messages to the child, the child is experiencing the receiving of those messages and making her own interpretation.

The Child ego state contains the experience of being a child in the family, environment or culture in which the patient lives. It is a set of feelings, attitudes and behaviours that are 'relics of the individual's own childhood experiences' (Berne 1961). When in Child ego state, the patient will replay the thoughts, feelings and behaviours from her childhood. The Adapted Child displays behaviour that adapts to the rules of the parent others. This may be a direct compliance or a negative response to the message. If the latter, it is the part of the adaptation that rebels (Rebellious Child). The Free Child is manifested by natural forms of behaviour responding to needs and gratification of them. Physis, or drive to survive, emanates from the Child ego state. A child may rebel against eating food as a way of gaining power and self-mastery or because she does not like the food offered. The former may be seen as adapted rebellion. She rebels against the required adaptation to be servant to the parent's inability to give her space to develop her own sense of self, identity and individuation. Refusing food because of dislike of the taste would be a natural child response.

The Adult ego state deals with here and now reality. Responses from the Adult are commensurate with age and circumstance. The Adult ego state will observe and make appropriate meaning. Therapeutically the Adult is used to make meaning of past experience in relation to the present and to make new decisions for the future.

The different ego states may be in our consciousness simultaneously. A patient may hear her mother's voice in her head saying 'Eat up, think of the starving millions' and at the same time be aware in her Adult that she can deny that command from a rational sense of the here and now. However, she is compelled to eat by the Child that needs to obey the Parent regardless of her Adult understanding that eating everything on her plate will not help any starving nation. In the same way, though more subtly, a patient may feel the pain of her overeating and her size in her Free Child ego state and laugh from her Adapted Child whilst describing it.

When a patient speaks from an adaptation as if she is in the present and using Adult thinking she is said to be speaking from a contaminated Adult. The contamination may be by the Parent self or the Child self. The therapeutic direction would then be to bring the contaminations into awareness in order that the patient may decide how she wants to feel, think and behave in the present.

Not surprisingly most of the behaviour met in patients with eating disorders will be Parent and Child. The ultimate aim is for the patient to make decisions from her Adult ego state about her eating and her size although it may be that internalizing a new parent figure (the therapist or practitioner) will be sufficient for the patient to change her behaviour and effect a more comfortable lifestyle.

The Child ego state is most influential. The patient can only internalize a new parent figure if that parent figure is agreeable to the Child self. The Adult can only make new decisions and put them into practice if the Child has already been convinced of the efficacy of those decisions. Hence there is little point in a patient dieting if her Child holds fears and fantasies as to what will happen if she loses weight. The Child fear will be stronger than any Adult assessment of the situation. This is why diets fail or patients do not maintain weight loss. Until the Child self is convinced of the safety and efficacy of losing weight, the patient cannot achieve it.

As previously noted, when past experiences are evoked they will be re-experienced with the associated thoughts, feelings and behaviours. The patient may see the scene, hear the voices (or other sounds) and re-contact the emotions. She may smell the smells, sense the textures, taste the tastes and clearly hear the actual words spoken at the time. If these are positive, they will make the patient feel good, unless the person associated with these feelings has gone, in which case she may experience grief for that loss whilst still maintaining the phenomenological sense of warmth, comfort etc. If they are negative, the patient will feel the pain and fear again. This dynamic of the patient's unconscious experience can be brought into awareness through enquiry.

It is interesting to observe that any of the five senses may be the catalyst for regression. Smells are particularly powerful in the involuntary recollection of past events as are tastes. This is particularly significant in the experience of the overweight patient, who will be rubber-banded back into the past by the sensory encounter with food. Likewise she will use the taste and the smells of food to regain the associated desired experiences.

Contamination of the Adult ego state

The following chapters will refer to the decontamination process. Contamination is seen as the patient operating from unscrutinized belief systems and feelings from the past as if they are still appropriate in the present when they are not. Parts of the diagnostic questionnaire in Chapter 5 are aimed at revealing some of these beliefs. Contamination is represented in Figure 6.2 below. Though the figure displays a double contamination, it is important to focus on either a Parent or a Child contamination as a starting point in the therapeutic process of decontamination. This means specific work with either the Parent or the Child in ways described in the following chapters. However, as our psyche is not psychologically actually divided into such neat and discrete sections of self and my own belief is that changes in one ego state must affect the energy in others, movement in the decontamination of the Adult by freeing it from Parent introjects will also affect the Child response. Likewise, shifts in releasing the Adult from Child beliefs will have repercussions for the Parent. This way of thinking about the psyche recognizes the wholeness of our being.

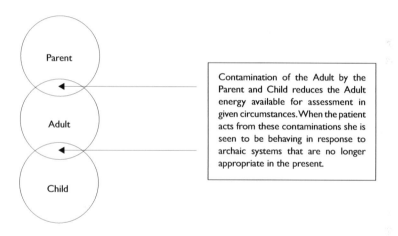

Figure 6.2 Diagram showing contamination of Adult by both the Parent and Child ego states

The following chapters describe working with the three ego states. You will note that when I describe the ego state I use the capital letters P, A and C. For the actual person of the parent, adult and child, I use lower case initial letters.

Chapter 7

The Parent Ego State

The Parent ego state contains the historical record of the influential figures in our lives. The most significant of these are mother as the usual primary carer and father. Other parent figures may be grandparents, school teachers, older siblings, aunts, uncles, neighbours, in fact anyone with whom the child interacts. The Parent ego state also contains the rules, norms and values of the community and culture within which the patient lives. The thoughts, feelings and behaviours of the significant other person as experienced by the child may be 'swallowed' whole. This is called introjection. This would mean that the child and later the grown-up would clearly hear and use the language that the parent figure used. When we hear someone say 'You won't have pudding unless you eat up what's on your plate', it is likely that that person is repeating the exact words of her mother without thinking whether she believes that it is the right thing to say to her own youngster. In addition, it may be that that person is also still responding to the message without scrutiny, believing that it is not right to eat a second course if the first has not been finished up.

New information can be incorporated into the Parent ego state at any age. The Child self needs to be sure that the parent figure from whom new information will be assimilated is dependable, trustworthy and in most cases more potent than the original parent. The patient will only replace old Parent introjects in an environment of safety and will only re-decide when it feels anodyne for her to do so, when the Child is convinced that there will be no adverse repercussions that she cannot handle with the aid of her positive Controlling Parent, Nurturing Parent and most significantly her Adult. This clearly has consequences for the therapeutic relationship and the transferential phenomena in the therapy room.

An initial stage in the analysis with the overweight patient is to discover parental messages from actual parents with regard to food, to eating and to size. The diagnostic questionnaire traces these messages. The purpose is two-fold. First, to ascertain what the patient may be hearing in the internal dialogue or monologue and whether she is still responding from outdated commands. Secondly, to determine the patient's responses to the idea of changing these Parent introjects. When the patient readily sees that she is responding from outdated instructions and has Adult energy to observe herself and assess the situation, and if her Child is not threatened by change, she will be able to think differently about her eating. The Parent message will no longer be effective. This patient will not feel anxious about 'disobeying'. If, however, the patient displays anxiety she will not be able to change her eating practice until the underlying fears are faced and resolved.

Case study: identifying introjects

Alison was a patient who presented with the problem of her weight. She was about 42 lbs overweight and had dieted numerous times. Early in the therapy I was able to work with Alison to identify her Parent introjects because she seemed to demonstrate a good level of Adult energy with regard to exploring the issues around her weight and eating habits. She did not display undue anxiety.

I asked Alison to think of her family sayings. Amongst these was the guilt engendered by the notion that there were millions without food and that she had the selfishness to want to leave food whilst others in the world were starving. Her mother also told her she could not have a pudding unless she ate all her first course and that she would not be allowed to leave the table until she had finished her food. The outcome of these directions was that Alison still did not leave food on her plate, but if she did she would feel guilty and would certainly not eat any pudding unless she had cleared her plate. She cleared her plate and ate pudding.

Therapist:	What do you think about these instructions now?
Alison:	I think they are silly. I know that food left on my plate won't help others at all, but somehow I feel pushed into still eating stuff I don't want to eat.
Therapist:	Why do you think you do that?
Alison:	I don't know. I hate it. I don't seem to have control. I suppose I do it without thinking.

Therapist:	What would happen if you did think about it? If you take time to think.
Alison:	Are you thinking I might be able to leave some?
Therapist:	What would happen if you did?
Alison:	(*Laughter*). Nothing. There is no one to make me eat any more, well not when I'm at home.
Therapist:	And when you are not at home?
Alison:	No, no one else can force me to eat can they? It makes no sense that if I leave something anyone else is going to be better or worse off really. I am not going to send the food to anyone, am I? And it is up to me if I want pudding.
Therapist:	Yes.
Alison:	Is it that simple?
Therapist:	What are you feeling now?
Alison:	OK. I feel quite together.
Therapist:	What did you feel when you were obeying those Parent messages?
Alison:	When I finished everything on my plate you mean?
Therapist:	Yes.
Alison:	I don't think I was aware of feeling anything, I just did it.
Therapist:	And afterwards?
Alison:	Resentful I suppose. Certainly uncomfortable. I wasn't aware of this. I mean, I didn't know I was... Well I did... What I mean is, I obviously had that message to eat up but it was sort of quiet, in the background and I didn't know about it.
Therapist:	What would your mother say now if you decide not to finish your plate, or to have some pudding even if you hadn't eaten your entire first course?
Alison:	Well, I don't think she would say anything now. I don't even know if she still holds by it, to tell you the truth. Isn't that odd? I just don't think she would say anything or if she did, she would say it in a careful way... No, I don't think she would even comment... How strange! Huh!
Therapist:	Just suppose she did, what would you do?
Alison:	I would tell her it is my business what I do and that I am a grown woman. But I really don't think she will.
Therapist:	What does that mean to you now...that your mother will not say anything about leaving food?

Alison: I can do what I want. I can leave anything I don't want.
                 Yes, I can.

In this case, Alison used her Adult to consider what she was doing and why she was doing it invoked by my interventions inviting her to think. She traced the obligation to finish her food to her mother's pressure and was able to recall actual words her mother said. She realized that she had internalized these messages to the point of such familiarity that she did not recognize what compelled her to eat in this way. It may have been that her mother also carried these messages from her mother. Alison realized she used such words with her own children from time to time and was intrigued to realize she had never questioned them. Alison's Child self was not threatened by her decision to act differently. This was apparent in her clear response, her physical posture and her Adult tones. She did not exhibit any hesitation that was not part of her thinking process and did not show fear. After this session, each time she ate, Alison was aware of the voice in her head that said she must eat all her food and she refused to comply. Eventually the 'voice' in her Parent gave up. She also started to listen for other messages she might be obeying about food or about being at the table and eating. She called it 'clearing out'.

Alison felt a release from binding introjects, a release that she said felt to her far greater than the piece of work we had done seemed to warrant. In fact the essence of the work was not only about her need to free herself from messages that seemed to coerce her to eat extra food but about her ability to take her role as an adult in the here and now. To be herself. The decontamination was more than the fact that she realized she was responding in the present as if in the past in relation to her clearing her plate. She simultaneously understood her right to autonomy and sensed a strong physiological reaction that she described as excitement: 'It is like I have come out of a cage' was her description.

Though decontamination implies a renewed understanding of the patient's behaviour in response to internalized others, and in this case the recognition of the contaminating Parent, I do not believe that it ever clarifies the Adult without there being a corresponding freeing in the Child. In fact, change in one ego state will effect some change in all other parts of self, or ego states. Freeing the Child must also have some meaning in the Parent self. For Alison 'coming out of her cage' meant a freedom for her Child self even though the decontamination of the Adult rested with recognizing Parent messages.

Alison had significant Adult energy available to work with this aspect of her eating and her size. This together with the unthreatened Child within meant that she responded positively to this treatment process. There was no stuck place or impasse once Alison had brought the subconscious process to consciousness.

When a patient does reach an impasse (a stuck place) this line of empathic enquiry will serve to reveal the subconscious or unconscious process that is keeping the patient eating or fat. I will see and hear the resistance to think and engage Adult energy to make a new decision, though the Adult may still be available as an observer to the process. The work involves all three ego states with particular acknowledgement of the scared Child. This work cannot be done without a well-founded working alliance and established therapeutic relationship between patient and clinician.

The focus with another patient who was obeying the same archaic command developed very differently as can be seen in the next case study.

Case study: a shift from passive adaptation to active rebellion

Pat had been in therapy with me for about 20 weeks when I worked in this way with her Parent ego state. She had been in therapy before and had tried various alternative therapies for a number of health and psychological matters. The knowledge of what, in general terms, therapy entails, allowed her to establish a good enough relationship with me to work at deeper levels of meaning and understanding. However, I did sense at times that her Parent self was watching and waiting for me to let her down or get it wrong for her. She particularly transferred her experience of her mother on to me. She would become impatient and questioning. She was also waiting for me to cure her. She would ask me how she was getting on and whether this process was what I would expect. Gradually she was able to see that she needed to be active in her treatment direction rather than passive. It is not unusual for patients to come to 'the expert' for help and to expect in some way to be told what to do as they have always been told before at the slimming clubs and surgeries, by the diet books, magazines and media and by well-meaning relatives and friends. The therapist or practitioner can also experience the powerlessness the patient feels as she projects this feeling onto the practitioner within the unconscious process. This is called transference and is dealt with more fully in later chapters. I strongly felt and jostled with, both the challenge to my potency that I perceived as being the powerlessness Pat was projecting onto me and the pull to come up with a solution in order not to let her down as her parents did. Her Child wanted me to succeed, whatever that meant, whilst her Parent waited for me to fail.

The work I describe here followed an enquiry by my patient about how she was getting on and whether things were developing as I would expect. There is certainly a pull to take up a Controlling Parent role. I shared my thoughts on her process and my observation that she expected me to be the sole monitor of her progress towards change. Her own measure was that she had not yet lost weight. She said I was the expert and had more idea of what was needed.

In the discussion that ensued I realized that Pat was too vulnerable to open herself to confrontation of her passivity. A passivity she had had to develop when sexually abused. I therefore decided to respond to her need for me to choose a therapeutic intervention that felt safe for her. The fact that she would initially see the intervention of exploration of Parent messages as an experiment provided her with a boundaried framework that she felt safe to enter. This was a recognizable pattern. Pat would invariably seem to submit fully to the process whilst keeping a part of herself out of it. This was a behavioural process that echoed her management of her sexual abuse.

I suggested to Pat that we might again investigate her Parent messages concerning eating and food. When I asked Pat to bring to mind one of her Parent messages, she said the most obvious one was 'Finish your plate, think of the starving millions'. I noted that she was not yet fully engaging in the process and felt that she was indeed playing along with an 'experiment'. Pat clearly enjoyed the attention I gave her and specifically when she saw me as the one who would take control, something her mother had never done. I was also aware that underneath was the frightened child who had been let down by her parents and who had had to find her own containment for her abuse. She had been sexually abused by her father, which was ignored by her mother and older sister. Trust was as yet still in the balance.

Pat showed no sign of recognition of the absurdity of the statement she had chosen as a focus. I asked if she was still responding by obeying the directive. She thought for a while and said she supposed she was. The work continued as follows:

Therapist:	Who is it you hear saying 'Eat up, think of the starving children'?
Pat:	My mother.
Therapist:	Do you still want to obey your mother?
Pat:	(*With a little heightened energy.*) No, I don't, not at all. But…I am not sure I can do any different.
Therapist:	Why?
Pat:	I don't know. I just feel…I don't want to obey her. It would give me great pleasure not to obey her. I could try. (*Her use of the word 'try' and her tones and body language suggested that she was not convinced of her ability to think or behave differently.*)
Therapist:	How about you close your eyes and imagine you have a plate of food in front of you. (*Pat settled back in her chair and closed her eyes.*)
Pat:	Mm. Yeh.
Therapist:	Now imagine yourself leaving some of that food on the plate. (*Pat became agitated. There was a long pause.*)
Pat:	I can't leave the food. It is signalling me to eat it. It feels like I have no choice.
Therapist:	What do you mean when you say 'signalling'?
Pat:	It is as though someone is speaking to me from inside the food.
Therapist:	Do you know who is speaking to you from inside the food?
Pat:	It is my father. (*Pause; Pat looks both agitated and confused.*)
Therapist:	Your father.
Pat:	Yes. It is as though he is saying 'Come on, eat me, you can't resist can you? You have to eat me.' I have to obey. (*Pat showed signs of losing energy.*)
Therapist:	What are you feeling right now?
Pat:	Powerless. He controls me. He wants me to eat so he can keep control. It is another way that he has power over me.
Therapist:	When else did he have power over you?
Pat:	When he abused me.
Therapist:	When he abused you, you felt powerless.
Pat:	Yes…but I would just give in and detach from what he was doing. I would wait for it all to be over. There

Therapist: was nothing I could do to stop him, so I disconnected until it was over.

Therapist: Do you detach from the food when you eat it?

Pat: No. I enjoy my food. (*Pause.*) I don't think about what I am doing though. When we talked about being in touch with my body sensation enough to know that I have had enough, I couldn't do it. I can't think about these things when I eat. I get on with eating. I suppose in that sense I detach because I am not thinking about what I eat. I just eat, enjoy the food and don't think about what I am doing or what we do here or anything.

Therapist: And the voice behind the food that signals you is your father's.

Pat: Yes.

Therapist: What would happen if you didn't eat all the food on your plate, if you left some? If in fact you disobeyed?

Pat: (*Giggles.*) That would be good. I like that idea. (*Thinks with an amused grin.*) Yeh, that would be good to do.

Therapist: So we have two aspects to this now. One is your mother's message about eating because of the starving nations and the other, which is your father gaining power over you.

Pat: Yeh. I sort of have to deal with both. I could disobey both of them. As I said, she never acknowledged that I was being abused; she must have had some idea of something going on, but never did anything about it. It's like I would gain some power over both of them if I refused to clean my plate. (*Pat thinks for a while.*) Yeh, I think I could do that.

Pat decided on a plan to test out her response to food on her plate from time to time. She felt excited about her sense of rebelliousness and felt some power in this. She was curious to see whether she reacted differently to the food and her need to eat large quantities and finish it all.

In the course of this piece of work, I started with attention to internalized Parent messages. There is, of course, no power in those messages unless the Child adapts. Pat began to feel her own potency when she was amused at the idea of rebelling and felt that it was safe to do that. Rebelliousness is active energy rather than the passive energy that is in the adaptation. It is therefore useful energy. At this stage it was important for Pat to feel that she has some potency herself even if it is in 'getting one over' her father and her mother. In reality neither her mother nor her father has this influence now. She never sees her father and her mother does not repeat the seemingly universal slogan. It is her internalized Parent that she is defying in choosing to leave food on the plate.

Pat chose rebellion. Rebelliousness is an active response rather than the passive alternative of adaptation. It is not always possible for the patient to rebel but the work Pat and I had already done together had resolved some of her position of impotence such that she was able to switch her energy in this instance from passivity to activity. She still had unresolved issues relating to the sexual abuse and self-empowerment was a precondition for effective resolution. Gaining power over eating, even though initially through rebellion, would strengthen her Adult and her positive Parent ego states, which would in turn provide a self-supporting internal structure that would allow her to free herself from limiting Child beliefs.

Of course this work was only a small step towards a cure for Pat. What was revealed was how she felt that she was being compelled to eat by forces she experienced as external to herself. She was describing 'the other in me'. When she decided she could rebel against the other she felt more potent and recognized that her rebelliousness rendered her more powerful. Though she saw this as rebelling against actual parent figures she was in fact shifting internal ego state energy away from this negatively influential Parent. I expected some repercussions since she had related the voice calling her to overeat to her abusive father and she clearly had not as yet resolved all she needed to in respect of that sexual abuse.

Her Child immediately found a way to maintain the status quo by suggesting she take more food onto her plate so that she could have as much as she wanted and still leave some. However, as long as she upheld her sense of power through rebellion she was able to stop putting extra food on to her plate and to eat less whilst maintaining that she now had a choice.

Later focus in Pat's psychotherapy centred on her continued acceptance and integration of her sexual abuse. She did manage to leave food on her plate and as she did this, she recognized that she could exercise her potency in other spheres, a potency that had been lost to her as she necessarily gave her self up to the abuse. She began to re-associate with her body self and thereby with the physical sensation that would inform her of the difference between hunger for food and other psychological hungers. She developed a renewed level of body awareness that would allow her to know when she had had enough food before she felt overfull and distended. She found this intriguing.

Through attention to a simple parental instruction relating to clearing her plate, Pat shifted into a reorganized ego state energy system that permitted us to work with her Child ego state. Part of this work was geared to body work as described in Chapter 12.

Working directly with the Parent ego state

There are several ways clinicians can think about working directly with the Parent ego state. Before embarking on any of the methods of working, the therapeutic relationship, working alliance and trust must have been established. The timing of such work will depend on a number of factors including:

1. The competence and expertise of the therapist and his or her familiarity with this methodology.

2. The level of trust in the therapist.

3. The potency of the therapist as perceived by the patient, particularly in relation to the power of the parent figure and thereby the internalized Parent. The therapist must be experienced by the patient as more powerful than the original parent or internalized Parent such that where necessary the therapist can interpose herself between the patient's Parent and Child ego states.

4. The skill of the therapist in working in this way and his or her trust in self to hold the process and provide a safe environment in which to enable the patient to confront either the negative aspects of her Parent ego state or her demonic self that lies within the Child ego state and regulates her behaviour through fear.

5. The length of time the patient has been overweight or overeating and thus the depth of the pathological belief system that supports the need for food or size as a defence.

6. The awareness of both the therapist and the patient with regard to the meaning of working in this way.

The following are some methods I have found useful in working with obese patients. I illustrate each using patients' material.

- *The patient role-plays the actual parent figure (the Parent Interview)* from whom she knows she has received a certain limiting message, which she is still responding to but not wishing to do so in the present. The therapist works with the patient in the role of her parent, which essentially represents the patient's Parent ego state.

- *The therapist enables the patient to interview her own parent figure in two-chair work* where the patient remains herself in the present in one chair and the other chair is the chair that will represent the actual parent figure. The patient moves from one chair to the other cathecting the energy of that parent in the parent chair. She responds from that Parent ego state to her own questions and discussion. In this way she produces a dialogue between herself and her internalized other.

- *The patient may imagine that she is dialoguing with food as the Parent* * and will put her image of the food on the other chair and work in dialogue with it.

- *The patient may 'put' the weight on the other chair* as the Parent* and dialogue with it.

- *Three-chair work*, where the patient chooses a chair for each of her three ego states: Parent, Adult and Child. There follows a three-way process. With her Adult she becomes observer to her own dialogue, which she then discusses with the therapist. She is also encouraged to speak from her Adult to the other ego states as an observer to the process, an informer of here and now reality, as an assessor, mediator and as a potential integrating influence.

The Parent interview and the two-chair work that set up a 'dialogue' between the patient as her perceived parent and herself are different techniques from the three-chair work where the patient represents her internal dialogue between her ego states. Each way of working attends to the patient's belief systems and both the content and internal functional dialogic of her ego

---

*   Clearly food and weight are not ego states and neither are they representative of any one else's ego state. However, their significance is in providing protection and feeding hungers, which may be translated as parent functions. To this extent, I take the liberty of including them here.

states. *A caution*: multiple-chair-work is contraindicated or needs to proceed with extreme caution and only after a lengthy period in therapy for those patients who display bipolar traits or disorders. This is because the patient's bi-polar presentation may be reinforced by a process that separates the different representations of the self.

The purpose of multiple-chair techniques is for understanding the internal dialogue that keeps the patient in script, a recognition of the option to use ego states other than those the patient is using or normally uses in similar circumstances and integration of all the ego states. Shifting chairs assists Adult awareness. The patient is often surprised by the power of the energy or lack of it that she feels in each ego state. This is clearly about awareness of the psychological processes that govern the patient's choices with regard to thinking, feeling and behaving. Before the chair work, the patient has little idea of her distribution of ego state energy.

When the patient plays the part of an actual parent she talks from her own understanding of that parent's patterns of communication and meaning, which involves her own interpretation of them. She is therefore responding from an internalization of that parent into her own Parent ego states. When I work with or 'interview' this parental representation I am working with the patient's Parent ego state.

The Parent interview

The therapist needs to think carefully about what is to be achieved from this type of intervention. The Adult ego state of the patient needs to be available even if the patient submerges herself in the Parent role. This has implications for when this might be a pertinent operation in a patient's treatment plan. There is no hard rule about when to use this technique once trust and relationship have been sufficiently established. This is, like any other intervention, guided by the expertise and awareness of the therapist.

This is a technique that is more in the control of the therapist than the others described in so far as she is able to monitor the Parent responses, and provided the clinician is seen by the patient as more potent than the internalized Parent she can use whatever methods she chooses to effectively guide the interview. The patient, whilst playing the role of mother or father will also be watching from her Child and her Adult. An attuned therapist will feel the presence or absence of these energies, giving her additional information on her choice of interventions. She may feel the patient's Child enjoying the discussion between the therapist and her mother or the Child's scare as the process develops. This scare, which may be detected in the body language, tones and gestures of the patient, indicates a fear of change. Since from infancy the patient developed strategies for survival in response to her environment, challenge to some of these strategies will feel 'scary' to the patient. Generally, the patient is initially unaware of the reason for her scared feelings, but they are certainly indicative of a need for the therapist to address the scare. I associate this scare with the Child ego state that indicates that the patient has reacted from her Child self to something that has arisen in the process of the Parent interview.

The purpose of the interview is not to humiliate the Parent. The therapist needs to remain respectful and empathic with the Parent as much as she would with the patient herself. She may allow herself the same firmness she would allow herself when working with the patient in any other challenging circumstance.

Prior to the patient becoming her perceived parent, there needs to be discussion about what the purpose of the piece of work is. This must not be done within the process of the work once embarked upon as this would lead to role confusion.

The patient may be able to hold an observing role whilst the interview in role proceeds or may be able to cathect enough Adult to examine the process subsequently. Or the patient may need to watch from her Child ego state in which case the therapist needs to be potent enough to conduct an effective and productive exchange with the patient's representation of her parent figure. It is therefore necessary to use this technique when the therapist has a sense of the power of the parent in question and her own potency with regard to that power. In my view this potency resides in an integrated sense of self and the Adult ego state, though the therapist may at some stage use her Parent ego state should this be necessary and provided her Parent can meet the strength of the patient's actual parent. Such work is counterproductive if the therapist is overpowered by the patient's introjected parent other.

The patient needs to sit in a different chair from where she normally sits. This is important to provide a separate space in which she can become her Parent and as far as possible leave behind her usual therapy persona. The more the patient feels her Parent energy the more real will be her responses. If the patient displays signs of agitation as the parent figure and this is not part of the behaviour of that parent, then the work needs to stop and be investigated. The aim of the work is to release the patient from limiting and/or harmful introjects and to enable her eventually to make a new decision in the here and now.

Case study: Parent interview, Sal

Sal elected to be her father. Her father had always been critical about her weight, taking, what at times, seemed an inappropriate interest in her body development. He started weighing her every week, some-times even more often and kept a record of her weight. When she was able to go to the chemist to be weighed she was sent with her weight card to be filled out and her father checked it each week. Sometimes he would put the record of her weight gains on the fridge door. This petrified her. Sal ate throughout the week as she panicked about the next weighing session. She found sources of sweet stuffs with neighbours, her friends and her mother's cupboard. She bought food with the money she was supposed to be saving in her piggy bank and even at six years old would occasionally steal sweets from the local shop. In adolescence her father seemed to take a disturbing interest in her body development. He was reluctant for her to have a bra and discussed her menstrual cycle with her mother.

Sal felt anxious about the role she was about to play and we discussed her safety, her ability to stop whenever she wanted or needed to and what my responsibility would be if she became distressed.

When Sal became father, she changed within moments. She took on the role of a dominant, impatient figure. His name was Jack and I introduced myself to 'him', calling 'him' by name. The first response from Sal as her father was to say what nonsense this is. Sal should be getting on with her life not spending precious money on 'this indul-gent crap'.

I said that Sal wanted to get on with her life but felt unable to do so in the way she wanted. Part of the problem for Sal was her weight... Sal, as Jack, interrupted and in angry tones, shouted that Sal had always been fat and that he had tried hard to get her to lose weight.

I said I knew that he weighed her weekly and asked why he did that.

He said that it was the only way he knew how to help her. The doctors had taken no notice.

I commented gently, that he would get angry if she put on weight.

He replied that it was so frustrating. He felt defeated.

When asked why it was important to him that Sal was thin, he at first gave pragmatic replies about health and success. His physical signs and his verbal tones, suggested it was something more than this.

I empathically observed his hesitance and sense of discomfort and asked what he was feeling. He struggled for a while. I was not sure whether this would have been father's struggle or whether it was in fact Sal's.

After some time, he was able to say that he wanted his daughter to be attractive like her mother. It was important in a woman.

I asked what he meant by attractive. He replied again with discomfort that he meant attractive to men. 'No man wants a fat woman, it doesn't matter what you do-gooders think. Understand this, I don't want her to be fat.'

There was something in Sal's father's tone that seemed to belie his statement. It seemed that Sal herself had noticed this.

At this point, Sal/father went quiet. Father became more uncomfortable. Sal was moving out of role. I said I wanted to thank father for being here and in role, Sal acknowledged that. She returned to her original seat.

Sal seemed to understand something very important in what had just happened and the change in her father's presentation. She recalled times when her father was flirtatious with her teenage friends and that her parents often invited Sal and her teenage friends to their parties where they were plied with drinks in the same way as their adult guests. Now Sal associated this with her father's interest in her developing body. Since the message she had taken from father was that fat is ugly, she felt that she had needed to be fat in order not to be a sexual target.

Sal had always had a sense of being sexually abused but without memory of it. She now believed strongly that her weight was her defence against sexual abuse, believing that she would not be a victim if she were fat 'and ugly'. Sal believed there had been incidences of sexual abuse in her father's family. It was her weight and large size that was the armouring defence for Sal, not the food she needed in order to be fat. Sal believed that she was rebelling against her father because of her own subconscious fear of sexual abuse. There was, however, a sense for her that this was not the whole story. In later analysis, Sal worked further with the anomaly that her father was always so angry with her weight to the point of inflicting physical pain and yet she would not comply with his wishes. What she concluded was that she was protecting her father against his fears of finding his own daughter sexually attractive, and perhaps his fears about acting upon that attraction. His extreme behaviour ensured Sal's rebellion and that she remained overweight. In this way they both fulfilled a need of avoidance of sexual attraction and involvement.

The parent interview with Jill as her father was less complex. She wanted to resolve her ongoing need to be what she perceived he wanted her to be. She felt that she still needed to please him and she wanted to be herself.

Case study: Parent interview, Jill

The interview started with my use of her father's name, Ivan. Ivan was not reluctant to be part of this process. My focus with 'him' was Jill feeling she needed to please him and that this was restricting her ability to be her grown-up self. I explained that she often felt fearful of his anger and scared that he would abandon her.

Jill's response as her father was one of astonishment, which developed into sadness. With continued discussion about Jill's past experience, 'he' became remorseful. He explained something of his troubled past and insisted he had no idea that Jill felt this way. He would never have wanted her to be scared of him. In a further session, Jill chose to do two-chair work where she 'talked with' her father whom she placed on the second chair.

It is important to bear in mind the impact on the patient of the therapist being in communication with her parent figure. The patient will expect that the therapist will be on her side. It would not be therapeutically beneficial to 'side' with the parent figure against the patient and the therapist must be seen to be working on behalf of the patient.

Two-chair work

Here, I will outline the approach where the patient remains herself in the here and now whilst talking with her own internal Parent whom she 'places on the other chair'. The patient moves physically from one chair to the other. In so doing she is both the Parent and the Parent's interviewer.

The patient needs to decide which chairs in the room best fit the energy of the Parent and herself and then to arrange them in proximity to each other such that she can move from one chair to the other and dialogue between them. She needs to be comfortable with the distance between the chairs and their position in respect of each other. Face to face may be too confrontational. It is therefore necessary to allow the patient to arrange the chairs. It is also necessary to negotiate where the therapist sits in relation to those two chairs chosen by the patient.

Before commencing the dialogue the patient and therapist will discuss the focus of the work, which may be investigatory, and consider the opening statements or question. The patient will then commence the work as herself, opening the dialogue with her Parent on the other chair.

The therapist's role is primarily to watch the process and be ready to make meaning with the patient subsequently. If, however, the patient becomes stuck, the therapist's role is to enable and empower the patient.

Case study: two-chair work, Jill

Jill chose to 'be with' her father in the therapy room by way of two-chair work. She was able to relay to him how scared she was of him at times and how she hated being sent to her room. She wanted to hear what he had to say about that. The following is a summary of Jill's two-chair process.

When Jill moved to the Parent chair where she took on the role of her father, he was contrite about his behaviour, regretting some of the decisions he had made. With further questioning by Jill he declared he was sad that she was still feeling hurt and said that he had always loved her.

Jill moved back to her own chair and said she wanted to be herself and not to have to continue to try to be what he wanted her to be. This time she was displaying signs of anger. His acknowledgement of his love provided a space for Jill to feel her anger that she had repressed for fear of his rejection and abandonment.

For a moment, Jill seemed stuck. She did not feel an urge to move chairs, and she looked at me. I did not try to engage her in here and now assessment as that would have shifted her out of the process and so I suggested she ask her father what he wanted from her. Jill had held on to the idea that she was not allowed to be herself because of her father's demands on her. It seemed now that Jill had ascertained from him that he loved her and that he regretted some of his past behaviour, that she could be released from the injunction against being herself that she believed her father had imposed. My hunch was that by asking this question, she would gain this release. She asked the question and, regaining energy, moved immediately to the other chair. She thought for a while and then replied, 'I just want you to be happy. I want you to do whatever you want so you can be happy.'

Jill was very moved by this dialogue and felt that it was actually what her father would say. She felt a release. Change in Jill's eating behaviour of course, was not immediately apparent. She could not actually say what this meant to her, other than she felt a huge relief. As time went on, however, she became significantly more self-accounting and assertive and her relationship with her father became closer, richer and age-appropriate. This in turn freed her further from the transferences she had with her husband and boss. She reduced her eating because she had changed the circumstances that engendered the stimulus to eat. When she did revert to a binge-eating response, she was able to recognize what was happening and either allow herself an amount of food and tolerate her relapse or find another way of calming herself. She developed a way of understanding her bingeing in relation to her stressors and to accept the lapses in her eating behaviour as normal in her own life flow. In this way they became reframed as phases that she was able to manage rather than her unmanageable lot in life.

Patient dialogue with food

As mentioned above, a further development of the idea of the two-chair work is for the patient to imagine putting food on the second chair and dialoguing with it. This is a more intensive way of finding the meaning of food for the patient. The therapist needs to be vigilant and in that vigilance provide a sense of holding and safety for the patient. This can be distressing work.

Once the patient has 'put' her food image onto the other chair she may start by talking to it in whatever way she is driven to do or she may need to express her feelings on being confronted with this addictive substance. Most of my patients have felt both hatred and neediness. They need to be able to express and integrate both their repulsion and their need. They need to accept that this is the position at present and serves a purpose that patient and practitioner can endeavour to discover. The therapist's role is to encourage this integration. This reduces the sense of the 'battle'. Battles have to have enemies. Whilst food is the enemy, the battle has to continue. The patient needs to understand that she is using food as a defence, cleverly worked out by her Child as a way of coping at a time when she was unable to use logic or even symbolism to do this.

The patient may dialogue with the food without moving from her chair or she may become the food and talk from that perspective. This latter technique is more emotionally demanding but provides better options for synthesis as the beneficial intent of the use of food is likely to be more clearly heard by the patient when she is not sitting in angry opposition to it.

The meaning of food may be anything from survival where the patient feels that she will die without the excess food, to recognizing that she is mindlessly following someone else's prescribed pattern of eating and beliefs about food.

The therapist needs to closely observe the dialogue and listen for the story the patient will be narrating overtly and covertly in the process. She must bear in mind the psychological hungers described in Chapter 10.

Because of the tug of war the patient feels between eating and not eating, between the desire or need for food and the yearning to control her consumption of it, the patient is likely to feel confused. She may become overwhelmed by her internal sensation of hatred of the substance on which she depends. A clinician who senses she may herself become overwhelmed should not enter into this work.

Patient dialogue with weight/fat

This again, can be highly emotional work. The patient often experiences fear and needs the therapist to provide a safe and holding environment. The therapist must have investigated the meaning of food and size with the patient earlier in the psychotherapeutic journey so that she or he has some knowledge of the depth of the pathology and beliefs relating to the patient's need to eat or be fat. This work is used when a patient has the potential to gain self-empowerment from the process with the support of the therapist.

Case study: patient dialogue with weight, Hazel

Hazel considered my proposal of putting her extra weight onto another chair and discoursing with it. Her immediate response was one of fear. She was both apprehensive and intrigued by her fearfulness. She had a sense of being naked and vulnerable without the extra body protection. I suggested that she should think in terms of taking off a thick coat that she could easily put back on. She said that she needed to think of it as a protective suit, rather like a space capsule that would seal itself when she put it back on. She needed reassurance that she could replace the 'fat body'. She was then ready to enter the process.

Hazel:	*([Chair 1] Silence, staring at the other chair [Chair 2] in which she had 'placed her fat'. She stared at Chair 2 silently for a long time.)*
Therapist:	What are you experiencing?
Hazel:	I feel cold and small and vulnerable...and scared *(small voice)*.
Therapist:	Cold and small and vulnerable.
Hazel:	Mm.
Therapist:	And scared.
Hazel:	Mm.
Therapist:	What are you scared of?
Hazel:	I don't feel safe. I feel as though I want to grab the fat and put it back on.
Therapist:	And you can do that. Are you willing to stay with the scare for a while knowing that you can put this fat back on?
Hazel:	Yes. *(Continues to stare at Chair 2.)*
Therapist:	What's happening?
Hazel:	I am seeing that the fat has a purpose...and I am ...I'm trying to work out what it is.
Therapist:	How about you ask it. Ask it what it does for you.
Hazel:	*(Addressing the chair)* 'Why do I need you?' *(Hazel waited to sense the reply. She did not move to 'become' the fat.)*
Hazel:	It says that it protects me *(pause)*.
Therapist:	How does it protect you?
Hazel:	*(Listens again to the response from the fat on the chair, looking intently at it.)*
Hazel:	It says it protects me from my mother *(pause)*. She needs me to be fat. I won't survive if I lose the weight...or she won't...no, I think I will disappear... Or she'll...no, she won't die...she just won't be anything. *(Hazel's body became tense and closed. She seemed very young. She started shivering.)*

I asked Hazel what she wanted and she said she wanted to put the fat back on. She imagined getting back into her 'capsule' of fat. In this brief work we had discovered something of Hazel's illogical, early decision that she needed to be fat in order to survive herself or for her mother's ability to be there in some way. This exposed the necessary therapeutic direction. Hazel's maintenance of a large size was a survival issue. Her fantasy was that either she or her mother would not thrive if she lost weight. We needed to find meaning and resolution to these beliefs. It seemed that the weight was the Parent created by Hazel's Parent in her Child, P1 (see Chapter 6). It was both critical and containing.

> Hazel's mother made extremely prejudiced remarks about fat people. Hazel's understanding much later in therapy was that her Child self found a way of staying in relationship with mother through being fat whilst psychologically protecting herself from both mother's intrusive and impossible demands of her to be the daughter she wanted her to be and from her fear of her mother's emotional abandonment of her. Whilst believing she was not good enough because she was fat, she could avoid the possibility that she was not good enough as a person. Hazel needed to face and integrate her shadow side. If she lost weight she felt she would have no protection against mother's demands of her and would lose herself. If psychologically her weight also represented her mother, she would also lose her. Her image of herself without the fat was of a 'will o' the wisp' having no substance and no sense of contact with any surface or being. This she found frightening. Until Hazel resolved these issues she would clearly not be able to lose weight.

Three-chair work

In three-chair work the ego states of Parent, Adult and Child are each represented on three different chairs. The patient needs to be able to choose which chairs she sees as appropriate for each ego state. These may not be the same as the therapist might have chosen. The process continues in much the same way as with two-chair work except that the Adult self is encouraged to take an active part in listening and evaluating the dialogue between the Parent and Child. In the position of Adult she may also speak to the therapist about the process. The therapist may ask the patient to move to the Adult chair to dialogue with him/her if she/he feels the patient is stuck.

Three-chair work is used when the patient's stage of therapy allows her to take charge of her internal process. Having said that, discussion of the work with the therapist will invite further Adult energy. Patient B who I included as an illustration of the use of the diagnostic questionnaire was able to enter into three-chair work and follow her own internal dialogue, making meaning in the here and now. She realized that she was highly self-critical and that this was one of the reasons why she reached for food. Her Child self was diminished by the very critical Parent self. Interestingly at times she was unable to speak from the Adult chair within the process, finding that her Adult too was diminished by the overpowering Parent self. However, when using the chair to communicate with me, she was able to reflect on the process and how dominant her Critical Parent was. She gradually became more able to use her Adult within the process, thus strengthening her Adult and reducing the potency of the destructive Parent ego state. As she became less self-critical, she also reduced her stress levels and found that she was more available as a loving partner within her relationship. Both these shifts lead her to monitor her eating patterns. She not only began to eat less but also changed to a healthier regime.

Summary

The Parent ego state contains the introjected parent others including the family, social, cultural and global elements described in Chapter 2. When considering the internalization of the parent figures it is necessary to bear in mind that those introjects will include the Parent, Adult and Child of the other person since those parents and parent figures necessarily had ego states. So, in working with the Parent ego state the process also attends to any or all of the ego states of the actual parent. This explains why some bizarre and conflicting messages form within a patient's belief systems. For instance, Sal's father professed that he wanted her to be slim whilst at the same time in his own Child ego state he needed her to be obese in order for him to contain his own sexual desires towards his daughter. At a more overt level when Jill sulked and withdrew she was exhibiting the same Child response her father had used to control his world. When she fed herself with compensatory food she was copying her mother's style of Nurturing Parent behaviour.

As can be seen from these illustrations of work with patients the Parent ego state plays a major part in their need to eat or maintain a large body size. Working with what might seem a straightforward and attributable parent saying may provide a level of clarification for the patient that leads to a re-decision with regard to eating or it may guide the therapy into focusing on deeply entrenched psychological decisions and defences.

Patients who are less dependent on food and are generally not morbidly obese or who have a shorter history of overweight are less likely to need to work at these deeper psychological levels. Their defences are not as profound and they do not cover such debilitating early deficit such that food or size become survival issues.

Focus on the Parent ego state is a way of thinking about and understanding the beliefs and decisions made by the patient in order for her to cope with the world. The Parent is only a part of the whole self and must be seen in the context of the whole person. Whilst working with the Parent as a focus the therapist is also working with the patient's whole self. The Parent does not function in isolation, though at times it may seem that it does. Its energy may reduce the energy in other ego states or even exclude one or more but this does not rule out the presence of the other ego states or parts of self represented in them. The whole picture includes the exclusion or low energy in those other ego states. When a patient is operating from her Parent something is happening in all other parts of the self, even if that something is inactivity. The same truth applies when working with any of the other ego states. This should be kept in awareness as I introduce the Child and Adult ego states in the following chapters.

Chapter 8

The Child Ego State

The Child ego state is the part of self that is intuitive, creative, playful, spontaneous and holds a huge capacity for intimacy. It is also the part of self that contains non-age-appropriate scare, archaic hurt, and unexpressed and unresolved anger. It holds decisions made in response to its environment of how best to be in the world and the means to enforce them with what have been experienced as real or have developed as fantasized sanctions. In other words, the Child ego state has the capacity to scare the patient into behaving in a certain way that has been expected or perceived to be expected by the parent figures in her life. And it holds the capacity to rebel against the parent figures.

The Child ego state develops from the earliest experience of life, that is, birth, perhaps even in utero. From then onwards the infant experiences a series of related or unrelated events with associated affect and responses to form a multitude of Child ego states. These will be positive, negative and benign. Some of these will interfere with our ability to assess in the here and now and to use our Adult reasoning and thinking self in making appropriate choices with regard to who we are and what we do. Some will enable that process.

In infancy the actual child obviously needs to be in contact and relationship with another person, usually mother, and later others, in order to thrive. This need perpetuates throughout life but is clearly most necessary when the child is unable to do anything for itself and is not yet adept either physically or psychologically to cope with what begins as an unknown environment. More detailed analysis of child development, which is particularly significant in understanding and working with the overweight patient and her choice to use and abuse her body and her eating function is the subject of Chapter 12. However, some basic tenets need to be included here.

A young child who is responded to with patience and attunement, who is loved, accepted, allowed to express herself and is free to evolve within safe boundaries will develop a Child ego state and a correspondingly healthy Parent (and later Adult) ego state that guide her through life with enough self-esteem and self-mastery to tolerate and manage trauma, disappointment and loss. If she does not have this level of attunement but is met with anger, frustration, abandonment or engulfment, neglect and abuse, she will not grow with a sense of self-worth or have an integrated sense of self and wholeness.

Developing children, whether met with attunement or otherwise, will make meaning of their worlds and respond to their environments in ways they perceive as best in order to please their carers. The abused child will need to develop strategies for survival in a frightening and negative world. The child who is insecure and vulnerable because of abuse or ill-attuned parenting is likely to perceive herself as bad and 'not OK' rather than the carer. It is more tolerable to make herself bad than to depend on a bad carer, for the infant cannot abandon her carer in the way that the carer can abandon the infant. As time goes on she may change her position. However, in my experience over-weight patients are more likely to see themselves as 'not OK' and the other as 'OK' or the other as also 'not OK' rather than see themselves as 'OK'.

The patient's beliefs about being bad and hiding their bad selves behind their layers of fat is a coping strategy that has been built up in the Child ego state. The inappropriate use of the body self or physical body is also a defensive and protective structure created by the child and lodged as an available process in the Child ego state. The actual child works out numerous strategies to help her live in her environment. Some are benign and beneficial, others are destructive but seem to be better than any real, imagined, perceived or self-created threatening alternatives. The production of these strategies clearly does not involve logic or reason. Many are developed before the child has such capacities. They are built on sensation, intuition and primitive perceptions of what is going on and remain in place until the child, adolescent or grown-up discovers and chooses to change her belief system in the light of new and different encounters. One such encounter might be psycho-therapeutic intervention.

A major therapeutic direction therefore, in working with overeating and obese patients is to work with the Child ego states. This is particularly so with regard to long-term sufferers. In the psychotherapeutic process there is clearly focus on the pathological nature of the Child ego state constituents. However, the therapist must also keep in awareness the power of the positive in establishing balance. Trauma at any age can be significantly devastating to render the patient incapable of seeing that life was ever any different. Finding positive events can be a catalyst for movement away from debilitating aspects of script. A patient's tendency in negativity is to find all supporting information and messages that support her negative beliefs. She will discount (ignore) information that indicates otherwise. So the obese patient whose being centres on her eating and body size may see very little that is positive in her life or history.

Most parents have positive and good characteristics, although at times it would seem that they are cast as all bad. However, patients have to be ready to see the good in their parents without adapting to a cultural or parental demand or to a perceived invitation to do so from the therapist. When a patient is in her needy Child ego state wanting to be met with attunement and understanding she may see the therapist who invites her to consider the good in her parents as siding with those parents against herself. The patient will only reach the understanding that her parents were not all bad through the release of positive energy in the Child ego state.

When Jill dialogued with her father in two-chair work (see the case study in Chapter 7) she responded emotionally to the realization in her Child ego state that her father wanted her to be happy. She was released from a belief that her father was restraining her from being herself and therefore being happy. She had compensated her disquiet with food, binge-eating whenever she was triggered back into a real child experience in response to which she had made certain conclusions and decisions about herself. At these times she would also reconnect with the phenomenological experience of those childhood events. The deprivation and confusion she re-experienced at these times were of course only briefly met and calmed with food. Her observable physiological and psychological shift in the process of the therapy indicated a release in the Child ego state. She described it as a relief. It meant that she was able to see her father differently and for who he was rather than seeing him in the light of an introjected experience of him from the past. She then was able to make a new here and now relationship with him, and to stop attributing aspects of her archaic father figure to her boss and husband. She thereby released herself from circumstances that compelled her to eat.

Free Child, Adapted Child and Rebellious Child

In the work with patients, the therapist or practitioner will witness three fundamental types of Child ego state functioning: Free Child, Adapted Child and Rebellious Child. These correlate with intrapsychic processes that can be traced in the patient's internal dialogue. For instance, the patient who 'hears' her mother's voice telling her to finish her plate and the internal Child who responds by adapting to the command without Adult assessment. The command and response go unnoticed because the pattern of behaviour has become automatic and an unconscious process since being established in early years.

Free Child functioning involves natural and uncensored procedures. The infant is born with natural propensities and drives that are then shaped by the carers and parent figures in order that the child learns the rules and norms of the world, her culture, her family and her parents. Censorship may be in the child's best interest, in which case it is positive or in the carer's best interest, in which case it might be positive, benign or toxic for the child. Behaviour that is left uncensored may be behaviour that is appropriate and acceptable in the culture or it might be detrimental to the acceptance of the child in her environment.

Overeating can be seen as uncensored Free Child behaviour for someone who was never been taught to monitor either her food intake or the types of food she ate, such as my patient whose mother gave her anything she wanted at any time of day and who felt almost orgasmic excitement in planning and eating her evening meal. Her delight and even sense of existing centred on this aspect of her day and in other spheres she reported having little or no affect. Most of her childhood was spent playing with mother who rarely allowed her to play with friends. Thus her Free Child energy had few outlets in other spheres. In her adult life she continued the pattern of staying at home, rarely seeing her few friends and realized that she joined in hardly any fun activities. Her channel for Free Child energy seemed to rest with her food intake, hence the intensity of her childlike excitement when planning, buying, cooking and eating her meals.

The Free Child is modified and contained in the process of both necessary and unnecessary socialization. That is to say, aspects of conditioning and socializing are necessary for us to survive and to live in the cultural environment we are born into. Other aspects of parental censoring are not in the

The Child Ego State / 113

child's interest but in the interest of the carers. Pertinent to this work, for instance, is the early modification of the knowledge that the child is born with a sense of when she is hungry, when she actually needs food and when she is replete, since from infancy she is regulated into eating at certain convenient times that generally suit others rather than her own biological rhythms. In early infancy, feeding patterns are paramount in the process of the child's developing sense of self. A child who has been forced to eat when she has no need or desire to do so will form a poor relationship with food. She might also be deprived of the sense of effectiveness and self-mastery that would have been her right had she been able to eat and not eat in accordance with her own body rhythms and be fed in response to her indication of these rhythms through the normal channels of communication with which a baby is born. Her confusion over the meaning of food and her decisions about herself in the process of her thwarted attempt at primitive effectiveness will reside in the Child ego state. She will react in future in Adapted or Rebellious Child mode.

In a child's socialization, food may be used for reward and punishment, which adds a physical, social and psychological dimension far removed from needing food to fuel the body. Many children are forced to eat foods they don't like. Food can become currency within the family and often develops into a powerful source of control. In these circumstances the energy from Free Child shifts into Adapted or Rebellious Child, the parts of the self that concur with (Adapted Child) or rebel against (Rebellious Child) parent demands.

The Free Child self lets the patient know when she is hungry for food and when she has had sufficient food. If early feeding patterns and related caring and attunement have allowed enough space for the infant to maintain sufficient mastery of her own biorhythms she will not be unduly affected by later imposition of meal times or indulgent celebrations. The Free Child eats to live, which means she eats to fuel her body in order to have the energy to fulfil her daily task. Because of this, it is easier for the person with Free Child energy to say 'no' to food. The person who has this Free Child capacity, is in tune with her body self, enjoys food and eats it guilt-free. She responds primarily to her own needs and assesses the consequences of responding to others' demands in lieu of her own. When she decides to react in response to others' needs, she does so with calm and decision and does not hate herself for doing so.

For the overweight patient there is little or no Free Child energy available to inform her of when she is hungry and when she is replete. She operates from her Adapted Child who does not have a sense of being replete until she is overfull. The sensation of bloatedness or even feeling sick is her indicator to stop. This patient is usually out of touch with true body sensation, always in respect of food and often with regard to discomfort, pain, body-surface eruptions such as rashes, bruises etc., and sometimes in relation to warmth and cold. Her 'need' for food is triggered by sensations relating to psychological, not physiological hunger. Pleasure in eating is quickly followed by guilt and self-loathing. For the overweight patient food becomes so important that it seems she is more likely to live to eat than to eat to live. However, if early deprivation forces her to use food to quell psychological hungers, the compulsion to eat or maintain a large body size will feel like a survival issue, that is, that she needs to eat in order to survive.

The Adapted Child uses the body as defensive armouring. The decision to do so can relate to any stage of development of the self, though it usually has its essence in infant development between birth and 18 months, when touch, sensation, attunement and accurate enough mirroring by mother and later other carers are paramount. Feeding, ingestion, digestion and elimination, distention and vomiting are all highly sensate body activities experienced by the infant. These events are associated closely with the caring other. The patient may subconsciously aim to re-contact those sensations through over-eating, vomiting, and purging in an attempt to reconnect with those early experiences and her encounter with or her yearning for the good mother. Though the elimination and purging behaviours are more significantly associated with anorexics, many obese patients will use them as a bid to control weight. They are shortlived, unproductive episodes.

The Free Child enables a patient to be attuned to her body self and to have a sense of integration of both her psychological and physical selves. For this energy to perpetuate she will have developed a positive body image, which is a necessary process in developing a cohesive sense of self (see Chapter 12). The Adapted Child forces the patient to dissociate from the body she has not integrated into her sense of self as a physical and psychological being. As a result she avoids looking in the mirror at her body. Some patients report not looking at their faces either. The self-loathing is too virulent to face this physical manifestation of the 'bad' self.

The Adapted Child responds to what her internalized parent others want, or the perception of what they want, either by compliance or rebellion. Eating excessive food and obesity may be compliance or rebellion. The therapeutic work is to find out which and why.

The Adapted Child self buys love and friendship through compliance. Friends and family appeal to the Child ego state when offering extra delicious food, saying things like 'I made it just for you' or 'I have been in the kitchen all day preparing this' or 'Don't make me eat this alone'. There is a power play. The person who says these things has her own agenda for wanting to beguile the other to eat. The obese patient becomes the obliging child whether this suits her cause or not.

It also plays a major role in the dieting regime. From the internal Parent or an external source comes a message 'You should diet'. The Adapted Child complies, going on a diet, joining a slimming club or other chosen adapted response. For some time this works. Then the Rebellious Child kicks in to say 'Sod this, I am going to eat what I want'. Lister, Rosen and Wright (1985) call this the diet–binge cycle. They suggest that the moment of change is when the Free Child experiences deprivation that she relates to similar archaic feelings of there 'not being enough'. Enough of *what* needs to be explored with the patient. It is usually associated with the perceived or actual availability of love or recognition by the caregiver(s). Lister *et al.* suggest that the stopper in the diet–binge cycle is Rebellious Child energy in protecting the Free Child that feels the deprivation. I do not always see such righteous rebellion. At times the fear that wells up in the patient causes depressive withdrawal rather than active rebellion.

If a patient is fearful of losing weight because diets and weight loss rubber-band her back into re-experiencing, albeit phenomenologically at an unconscious level, early deprivation where her survival seemed to be at risk, she will not lose the weight or will lose some and then regain it and more besides. This early sense of scarcity will relate to the absence of a sense of being loved or a sense of only being loved conditionally, of not being mirrored or attuned to and/or being in a second order symbiosis where the infant senses she needs psychologically to take care of the carer(s). The needs of the infant are only secondary to those of the carer leaving a deficit in the psychological hungers of the infant that will then perpetuate into adult life. The strategies become centred around feeding the psychological hungers with food rather than appropriate methods of satisfying those needs. These experiences are logged in the Child ego state and it is within the Child ego state that strategies are formed to deal with them. Each time the patient diets and 'fails' she will reinforce her belief system.

My observation of my patients is that few have real Free Child energy to enjoy fun activities unconditionally. Their laughter is often at their own expense and they play the entertainer to other people. They rarely 'let themselves go' in an unadapted and uninhibited safe manner.

Therapy with the Child ego state will result in shifts of energy in the Adult. As the Child within is released from the 'spells' of childhood perceptions and decisions, energy shifts into the Adult ego state. She begins to understand and make meaning of her behaviour and becomes free to make new decisions. All the ego states need to support a decision for change. The Child self, however, is the most influential in the process as it is the Child self that made the decisions that she perceived as being necessary to operate or even survive in her environment.

Until there is change in all the ego states in support of different behaviour, the patient who is caught in the diet–binge cycle cannot be released from this repetitive synopsis. If the Child is not convinced that change is right and safe, the patient cannot change or maintain change. When a patient diets and loses weight without the Child being convinced that it is the right thing to do, there will be a limited time before the extent of the scare in the Child will be felt and when it is, the patient may eat as if there is no tomorrow in the same way that a person starved for days will attack food. What the patient is experiencing in these circumstances is clearly not biological hunger, for most diets give the patient enough food to feel reasonably well fed, it is psychological hunger.

The patient is not aware of this sense of scarcity in a logical way. She is aware of the urge to eat and the lack of ability to stop herself. Focusing in therapy on the sensations the patient has before reaching desperately for food is a way into her understanding what she is attempting to feed with the food she consumes. She may be aware of some form of agitation that she will feel in different parts of her body. Tracking these physiological responses is important. Just as the body of the newborn infant is at the core of her sense of being in the world, so the body continues to involuntarily have its own physical response to events. The body often 'speaks' before the patient is aware of the stimulus to which it is responding. Body sensations can alert her to real or imagined danger or conflict, and can inform her of when she is angry or sad, agitated, excited and so forth. Though the overweight patient is generally out of touch with her body self, she can usually recognize symptoms of agitation that lead her to eat compulsively or continuously. If she cannot trace these feelings, then she can learn to reconnect with her body self in order to heighten this awareness. I refer to body sensations as a means to understanding the patient's need for food in this chapter because I see the body self residing in the Child ego state. In working with the body self the therapist will be working in a non-verbal domain of the Child ego state.

I have proposed that a patient may relinquish a diet through rebellion or deprivation. In the chapter on psychological hungers I expand on this sense of deprivation, as each of the hungers when inadequately met may lead to bingeing or stopping a diet regime. At its simplest level, something that happens in a day such as criticism by a boss, anger from a partner, an argument with a friend or even something not turning out the way she planned can thrust the patient into negative beliefs about herself and/or others, as a consequence of which, she feels inadequate or a similar, familiar destructive feeling. This feeling will be what compels her to eat. A focus of therapy is to discover these feelings and their associated origin and in doing so the therapist works with the Child ego state.

Dieting is a precariously volatile activity for those whose need to eat and be big in order to meet psychological needs. Their decision to use food and weight is irrational. It is Adapted Child behaviour and Adult thinking is not involved. Diets are promoted as quick-fix solutions and I have known few people who are content with losing a little at a time if they have a lot of weight to lose. I believe healthy eating and understanding the body's reaction to certain foods is the best form of weight control. The Child needs to feel content and 'stroked' by the level of self-care this regime involves. A stroke is a unit of recognition and is called this because of the infant's early contact with the world through touch (see Chapter 10). The patient's Child self needs to feel recognized and 'attended to' if the healthy eating option is to be successful. Clearly reaching this level of clarity is a long way away for the long-term sufferer who needs food and weight to survive. If the Child is agitating for foods that were used as treats or reward in childhood such as chocolate, crisps, cakes, sweets, biscuits and chips as remedies for non-biological hungers, she will not be able to keep to a healthy eating pattern until her psychological needs are understood and met appropriately.

In working with the Child it is necessary to make the links between the patient's behaviour and the decisions that she has made about herself, others and the world. When a child experiences parental behaviour, she logs some or all of that in her Parent ego state and at the same time makes some meaning of it in her Child ego state. An internal dynamic of stimulus–response is established. Without Adult assessment and scrutiny, the stimulus–response dynamic remains in tact. Each time the various stimuli related to a response of eating are present, the patient will automatically eat. Understanding the patient's stimulus–response system is vital if she is going to change it.

In the meantime, the patient continues subconsciously to respond to introjected messages even after there is no cause to do so. To perpetuate the myths of outdated parental demands she needs to discount any information that would inform her that she has a choice to do otherwise. The strength of this discount will depend on the potency of the original message or message giver, and the sanctions she knows or believes will be executed if she disobeys.

Let us take, for example, the now familiar demand that a child must clear her plate or else some sanction is threatened or imposed by her mother. If going without pudding was the only punishment, that child may integrate the experience, the sanction being mild and irritating rather than frightening. The child, however, who was shouted at or beaten, or perceived herself as threatened with losing mother's (or father's) love, would feel fearful of the physical punishment and terrified at the threatened abandonment. The sanctions in this case were severe and would have a greater impact on the child. This would be logged in the Child ego state with, in the case of the subsequent over-eater, the decision to clear the plate faithfully. The child may also have concluded that the bigger the plate of food to be finished, the more pleased mother would be.

In Alison's case (see case study on identifying introjects, Chapter 7) she had discounted that circumstances had changed and that she had the right to autonomous thinking. She had not assessed why she would still be obeying mother's historical demand even though she is now an adult and able to do as she decides. Neither had she thought whether mother would want her to continue to obey or whether she still held this view anyway. The absurdity is only apparent when the situation is brought into awareness. Alison continued a familiar pattern of behaviour in response to an early and outdated parent introject. When invited to think, she shifted from her Child ego state into her Adult, which brought the compelling subconscious forces into awareness and available for scrutiny. With this awareness came the opportunity to exercise choice. She chose to stop responding to outdated commands. Alison had not been threatened with physical punishment and did not appear to fear abandonment, nonetheless her mother's words, introjected into her own Parent ego state were still highly influential. How much more compelling would such commands be if accompanied by more severe sanctions as was the case with patients Pat and Hazel.

Let us now consider some of the patients I have introduced in this and previous chapters. Pat had been sexually abused, had been the subject of intrusive and boundaryless parenting and had been ignored by her mother who was unable to attach. Sal had been an unwanted child, was subjected to inappropriate sexual attention from both her parents and her uncle, had a sense of a family parade of abuse and received conflicting messages about how she should be in the world throughout her early years, through adolescence and into adulthood. She had been unable to separate from a parent with whom she had never healthily bonded and struggled with her own right to survive in the face of believing that if she claimed her power she would destroy others. If she lost weight she would destroy someone else or sacrifice herself. Rowena (see later on in this chapter), whose mother died when she was an infant and whose father would not discuss mother for fear of upsetting her, had early issues of survival, attachment, lovability, belonging and deprivation. Hazel was unwanted at conception. Once her parents accepted the pregnancy they looked forward to a boy. She was a girl. This was fine whilst she remained an infant, her mother related to babies. She did not relate to children when they developed their own personality. Her mother wanted her to be consistently as she wanted her daughter to be or she rejected her. She was, however, inconsistent in her demands and Hazel had no measure of how to 'get it right'. Mother exercised rejection, with venomous tirades. Hazel constantly strove to feel a mother's love.

All these patients presented with long-term obesity and were either in the higher bracket of obesity or morbidly obese. They had all tried various diets and regimes to lose weight. Even those who had managed to lose significant amounts replaced it quickly with even more weight than they had lost. The complexity of their belief systems was very different from those of Alison, for instance, whose Adult was more available because she had less to fear from giving up archaic defences. Hence the therapeutic work demanded a correspondingly more complex programme of work with the Child ego state than that needed for Alison to make changes.

Throughout her childhood the patient will have taken in messages from parent figures, swallowing these messages whole, and will have subconsciously take these into adulthood and continue to act upon them. At the same time as a parent is communicating with a child, the child tries to make meaning of what is being said or done. She interprets her parents, and later others' behaviour to fit a developing sense of self with regard to her environment. She does this with illogical infantile assessment and conclusion, in the best way she knows. Her defences build out of these illogical conclusions, hence the fantasies available to my patients who believe that they will become oversexual if they lose weight and men will be waiting to have sex with them; that they will die or disappear if they lose weight; that someone else will die if they don't stay fat. Or that they were never loved, or are unlovable. These beliefs and the building blocks for them are contained in the Child ego state.

Obesity is about adversely using the body in the process of carrying out script decisions and beliefs. This may be the consequence of needing food to feed psychological hungers or it may be a direct function of the body to hide the 'bad self', or to protect the self from malevolent others or a malicious world. In effect, the Child of the long-term obese person uses the body as both a protection and a means to self-deprecate. Patients want to hide inside their fat and yet are noticed because of it. They want to be slim but fear the consequences of relinquishing their weight. They have little sense of self-worth and are always ready to self-criticize and punish. Most obese patients I see blame themselves for things that go wrong around them. Such is the struggle within the Child ego state.

Remembering that the Child ego state holds numerous subsystems relating to events occurring at different times in the child's life, clinicians are likely to encounter any number of these subsystems throughout the therapy. They will not be sequentially presented and the therapist needs to be aware of the consequences of working with deeper issues before safety, trust and alliance are established both interpersonally between patient and clinician and intra-psychically within the patient. In other words, the patient needs not only to trust the therapist but also to have a level of trust in herself that she can enter into archaic experiences and survive.

In order to please her carer the child constructs her own unique form of self-regulation that she has developed in response to her actual and perceived environment. Injunctions are part of this process of self-regulation. Each injunction starts with 'Don't'. The strength of each injunction is directly proportionate to the force of the negative experience that gave rise to it.

The self-regulating strategy of injunctions

Injunctions are passed to the Child ego state of the child from the actual parent's Child ego state. They are usually thought to be taken on board by the infant before she is able to speak and generally within the first few years of life. They are implied in the parents' behaviour and conscious and unconscious, verbal and non-verbal communication with the child. The child reaches her conclusions without the ability to question and logs the self-regulating strategies in her Child ego state. Injunctions can be both implied in the psychological process of communication between parent and child and can be created by the child as a way of limiting herself to fit into the world she perceives around her.

A nervous mother will handle her baby differently from a confident mother and a mother who did not want her baby or feels jealous of the attention the infant gets, will pass associated unconscious messages to her child through touch and tones of voice. Whatever the unconscious process of the parent the child will receive a corresponding message about her position in the world around her. Verbal communication has both a social and a psychological content. So if a mother does and says everything right for the baby but subconsciously feels negative towards her existence, then the psychological message relating to that negativity will be picked up by the infant. Some communication is of course obvious in its implication and if said enough times will carry a certain message for the child, such as 'I am sick and tired of you', 'Get out of my sight', 'I wish I had never had you'. The child will conclude from these communications what she can and cannot do. What she senses she cannot do she logs as an injunction.

The Gouldings (1979) found that regular themes emerged from their work with patients and drew up a list of commonly held psychological injunctions. I discuss these injunctions in the context of my work with obese patients. Patients do not necessarily carry all the injunctions though they do present as being heavily bound by restrictive messages, some of which concur with the culturally held injunctions in western societies. Woollams and Brown (1978) propose a scale for the gravity of each injunction on a range of one to ten. This is useful in order to maintain an accurate view of what might otherwise appear an overwhelmingly negative force of injunctions. In describing the injunctions and giving some examples of how they might be internalized in terms of verbal and non-verbal communication from the parent figures, I aim to raise the awareness of what is a central behaviour-determining force in the Child ego state. This is a way of thinking about what drives the overweight patient to be overweight or to overeat. Patients will have some of these injunctions and some will be far stronger in their influence than others. The severest level of injunctions and the most debilitating to social functioning will be held by those with a history of long-term obesity and those who are morbidly obese. Some patients may seem to be coping from day to day, indeed may appear happy with their lot but it is the internal experience of the patient that shapes her sense of being in the world and what she feels she can or cannot do, or what she does or not feel comfortable doing.

The injunctions of overweight patients

Don't Exist

A Don't Exist injunction is an injunction not to thrive. I would always consider the possible presence of the Don't Exist injunction in morbidly obese patients. Obesity is axiomatically self-harming. Extreme weight can cause death because of the strain on the heart, the cardiovascular system and other vital organs. It is not possible to agree a contract of 'no self harm' with the patient because of the intrinsic self-harming nature of obesity and the fact that the patient cannot cease using the addictive substance, that is, food, as she needs this to fuel her body from day to day. This is very different from other substance dependency in so far as these patients need to have the substance, food, in order to live. Because of the defensive nature of her body size and her psychological need for food she is unable to take charge of her eating until at least some of her issues have been resolved.

The Child then concludes that she does not have the right to exist from implied or actual verbal messages. For instance if a fraught parent says 'I wish I'd never had you', 'I wish you had never been born', 'I wish you'd drop dead', her child may conclude that her parent does not want her to exist. Likewise if her mother tried to abort her, was not available for the child or was herself scared of having a baby around then the Child of that infant may decide that mother doesn't want her to thrive.

My patients who have had Don't Exist injunctions have tended to use the body self as a defence either more than or in addition to the need for food to feed psychological hungers. Sal, being an unwanted baby whose mother tried to abort her, believed that she did not have a right to exist. Her weight became a way of potentially obeying that injunction. Because of the attempted abortion, the difficult birth and subsequent, albeit temporary psychological disturbance in mother, Sal extended her belief to 'Someone won't exist, either me or mum'. Sal's alternative was to go crazy (Don't Be Sane injunction). Her mother had a series of 'nervous breakdowns' and episodes of severe depression. Sal felt that she needed to comply with whatever her parents wanted her to be and do if only she could work it out. Though Sal's mother believed that her nurturing was at least adequate, her unconscious lack of readiness to be a mother would have been transmitted to Sal through her touch and holding, her tones and the physical contact with her own body self. Sal sensed that she was not supposed to exist and constructed ways of believing that she might be able to live. One of these was to please her mother whom she believed could not tolerate her daughter being 'as beautiful as her'. Her fairy tale script (the story that the patient most relates to) representation was 'Snow White'. Sal believed that this was a reason why she chose to be fat. She chose to live in the glass coffin, which she saw as her extended body, where she was encased from the world and yet the world could see her. In some ways, Sal also believed that there would be a magical solution when her prince would arrive to deliver her from her tortured world. At times Sal would report feeling as though her mother was tearing her heart out. Nonetheless she would not entertain negative thoughts towards her mother and in many ways was more concerned about her mother's 'survival' than her own.

Sal had never separated from her mother. The impaired early relational experience with a mother towards her unwanted infant meant that there was no secure bonding from which to safely detach. Sal continued to search for this bonding. She described her internal experience as being one of struggling to survive.

Sal needed to know that she had a right to survive before she could decide that she also had a right to live independently of her mother. Like many overweight patients, Sal's large body size was both her means of survival and her means of potential self-destruction.

Interestingly, 'Snow White' is referred to by many of my obese patients as the fairy tale representing their life script. The fairy tale character lived in suspended animation until her prince came and woke her up to live her life. When she became more beautiful than her stepmother, her stepmother tried in various ways to kill her and eventually her life was suspended. Obese patients feel as though they are waiting to live again or even start living when they lose weight. They would also like the magical cure that is swiftly administered by the kiss of the prince. The stepmother is of course the patient's own 'internal demon' that regulates her being in illogical and frightening ways. This demon is part of the Child ego state.

Rowena's (see later on in this chapter) Don't Exist injunction came from her mother's inability to care for her and her death whilst still an infant. It was not as severe as the injunction demonstrated in the work with Sal. Her need for a large body size was related to her sense that she needed to be big to survive in the world and to be noticed.

Both Rowena and Sal used their body self as protective armouring and at the same time both used food to feed their psychological hungers. Work with patients who use both eating and body size as defence mechanisms needs to be carefully balanced between reclamation of the body self and reclamation of the psychological self. Patients must come to know and believe they have a right to exist and they want to do so, before any conditions they have conjured that might allow them to exist can be addressed. Patients who hold a strong sense of a Don't Exist injunction, that is, on the upper end of the scale of one to ten, clearly cannot lose weight or maintain weight loss for long. To do so throws them back on to their Don't Exist injunction, which in turn compels them to eat again in order to survive.

It is important to be aware of the possibility of obese and morbidly obese patients carrying a Don't Exist injunction. It is not normally characterized by attempted suicides but more by progressive incapacitation that can result from the condition of being overweight.

Don't Be You

The Don't Be You injunction is characterized by the patient's sense of her fat self being her armour as well as her identity. Some obese patients do believe that there is another person inside waiting to be released whilst morbidly obese patients tend to believe that if they lose weight they will face a void. They fear that there is no real self inside because their true self was lost long ago when they had to try to be who and what their carer(s) wanted them to be. As a fat self they have some solidity and consistency.

Obese patients who carry this injunction have only experienced conditional love with perceived heavy sanctions such as abandonment if they try to be themselves. For instance, Hazel's parents wanted a boy. As a child her mother had dressed her in frills and ribbons to emphasize her female gender. Hazel presented in her adult life with a masculine appearance both in her postures and body language and in her choice of clothes. She thought she did this in order to rebel against her mother's need to make her ultra-feminine when in fact at an unconscious level she was fulfilling mother's desire for a boy.

She identified that one of her decisions was to be big like her father, the dominant male in the family. He seemed to be able to resist mother's constant demands and neurotic outbursts. She saw him as having a steely protective shell. Her mother was constantly nagging her to lose weight, accompanying her appeals with words and tones of disgust at Hazel's size. Hazel realized when working with her 'fat armour' on the chair, that she was using it as protection from her mother. Later she realized the complexity of her decision to fulfil her mother's wish for a boy by presenting as masculine and at the same time using her large body size to defy her mother's verbal demands for her to lose weight. She realized that she mistakenly believed that being fat was the only way she felt she could be herself, rather than what her mother wanted her to be.

Hazel needed to be free to be herself before she could lose weight. As she developed this sense of moving out of the symbiosis with her mother, a relationship pitted with non-acceptance and a need on both sides for unavailable unconditional love from the other, she began to claim her femininity. She subsequently lost weight without feeling that she was giving in to her mother or sacrificing herself.

Don't Belong

As we observe people around us in groups, whether at work or in social settings we can see that some people hold back and never seem to quite belong. To feel intrapsychically that belonging is taboo is painful and lonely. Many obese patients do feel that they do not have the right to belong and that their size justifies this. How my patient, Rowena played this out was fascinating. She was constantly striving to belong, having experienced an infant separation from her primary carer in the first few weeks of her life. Her mother was ill and hospitalized, her father worked away from home much of the time and she was cared for by both her aunt and her grandmother in their own homes over the period of her mother's absence. When her mother returned home, she was still not able to care for herself and the baby consistently and so now Rowena was shared between the three parents. All these parents had different views on infant care. Her mother subsequently died. She did not have a sense of belonging anywhere and continued throughout her life, experiencing, and later, setting up, situations that worked against her fully belonging.

She was late starting school; she did not attend the meeting organized for new pupils at her secondary school; she was late arriving at university and missed freshers' week where activities were organized for students to get to know each other and the environment. Subsequently she repeated the pattern in other learning groups, missing first meetings and keeping herself from full integration by absenting herself from time to time on the pretext of having too much work to do. She invited criticism by her absences, which reinforced her feeling of not belonging.

In her infancy, Rowena's aunt often forgot to take her bottle with her if she was going out for the day. If she had friends round, which was often the case, she would make Rowena wait to be fed until after their departure. Her feeding was unreliable and inconsistent. She experienced and tolerated the sensation of real hunger. Her grandmother on the other hand, always had a bottle ready to heat up and fed the infant whenever she cried. Grandmother enjoyed holding and 'snuggling' Rowena. Later Rowena had two methods of dealing with her sense of loneliness and bids to avoid belonging. One was to starve herself and re-experience the hunger pangs with some sense of comfort and even ecstasy. This she did for a while in adolescence. The other was to promote the phenomenological memory of her grandmother's warm and indulgent presence by eating. During these times she would eat almost constantly throughout the day, snacking between meals in a frenzy of deprivation. When she was slim, she felt she could belong but it was a hard task to maintain. When she was fat she re-experienced the familiarity of not belonging. It was this latter condition that she adopted from about the age of 20.

Pat, Hazel and Sal also carried this injunction. As can be seen in their histories earlier in the book, each of them was only conditionally received into the family as infants. Each uncovered a Don't Belong injunction in the process of therapy.

Let us look for a moment at how Pat played out this injunction and how she used her size for this purpose. Pat reported feeling an outsider all her life and certainly demonstrated not belonging in her family. She described the sexual abuse at the hands of her father as being carried out as if she were someone outside of the family. She was not her father's little girl. At the same time she experienced a sense of belonging to him within the sexual contact. She perceived a close relationship between the other members of her family that excluded her.

When she presented in therapy, she was living in a secluded house with her partner. She visited her mother as she would a neighbour. She had little to do with the rest of the family. Pat realized that she used her large size not only to protect her from sexual intrusion but also to keep herself from belonging. She became conscious of the fact that she had always felt she was 'odd'. She described feeling as if she was odd if she was part of what she saw as a dysfunctional family but that she must also be 'odd' because she did not have a space as a member of the family. She was a loner at school and became self-employed, working long hours by herself after completing her training. She realized she had seen the distance people kept from her as a function of her size but discovered that she had psychologically used her size to keep herself away from others. She realized that she felt she did not belong anywhere.

Belonging in a family, social or task-orientated group provides a possible rich source of strokes and recognition. Absence of belonging deprives the patient of this supply of strokes. As will be seen in the chapter on psychological hungers, many obese patients eat in order to meet psychological needs. If a patient carries a Don't Belong injunction she may use her body size as a way of not belonging. She will almost certainly use food to feed the emptiness and loneliness experienced by her decision not to belong.

It is not necessarily the case that patients with this injunction exclude themselves from social life, friends and family. They may be very active with others. It is however, my observation that they will play a part with others, put on a persona that suits the groups in which they operate whilst inside always feeling separate, unfulfilled and dispensable.

Obese patients can feel as though they belong in a slimming group. It is, however, a conditional belonging, conditional on them being overweight. Patients report on the dilemma they face in that belonging is a condition of being overweight on first joining the group and then of losing weight. If they do not lose they do not feel able to stay in the group but if they lose they automatically sense themselves as aiming to leave the group. Life membership as a reward for weight loss meets this need to belong. It has not, however addressed the psychological need of the patient to be independent of the group and to have a wider sense of being able to belong anywhere she chooses and to feel accepted as belonging in her chosen groups.

Don't Be Important

This injunction is passed to the child by the parent who does not have time for her or the parent who ignores the child in favour of her own needs and says things like 'Don't bother me', 'Go and play', 'You're too big for your boots' and other such messages that imply that the needs of the child are not significant and that they can only be around if they stay out of the way. Many obese patients have a sense of being big in the world in order to feel they can be seen. They get attention because of their size, even though this is often negative attention.

A Don't Be Important injunction challenges the patient's creativity in finding ways to be important enough to be acknowledged and recognized. For instance they might play the fat and happy person, keeping everyone amused and smiling when inside they want to be respected and treated as if they have something important to offer. They might be the one that always does things for others and is reliable in her availability and willingness to say yes. Most patients report that they feel they have to work very hard for the attention they feel they yearn. They do not feel they deserve to be important in their own right.

Sal found that she felt important when she was being given attention for being fat, even though it was extremely painful for her to be weighed and be shouted at for her persistence in being overweight. Her weight seemed to become a central issue in her family. Alongside the chastising there was a comfort from those like her mother, who would secretly feed her 'nice things'. In later life she also gained attention by being obese. Friends would tease her about her size as she made herself the centre of her own derisive humour. She used her weight as a focus in pastiming, which she saw as 'sacrificing herself for the slaughter' before others did it first (pastiming is spending time in inconsequential, but often, pleasurable, chatting and community with others, described more fully in Chapter 10). This way of thinking was a version of an existential position Sal held of 'kill or be killed', developed in early childhood and analysed in Chapter 12.

At work, however, she felt less in control. She adapted to her senior colleagues even when at times she knew they were wrong. She felt unacknowledged although she knew she was extremely adept in her job. Other team members would ridicule her, have fun with her, but never consider her expertise or opinions. The extra hours she worked because of her dedication seemed to go unnoticed.

The way Sal dealt with the injunction was to find active ways to feel the centre of attention. At times she chose quite extreme behaviour to achieve this. When first working therapeutically in this sphere she could not see how without her weight she would ever 'be seen'.

Rowena also felt unimportant. When in her Child ego state she felt that people 'who are unlovable' (like herself) 'do not deserve attention'. She was missed at school, overlooked at college and at work at repeated stages in her life. Supported by the Don't Belong injunction, Rowena could easily be passed over in the groups she attended and struggled to be seen or heard. She was aware of being unacknowledged but felt powerless to do anything about it.

Rowena had not felt important enough in herself or important enough to her father to ask him about her mother who had died when she was so young. She felt that it was her weight that allowed people to dismiss her and it was her reason for discounting herself. Rowena realized that she could blame her weight for being missed by other people because this was less painful than believing that they could see her inner Child whom she perceived as bad and unlovable. Since this is what she believed of herself, she feared others would see that badness too. The weight hid the badness but also gave people a reason to reject her.

Obese people report that they are ignored in shops and restaurants, and dismissed in many other spheres of their lives. I referred to such situations in Chapters 1 to 3. They are often treated as if they cannot think and as if their opinion is not worth seeking. They are treated as being unimportant. This confirms their self-belief. If a patient has a Don't Be Important injunction, then she will unconsciously communicate it to others and she will operate with the injunction as her guiding force. In other words she will invite others to ignore her by her unconscious submission to the injunction. The patient who reports being dismissed or ignored is inviting that response by presenting as discounting (ignoring) herself. If she discounts herself, others will do.

Don't Be Sexual

Obese patients tend to report feeling sexually unattractive. Sexual activity with a caring partner is rare and generally unsatisfactory. Patients may lie about their sexual activity in the early stages of therapy suggesting that their size does not affect their sex life. They feel shame in not being sexually active.

The patient who carries this injunction will use her body self to ensure its fulfilment. Even if her partner is not concerned about her size, she will be unable to relax whilst making love fearing every touch of her flesh will repulse her lover. Making love is traumatic and something she will avoid whenever possible.

The patient's fear of being thinner often involves a fear of being sexually active and a fantasy that her sexuality would lead her into trouble. The bizarre nature of this fantasy is exemplified by the image a number of patients had of there being men lined up outside waiting to have sex with them. Being fat keeps them away from such excessive sexual activity. They seem to discount completely that they would be able to refuse sexual advances, even if there were numerous men approaching them.

Children demonstrate a sense of their innocent sexuality early in their development. They need appropriate mirroring and acceptance of their experimentation with this newfound way of being. Girls will have their femininity and sexuality modelled by their mothers and validated by their fathers. Inconsistency and intolerance would be interpreted as a command against being sexual. The negative message may emanate from parents who themselves have an issue with sexuality.

Confusion, scare, disgust and shame are words commonly used in reference to my patients' sexual being. Confusion will also arise from mixed messages from the same parent who verbally warns against sexual behaviour whilst unconsciously transmitting messages of it being 'naughty or exciting fun'. It might also arise when mother and father give opposing messages such that father may be restricting his daughter's sexuality whilst mother is permissive.

Scare is often engendered through the scare of the parent, usually the mother of the female patient. Disgust seems to reside mainly in the mind of the mother who has herself been told by her mother that sex is disgusting. Shame is evoked both by the parent's messages to the child through their inability to discuss sexual matters with their daughter and the taboo on discussing sex that still prevails in cultures, particularly the British culture.

Sal had mixed messages from her parents with regard to her sexuality. Father, as we have seen, needed her to be non-sexual for his own safety though he still flirted with her as a toddler and through to adulthood. Mother was attractive, slim and sexy. As a female, Sal's understanding would have been to be like mum, sexy. However, mother also gave her a message that she should not be as attractive as her ('Mirror, mirror on the wall'). From both her parents' Child ego states she had an injunction of Don't Be Sexual whilst socially they displayed lax boundaries around their sexuality. In order to fulfil this injunction, Sal gained weight and maintained it, though later, at times her Child rebelled by engaging in inappropriate and unsatisfactory sexual behaviour at the same time, copying the lax sexual boundaries displayed by both her parents. Whilst being fat, she kept her mother's Child happy by not being as attractive.

Sexuality is an issue for overweight patients who see their weight as standing in the way of them being sexually active and sexually attractive. When a patient reveals her fears, doubts, shame or disgust in relation to sex I would be curious about the possible presence of this injunction.

Don't Be Close

This injunction is passed on to the Child ego state of the daughter if a parent is unable to show affection, is remote, unable to touch or who abandons the child through leaving or death. If a child reaches out to her parent but gets no response she will feel a painful rejection such that she will eventually decide that it is better to contain herself and stop reaching out. If a child has trusted her parent and then the parent leaves she may decide that it is better to keep a distance in order to protect herself from the trauma of losing someone. This was certainly the case with Rowena whose mother had died when she was very young.

The injunction is epitomized by the fear of forming close relationships. Extending body boundaries ensures some level of physical distance. Obese patients have difficulty being touched or held. They tell themselves they are too big to be embraced and indeed that to cuddle layers of fat would be repulsive. Even if someone cuddles them, they are unable to relax, being so conscious of their body size. They often feel, or actually are, starved of physical affection. The layers of fat keep others away both physically and emotionally. These patients crave for affection but cannot risk getting close enough to feel it.

Don't Grow Up and Don't Be a Child

These two injunctions are interesting as so often obese patients will indicate the existence of both. Most of the obese patients I have worked with have a lack of self-agency and discount their potency. They interact from Adapted Child in order to please others. They take criticism, ignorance and intrusion because they lack a sense of their own boundary and potency to create one for themselves. They lack a sense of self other than as an overweight person. They often play the little girl entertainer. They are sweet and charming whilst being used or put upon by others. They play Cinderella, only being big enough to go to the ball through the spells of a magical fairy godmother who never arrives. In the meantime, like Cinderella, they are often at the beck and call of those around them.

I have noted that many patients seem to have been elected the carer in the family from an early age. They have often needed to look after the emotions of their parents as infants and have had to 'do' for others as a way of being accepted. They have had to deny their own needs in favour of those of others and as such have had to 'grow up' rather than be a child. They invariably present with a strong Nurturing Parent towards others and a very weak Nurturing Parent towards themselves. In fact their internal Parent is critical and rejecting of themselves. Both the infant who has not been allowed to develop a full sense of self-agency and the child who has to look after others being burdened from an early age with grown-up responsibility are present in many overweight patients. When they have not taken up the carer role demanded of them, they have been rejected.

A high percentage of overweight patients feel that they should be looking after other people's needs. Most carry out this requirement, only a few rebel. Either way they have a sense that they have to be big to carry the burden of others' demands upon them.

They dare not exert their own authority for fear of being rejected or abandoned. Even those who have struggled against the role of carer, still feel the pull to find the loving relationship that they never experienced. They struggle with separation and feel guilty that they are not fulfilling a servile role. They too report being burdened by the continuing demands they feel from a needy parent, usually mother. Most patients have a history of parents who have been psychologically dependent on them whilst wanting to keep them as children in order for them to continue fulfilling this role.

Don't Feel

Obese patients feel and feel deeply. It is not that the injunction stops them feeling but more that it restricts their ability to show feelings. This is generally due to an intolerance of feelings by the parent figures and a lack of appropriate response to their feelings. Emotional display of anger, rage, pleasure, discomfort, sadness and fear are the ways infants communicate their experience and their needs. An attuned parent will respond appropriately and with empathic mirroring. Certain displays of emotion may be met with anger or non-response such that the child learns to suppress or contain these feelings.

It appears that a high percentage of adults will understand how eating helps to quell emotion because they have indulged in such behaviour at some time in their lives. For the overeater the inability to show feelings (and thereby avoid empathic response) is paramount. Many patients say that if they allow themselves to express what they really feel they will be uncontainable in their emotion. They have a sense of being too much and feel the shame of being so. Their body size, which is 'too much', reflects their sense of the extent of storage they need to contain their emotions and the extent to which they have had to eat in order to hold them down.

Food is a way of keeping feelings down. The patient has a physiological experience of swallowing food, which at the same time swallows down the emotion and blocks it from surfacing. Mentally, food diverts attention from the emotion, at the same time attempting to feed the psychological need that has given rise to the emotion. Unmet psychological needs cause a patient to feel sad or angry, lonely, lost, rejected, abandoned, scared, shame or any other emotion or condition that they have been unable to express. Food represents comfort, attempts to feed the psychological hungers and temporarily blocks emotion.

When patients eat compulsively, maybe binge-eat, they have a sense of dissociation from their surroundings. It is as if they are caved in their space, seeing nothing around them. Such binge-eating tends to be triggered by a surge of uncontrollable emotion that must be quelled. They rarely really taste the food, and the texture of the food is more important than the taste. The food needs to be of a texture that the patient perceives as fulfilling the task of feeding her psychological hunger and of holding her emotions at bay.

This way of eating does not necessarily entail large bags of food at one time or a persistent period of eating. Patients will indulge in mini-binges characterized by fast eating of large mouthfuls of food, cursorily chewed and swallowed in lumps. They usually do this in secret, when no one else is looking. They will also take large amounts of food at meal times and eat another helping when they do not need to. As the feelings prior to doing this are examined, patients report on a sense of urgency, of deprivation, of emptiness, sometimes anger, panic, loneliness, and nearly always agitation. When the feeling or experience that precedes such eating is identified, there begins to open up a sphere in which the patient may understand why she overeats. For those who gradually but persistently overeat the process is much more subtle than for those who binge-eat very large amounts spasmodically. Such binge-eating is a more obvious and identifiable behaviour with more ready access to the feelings and sensations preceding it. Nonetheless, it is necessary to think of the continuous mini-binge style as entailing the same triggers and the same sense of loss of self.

When they give themselves permission to feel, patients contact extremes of rage, fear and sadness. They have held down these feelings for most of their lives. By eating and being overweight they have turned anger in upon themselves and have justified their self-loathing by their large unacceptable size and the physical evidence of their overeating that torments them after each indulgence. Releasing these emotions can be scary as the patient believes that if she starts crying she will never stop, or her anger will become uncontrollable, or her sadness overwhelming. When the obese patient is allowed to show her feelings and to manage them with a level of emotional literacy she will not need to hold them down with food.

Don't Have Needs

Obese patients discount their own needs in favour of others' needs. They do not know how to get needs met even if they are aware of what their needs are. They perceive themselves to have been neglected and unmet in some way as children. They have generally been party to caring that has centred on the needs of the parents rather than their own and they have therefore learnt that life is easier if they respond to others' needs and repress their own. They resort to eating and obesity in order to meet their subconscious needs. These needs relate to psychological hungers that are the focus of Chapter 10.

Don't Make It

This injunction is passed on subtly from the parent who fears their child's success. There may be verbal encouragement to achieve but a psychological message that says 'Don't be as clever as, or cleverer than, me'. Disallowing self-expression and recognition of ability to think and to succeed may be received in such phrases as 'You are getting too big for your boots', 'Who do you think you are?' or 'Don't grow beyond your station'. The Don't Make It injunction can be seen to be fulfilled through the discriminatory attitudes of others towards obesity. This is significantly present in the British culture where fat people are still discriminated against as far as selection for jobs and promotion are concerned.

Don't Think

The Don't Think injunction is not about being unable to think, but more about being told not to think. Obese patients are perfectly able to think but may not have been stroked for their thinking. In fact a cultural expectation and a label still associated with fat people is that they are 'stupid'. Though it is not my experience that obese patients cannot think and they are certainly not stupid, they seem to respond to the expectation by discounting themselves for all the reasons so far described. They often feel they have no forum for their capacity to think.

I have found that patients who do not engage in thinking at times in the therapeutic process are those who are most defended against 'knowing' themselves and changing because of the fear that this holds for them. They will move into confusion, scare or agitation if thinking brings them too near to facing and confronting their script beliefs.

Patients with a Don't Think injunction cannot name and make meaning of their sensations, feelings or intuitions, which is why they act upon them with compulsive eating. They need to be enabled to locate and interpret their feelings in order to move from using food to feed psychological hungers.

Those patients who have less or no fear of losing weight will respond more readily to cognitive and behavioural interventions that require thinking, discussion and reason, such as I have demonstrated in previous chapters. These tend to be the patients who have experienced a shorter term of obesity and who have less weight to lose. They would not carry a Don't Think injunction, or if they do it will be on the lower scale of intensity.

Don't Have Fun

Though the overweight patient often seems to fulfil the myth of 'fat and happy' I have found that this is a pseudo and defensive representation of the self. It is not a natural way of being, emanating from a core sense of self that has a right to laugh and have fun. The patients I have described in this chapter had little opportunity to have fun as children. They all had to bear socially and psychologically demanding environments with parents who were physically or psychologically absent.

I was very moved by a patient who wanted to play with her young daughter but said she had no idea how to do this. Her therapy centred on her learning not just how to play, but what to play and while she learnt how to play with her little girl, she learnt how to enjoy play for herself. She felt a marked and noticeable relief in her Child ego state, which was an important landmark in her reclaiming herself.

Another patient had had to care for a baby sister from a very early age and was given an undue amount of responsibility that extended to her later being put in charge of neighbours' children when she was about eight years old. Some of these children were older than her. When she was sexually abused at the age of ten by a stranger, she felt she needed to cope with it by herself and never told anyone. She had been bound into a position of caring for others, including the psychological well-being of her parents, from an early age so that childhood eluded her and fun was absent.

Obese patients feel that they are restricted in the way they can have fun because of their size and because they believe that cultural injunctions stop them having fun. It is like a collective voice that says: 'Fat people don't dance, don't play sports, don't go to the beach unless fully clothed, don't swim, in fact don't join in any physical activity that is fun because it displays their large size, which is uncomfortable for the observer'. The overweight patient will also believe that it is uncomfortable for the observer but that it is also uncomfortable to perceive themselves as displaying their bodies in any way.

The injunction against having fun that they have internalized from their childhood experience gets played out in their adult life through being obese. I would not say that it is an injunction necessarily central to a patient's decision to be overweight but it is well played out by that decision. However, I would say that to have fun in a Free Child way is important in releasing the patient from her binding introjects. It releases Free Child energy that is vital in the patient's recovery of her self.

Counter-injunctions and permissions

To counter the injunction, the patient creates conditions that allow her to operate without giving in fully to those psychological messages she has internalized. For instance, someone who has a Don't Exist injunction and who is still alive is clearly not obeying the injunction. As can be seen in some of the examples above, the patient will create a way in which she can exist. This may be characterized with an expression such as 'I am allowed to exist if I... ' For instance, Sal felt she was allowed to exist if she stayed fat, denied her self, played the happy clown role, remained submissive and didn't rock the boat. Sal felt that her body size was hiding her bad self that would otherwise have destroyed someone else (mother) or would have had to sacrifice herself. Rowena also felt that she could exist as long as she was fat. For Rowena however, it was more that she was protected by her large body size, which informed her that she did exist and that people around her confirmed that through their negative attention. Both these patients covered the primary injunction of Don't Exist with other injunctions that would have seemingly less destructive or potent sanctions.

Injunctions are all absurd demands lodged in the Child ego state. Parents would be amazed at the thought that their child felt they did not want her to exist, succeed, to feel, to think etc. as can be revealed in the Parent interview (see Chapter 7).

Injunctions are created at an unconscious level and the patient is unaware of them though she may be aware of the constraints she feels in both being and doing. For each injunction there is a corresponding permission that psychotherapy will work towards. Permissions are simply the opposite of the injunction under consideration. For Don't Belong: You Can Belong; For Don't Be You: You Can Be You and so forth.

Patients need permissions. Permissions balance the injunctions. An attuned and empathic therapeutic relationship and the trust encapsulated within it, provide ground for permissions for patients to exist, be who they are and be important. Throughout the therapy they are encouraged to feel and think and know that these capacities are not mutually exclusive. They are allowed to have needs and eventually know that they can ask for what they want. They get a sense of belonging to the human race as they experience positive regard, respect, empathy, interest and attunement. The success of the therapy with long-term sufferers of obesity depends upon the commitment to the relationship and trust.

Contacting the inner Child self

The Child ego state plays a major part in the long-term sufferer's need to maintain their large size or for the chronic overeater to continue using food to feed psychological hungers. In reactive or shorter-term obesity this is not necessarily the case. The reactive obese patient will usually make significant shifts by working with the Parent ego state and the Child ego state with the Adult always in control. The emphasis is on Adult to Adult transactions as a means of understanding the persuasion of either the Parent or the Child or both.

For long-term sufferers and for those who use their body as a defence, working directly with the Child ego state is necessary. As demonstrated, the questionnaire enables the therapist to find key areas of Child fears. Physiological displays will indicate Child discomfort. From there the patient's belief systems and of course her fears of what she believes or fantasizes will happen if she loses weight can be discovered.

It is important for the patient to make a relationship with her inner Child self. It is not an instant procedure and resistance can be profound, but it is a vital goal. I invite the patient to see herself in the room as her child self and to describe the child she sees. There is significance in the age at which she appears to herself in this way. I encourage compassion for this child. When it is not forthcoming, I will provide the compassion until such time as the patient can supply it for herself. In this way the Child is protected from the demon within it whilst the demon can express its hatred and loathing.

When the patient forms a positive and loving relationship with herself she begins to see how she can care for herself. Sometimes a patient will choose a soft toy to represent her Child self when she is ready to make a relationship with, and reclaim her inner Child. The patient learns to relate to the self-object, monitoring her feelings as she moves further into this relationship with herself. I advise her to look after the toy, keeping it safe and comfortable as if it is her real child. The patient finds it harder to ignore an actual physical representation of herself than to discount that part of her ego self.

Issues of supply

Addictions, money issues, sexual inappropriateness are all presenting issues that can be related to the limited supply of love and attunement in infancy. They represent the patient's sense of deprivation and scarcity of love and stroking in the here and now.

Issues of supply relate to the first few months of life. Touch, food, comfort, mirroring, attunement and above all, love and welcome into the world, are preconditions for healthy organization of the self. A 'secure base', (Bowlby 1969) is necessary for the freedom to find oneself and explore the world. The long-term obese patients I have introduced throughout this book did not present with having experienced a safe base on which to develop a cohesive sense of self or to build up trust in themselves or with others in relationship.

If a child *feels* loved she can tolerate a level of disappointment and pain in her life. If she does not feel loved the patient will turn to food as one way of compensating for the sense of scarcity that arises from absence of love. The provision of food is one of the media in which the baby can sense the mother's ability to 'read' her. It involves touch, mirroring as the baby watches the mother's face whilst feeding, and attunement and tolerance of the infant's need to feed or let go. It is not surprising therefore, that the need for love, for instance, can become confused with the need to eat.

Free Child fun days

A Free Child fun day is where overweight patients are able to play at different ages, with guidance as infants and with choice and negotiation as older children. I run these at intervals so that patients can have an opportunity to let themselves enjoy Free Child activities in a safe and contained environment, with encouragement and without criticism. My aim is for them eventually to give themselves permission to have fun and to know how to do this as well as experiencing being met with empathy and developmentally appropriate attunement within a solid therapeutic relationship.

Rowena attended a fun day. At first she tested my acceptance of her by bringing filthy objects including dog mess as treasures whilst acting out her three-year-old aggression. (I give my diagnosis of the meaning of this behaviour in Chapter 11 in the context of the analysis of transferential phenomena and games.) Gradually throughout the day she allowed herself to play more and more freely. At the end of the day I provide a relaxation phase for reflection and calming. In this period my patients may practice holding and touching with each other in a safe environment, or they can choose to self-soothe. Both choices are appropriate. The former permits the patient to know and ask for what she wants; to redress myths of her being untouchable and to enjoy and reclaim her right to touch. The latter facilitates the patient's awareness of options for self-soothing. For the first time, Rowena wanted to be, and was, held. Being able to do this was highly significant in her development in freeing herself from her belief that she was unlovable.

As a result of these Free Child fun days, I find that patients become more self-accounting. They free energy in the positive Child ego state, reducing energy in the negative Controlling Parent ego state. Without thinking about it, they have given themselves permission to be who they want to be, and to do what they want to do in the context of the day and thereby recognize that they can act upon these permissions without incurring terrifying sanctions. Though at first they need support to cross the boundary of the Parent messages that say that they should not be acting like this as grown-ups, and then that their Child should not be having fun in this way, they soon develop a freedom that becomes their own. They recognize their right to do this, which is in itself empowering. Their freedom to be who they want to be and do what they want to do results in decontaminating the Adult ego state and deconfusing the Child. They understand that they no longer have to obey archaic Parent introjects without necessarily having to discuss them with the therapist because they know at an experiential level. The injunctions are challenged as they take permissions to be who they want to be, to have fun, to be important, to be a Child, to show feelings, to be close and to think in the safe environment created by the safe physical surroundings and the therapeutic relationship. The Adult becomes an observer to the process and recognizes the value of this reclamation of self. A patient will take from these fun days what she is able to, and which is dependent on the depth of her issues and the time she has spent in therapy before attending.

After one such Free Child fun day, Rowena reported feeling empowered. She confronted a taxi driver who had been rude to and dismissive of her. She confronted him in a congruent and self-accounting way such that the taxi driver became aware of his negative attitude. In that interchange she stopped presenting as unimportant. He apologized to her and the next day a bouquet of flowers arrived for her by way of acknowledgement of regret at his insensitivity. He saw her as important enough to warrant this apology. This was a huge challenge to Rowena's belief system. She realized that she had discounted herself for so long and so profoundly that she invited equivalent dismissal from others. Subsequently, Rowena said she was ready to work with her belief about her mother's death and her own lovability. It was to be a major turning point in her journey.

Working with the early Child ego state

Below I have included an example of working with Rowena, exploring her Child ego state.

Case study: Child ego state, Rowena

In a group therapy session Rowena asked to explore her feelings and relationship with regard to her mother. In the course of the work that followed, I asked if she would agree to reality test her belief that people didn't like her and that this was because she was unlovable since she had decided she was unlovable because her mother 'left her'. She agreed. I was asking her to engage in what appeared to be an Adult assessment, knowing that if she realized that in reality there was evidence to show people did like her, she would struggle to maintain her negative belief system about being unlovable.

I encouraged Rowena to talk about the positive units of recognition or strokes she had received recently. She became quite animated as she thought about all the times people around her had shown her that they cared for her. I reflected this back to her and said that she was in fact talking about how lovable she is. I said that something wasn't quite fitting, because she was indicating her lovability whilst maintaining she was not lovable. Rowena said that it was 'OK for others to let you know you are lovable, but if you say "I'm lovable", that's like blowing your own trumpet. Isn't it?' The work proceeded as follows:

Therapist: It didn't sound like blowing your own trumpet to me. Do you think that is what you have been doing?

Rowena: (*With some hesitation and loss of animation*) A bit, yeh...not as much as I thought (*Rowena seemed a little confused.*)

Therapist: So if you say 'My mother didn't leave me because I am not lovable, I am actually lovable' that would be blowing your own trumpet?

Rowena: Put like that, no. (*Rowena laughs.*)

Therapist: What happened there? Did I wrap it up for you?

Rowena: No, because when you look at it sensibly, er...how to put this... I suppose, yeh, because...it is wrapped up, because if you sit there and say 'My mum didn't die because she didn't love me' then that's a sensible thing to think, isn't it? That's a sensible way of looking at it. Because obviously...somebody doesn't die because they don't love you. (*Rowena now seemed very small and a little scared. Her voice was soft and hesitant. She realized what she had just said.*)

Therapist: Would you like to say that again?

Rowena: Somebody doesn't die because they don't love you. (*This was said slowly and cautiously.*)

Therapist: What are you feeling? (*Rowena now looked scared.*)

Rowena: Scared. (*Rowena's voice trembled and her body folded.*)

Therapist: Why scared?

Rowena: Because I just said it...

Therapist: Where are you feeling your scare? (*As Rowena seemed to be regressing, I felt it was appropriate to*

	connect with her body self. It was likely that she would regress to early infancy since her mother died when she was very young.)
Rowena:	(*Points to abdomen. Cries. She then suddenly looked at me.*) No. It wasn't scary. (*Still sounding scared and dealing with a confusion.*) I just felt like crying.
Therapist:	Would you be willing to say it again?
Rowena:	(*Sniffing.*) Somebody doesn't die because they don't love you. (*Very tentative.*)

Rowena seemed very young and it seemed that she would regress further. I felt she needed more safe containment and wondered if she wanted someone to hold her and whether she wanted cushions around her. She said she wanted another member of the group to hold her and she took up my offer of cushions. She wanted them all around her. She then felt safe. I asked her if she would like to say the words again. She repeated her words and asked if she could say them again. It was as though she was stepping carefully through each stage of her realization. She spoke softly and cautiously and seemed to test out the safety of what she was now saying and believing. There were long pauses between each statement. This is what she said:

Rowena:	Somebody doesn't die because they don't love you.
	Your mum doesn't die because she doesn't love you.
	Nobody dies because they don't love you.
	My mum didn't die because she didn't love me.
	My mum didn't die because she didn't love me.
	My mum didn't die because she didn't love me.
	(*Very peacefully.*) My mum didn't die because she didn't love me. I think my mum did love me.

Rowena wanted to stay with the peaceful feeling she felt as she engaged with her statement that her mother loved her. She did not now need to be held but could provide her own containment. She felt a peace that had long eluded her. Released from the belief that her mother died because she was not lovable, she became aware of her lovability. She could no longer maintain her script system. She was free to change the behaviours that had accompanied her crippling beliefs.

In this piece of work Rowena regressed to a very early developmental stage. She therefore needed me to respond to her within that developmental phase. I saw it as the stage of being that relates to birth to six months (Levin 1988). In ego state analysis, she was contacting an early experience of herself that she clearly felt in her body self (CI Somatic Child) when she indicated fear in her abdominal area. For this reason I paid attention to her body sensation and her physical sense of safety in the cocooning. Her mother was ill from her birth and it was likely that Rowena would sense her mother's frailty when entering that period phenomenologically. In Chapter 12 I analyse further the need for her cocooning at this time.

I relate the body self and the early sensation and knowledge of existence through that body experience to this early Child ego state. The somatization that results from early deficit I see as being part of CI otherwise known as the Somatic Child. The decision to use the body as a defence, as a way of a patient knowing she exists, and as a way of being in the world, I also relate to early childhood. Therefore to work at this level is important in releasing long-term obese patients from their self-destructive early script decisions.

Summary

In this chapter I have aimed to give a synopsis of various ways of thinking about the part the Child ego state plays in the overweight patient's need to eat or be physically big in the world. The Child ego state is a highly complex phenomenon and one chapter can do little more than scrape the surface of the information available to the therapist when considering working with this ego state with the patient. I have therefore chosen specific concepts and focus that I hope have indicated some useful ways for thinking about the script decision of the overweight patient.

Each time the Parent ego state is analysed, it is important to think about the response to that Parent influence in the Child ego state. To this extent they are inseparable as a focus of investigation. When the obese patient is eating excess food and maintaining her large size she is most likely to be operating from her Child ego state. She will have heightened energy in this ego state to the detriment of her Adult ego state, which will be reduced in energy. If she has a deep-seated issue such as believing herself to be unlovable and not having the right to exist, her major energy source and the pain, sense of deprivation and conflict that arises from wanting to be lovable and to exist will be in the Child ego state. If she is responding to Parent messages that she can hear and locate as being engendered by a specific parent figure in real life, then the energy is likely to be distributed between her Parent and her Child ego states and conflict that may arise will be between these ego states. In either case the

Adult ego state is low or devoid of energy when it comes to matters of eating and weight control.

Work with reactive overeaters and short-term obesity sufferers will focus primarily on introjected Parent messages and the work with the Child ego state will focus on the way the patient is still responding to these parent introjects. If the patient is successful in making the required re-decisions and behavioural changes to her own satisfaction there is no need to enter into deeper analytical work with the Child ego state. For long-term sufferers, the more cognitive methods of investigation will only form part of the treatment direction. The Child will be a major focus of concern.

Chapter 9

The Adult Ego State

Transactional Analysis is both psychoanalytic and cognitive behavioural and this is one of its major strengths as understanding why the patient behaves as she does may not be enough for her to effect change. The final stage in therapy with the obese patient is to aim for behavioural change. The key issue is that the patient feels she has a choice to lose weight. She has to understand that she no longer needs to respond automatically in a driven way. She also needs to understand that she does not have to depend on others to 'do it for her'. She may ask for help and create a partnership. She does not have to discount her ability to make decisions and take control of her future. She may choose to stay as she is, but it is her choice to do so. This is Adult thinking and making an informed choice is an Adult ego state activity. She needs to feel in charge of herself and responsible for her actions if she is to lose weight or if she is to be content with the weight she is. Having said this, the choice to stay the weight she is is an option more available to the moderately obese patient rather than long-term sufferers and morbidly obese patients.

The Adult functions largely in conscious awareness. It is the rational, thinking, problem-solving ego state. It assesses possible future consequences of present behaviours and can assess the effect of the past on the present. Age-appropriate thoughts, feelings and behaviours are associated with the Adult ego state. It can be dynamic and exciting.

The Adult has the capacity to observe, to negotiate, mediate and bring together information that leads to a decision. The Adult is used to do this interpersonally and intrapsychically. That is to say, in dialogue or communication with others and in the internal dialogue. If the Adult is contaminated by Parent or Child its energy is reduced and at times the patient will act from the contamination believing that archaic systems and strategies are present realities.

The Adult ego state qualities are important if the obese patient is to understand herself and the origin of her fat-making script decisions; if she is to assess them and the consequences of changing her behaviour and to take control of her future rather than replaying outdated behavioural systems.

What is clear is that the Adult ego state potency is reduced if the Child ego state is in opposition. This is why a patient may use her Adult to decide that she needs to lose weight for health reasons but cannot carry out the weight loss if her Child is not convinced it is the right thing to do. The Adult, in effect, needs the cooperation of the Child self in order to effect behavioural change.

The Adult should, whenever possible, be engaged in contracting with the patient for the treatment direction and therapeutic outcome. As previously noted, it is not viable to have weight loss per se as a therapeutic goal. What is appropriate is to find out why someone is using body size or food in such a non-self-supportive or self-destructive way. Once the patient understands why, she can make new choices and evolve new strategies for herself. This would be part of the final stage of therapy. The stage at which the patient finds new ways of being and needs support in testing out how this works for her.

I cannot work with weight loss as the goal, though it would certainly be an overall frame of reference. Such a contract would set up the pressures the patient experiences in her life outside the therapy room. Failure to lose weight would act as a sabotage to the therapeutic process. The therapist would be cast in the role of the parent who is to lead the patient into weight loss, and failure to lose weight would result in shame. Games would be set up ending in the familiar negative pay-off for the patient. If the underlying causes of her obesity are left unresolved she will not lose weight. This is the major reason why such a contract is not viable.

When the patient has faced her demons and understands why she eats or uses her body in this painful way, she can then consider her options and choose viable options for herself. She is then responsible for the choices she makes. The patient needs to feel empowered such that she can make these choices and she cannot feel this empowerment unless she releases her Child ego state from the defence strategies she has created. When she has done this work, she can make choices about her weight loss from her Adult ego state.

Until then she will operate only from her Parent introjects, her Adapted or Rebellious Child responses, and her deep-seated fears.

In psychotherapy the patient needs to understand her Child fears and how they arose; her Parent messages that bind her in a life she finds painful, where they came from and the fact that she is still obeying outdated commands and requirements; and by doing so to build up energy in the Adult ego state. With her Adult she can assess the situation, whatever that might be, and make an informed decision in the here and now. Other practitioners will offer exercise routines, weight loss regimes, dietary advice and other related guidance. When the patient is psychologically free to choose, she will decide from her Adult self whether she needs further help, or whether she has lost enough weight, or feels content as she is.

It is necessary to explain to the patient why weight loss as such is not a viable psychotherapeutic goal. Psychotherapy is not about providing diet sheets, weighing the patient, checking foods eaten etc. I explain to the patient what I can offer and she has the right to accept or refuse. What often happens is that in the course of therapy, the patient begins to lose weight without having consciously to change her eating patterns. She does not reach for extra food as often as she begins to understand herself and her needs. The goal is for psychological change that then allows cognitive and behavioural change.

The Adult needs to be engaged in an observing role wherever possible. As can be seen from the transcript of my work with Rowena in Chapter 8, she necessarily regressed to a point where her Adult was not available to her. She needed to sense the strength of my Adult to hold her process and my attunement and empathic response using all my ego states, to trust that she could enter her early phenomenological experience. Some sessions later however, she could make sense of that experience and its meaning and re-evaluate her belief system together with her corresponding behaviour with regard to food and size. She would do this from her Adult self.

When working with shorter-term or reactive obesity, I find there is more opportunity to work much earlier with the observing Adult than in long-term sufferers. In the main, the reactive sufferer does not have the complexity of script beliefs that keep her in obesity. The psychotherapy is about making meaning in the here and now as demonstrated in the work with Alison in Chapter 7 who quickly saw that she had been automatically, subconsciously, responding to outdated commands. She was immediately able to make meaning of this discovery and to change her behaviour. Her Adult was present in the process and she therefore recognized the Parent messages, assessed the absurdity of her continuing to respond to those messages and made a decision to choose an alternative behaviour. She did not experience opposition from her Child ego state.

Shorter-term and reactive obesity and the Adult ego state

A shorter-term sufferer is rarely morbidly obese. In the unusual situation where the patient has gained weight to morbid levels in a short time, then her treatment direction would be similar to that of the long-term sufferer. If the patient is eating in response to a life crisis, such as bereavement, divorce, unemployment, moving house or any other major life stressor the therapeutic work will focus primarily on the cause of the stress and her reaction to it. It may be that this work will be sufficient for the patient to relinquish her over-eating without specific attention to her need for food. A process of grieving such losses is age-appropriate and the patient may be seeking support in understanding her reactions. The primary cause of her overeating can be seen as the recent stressor and not archaic trauma. However, if this is not the case and the patient has a pattern of resorting to food in response to critical stressors, then the treatment direction will involve exploration and understanding of her need to reach for food at these times. As with short-term obesity, the therapy is less likely to involve early regressive work.

Sections I and II of the questionnaire at the end of Chapter 5 are particularly relevant when working with shorter-term sufferers and obese patients. They will normally not have the depth of emotional response I would associate with the long-term sufferer. Hence the final question in each section about the most impactful of all the questions in that section will tend to elicit a practical assessment in the here and now rather than an emotionally charged archaic response.

The therapist can invite the patient to be 'interested' and 'intrigued' and to make links between the past and her present behaviour, asking such questions as 'Do you still want to do this?' and 'What would be the consequences if you do something different now?' The Adult is able to see the absurdity of responding in the present as if she is still in a parent–child relationship and can 'write over' the 'parent tapes' with her own age-appropriate schema.

The word 'intrigue' appeals to the curious Child self and is therefore non-threatening language.

These patients can respond readily to putting distance between the impulse to eat and the action of eating. They can see the sense in waiting and making a decision as to whether to eat or not at this moment. The intervention of inviting the patient to put psychological distance between impulse and action is not primarily to stop the patient from eating, but to allow time for her to consider the pros and cons of doing so at any one moment. The patient may decide to put actual physical distance between herself and the food, for example, putting it back in the fridge or the cupboard with a view to eating it later. Or she may decide she does want to eat it immediately. The importance of the exercise is to begin to build up the idea of having a choice to eat or not. Most obese patients feel so compelled to eat that there is no concept of the idea of choice. I find the shorter-term sufferer can make this shift far easier. She does not have the dependence on food or weight for survival, safety or identity in the way the long-term sufferer does. Patients with high food dependence will not be able to sustain the operation of distancing action from impulse even by a few seconds until significant releasing work has been done. When a patient binge-eats with all the urgency that entails she will not have any Adult energy available to provide this distance for herself.

After administering the first two sections of the questionnaire in Chapter 5, each question can be followed by an invitation to identify the significance of the patient's answer with regard to her present eating behaviour. This will take some time but is a focused and productive way of working cognitively and behaviourally with the patient. The patient whose Adult ego state is not restricted by Child fears will work well at this level and make changes in response to her findings. There is generally not a need for long-term therapy or for specific early Child-orientated work.

The Adult ego state can be targeted in the therapy room and the patient can be encouraged to use it for herself in her daily life. It is appropriate to 'teach' concepts of TA to the patient if she is available to receive them as her own set of tools. Many patients are intrigued and excited by the information they get from working through the concepts. Such interventions clearly need the Adult to be present and functioning. The patient can then identify what ego states she is using when she wants extra food. She can identify her Parent messages and decide whether to listen and obey or choose her own course of action. She can tune into her Child needs and find appropriate or less self-harming ways of meeting them. She can translate the concepts into questions for herself. For example, she can ask herself whether it is food she needs or something else. If something else, she can find out what it is and find a way of supplying it. She can deliberate on whether she needs to eat instantly or whether it would suffice to have something later. She can question the need to say yes to others who may be persuading her to eat and she can assess the consequences of saying no. In fact she can have the tools that allow her to say no and remain OK. She can choose to nurture herself in a better way than eating excess food. She can choose to have fun in preparing attractive meals. In fact with her Adult energy stimulated she can discover her options and choose those that are viable for her. Once the unconscious driving forces are brought to consciousness the patient can weigh up the pros and cons of holding on or letting go.

The Adult ego state is excluded when someone is eating to excess and maintaining a large size. If the Adult were sufficiently charged with energy, the patient would not make a choice to self-harm or to respond automatically to Child fears and Parental introjects. It makes sense therefore to aim for decontamination of the Adult ego state. For the shorter-term sufferer, there is likely to be less opposition from the Child ego state. For the long-term sufferer that opposition is strong and dominant. For the long-term sufferer or the patient with deep-seated issues relating to her weight and eating, release in the Child ego state is necessary before the Adult can gain or regain executive energy. It is only then that a primary focus on Adult interventions will be therapeutically appropriate. Hence the difference in the therapeutic approach.

The Adult ego state and the internal dialogue

You will be aware that we all have an internal dialogue from which we make decisions. Patients can be encouraged to listen to their own internal dialogue and to differentiate between what the Parent is saying, what the Child wants and whether the Adult is around to assess the two points of view.

A way of promoting this internal process is by using multiple-chair work. The patient chooses chairs for her Parent, Child and Adult. She then moves from chair to chair cathecting the appropriate energy for each ego state. The role of the Adult in this case is to:

- join in the debate that is in progress between the ego states

- observe the process and comment on it to the other two ego states

- discuss the process with the therapist where necessary and to be the recipient of the therapist's observations when indicated.

In three-chair work the bias in the Parent ego state is often towards Critical Parent (CP) and that in the Child towards Adapted Child (AC) or Rebellious Child (RC). In this case it is useful to use a five-chair technique so that the Nurturing Parent (NP) and the Free Child (FC) can be present. I have observed whilst working with obese patients that both these ego states seem to be excluded or very low in energy leaving AC and CP in control. The obese patient is usually nurturing towards other people, sometimes overly so, because of her need to be liked and loved. She does, however, have a highly critical internal Parent and any Nurturing Parent is used to feed her psychological needs with food, which constitutes inappropriate self-parenting. This is negative nurturing since attuned self-nurturing eludes her. Her Free Child has lost the ability to distinguish between biological and psychological hungers and particularly in longer-term sufferers, fears deprivation. Balanced insight to any problem is achieved in the presence of all ego states. The Adult can be the assessor, mediator and negotiator in chair work where the aim is to resolve a specified problem. When a patient has little Adult energy available, the therapist must hold this energy for the patient indicating potency and protection.

Ways in which the Adult ego state can be used in effecting change in the internal dialogue are shown in Figure 9.1.

Though the diagrams indicate communication patterns using three compound ego states, the same dialogical process can be used with the five ego states, dividing the Parent into Nurturing and Critical Parent and the Child into Adapted and Free Child. The possible patterns of communication are across all the ego states. Such patterns may be limited by low energy or exclusions in some ego states. Exclusions means that one or more ego states has no active energy and is usually decommissioned by another overpowering ego state. If the Adult is excluded then clearly this therapeutic intervention is contraindicated.

The internal dialogue will of course govern the external communication system. If an ego state is being excluded, the patient does not have a full capacity to assess her situation. She has a limited choice of ego states to

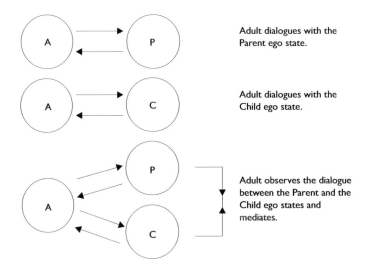

Figure 9.1 Possible Adult functioning in the internal dialogue

respond to and act from. For obese patients, it is clear that the dominance of Parent and Child ego states results in low energy in Adult, which then struggles to make informed choices when Parent or Child are in control of the eating function. For long-term sufferers and morbidly obese patients the Adult ego state remains overpowered by Parent and fearful Child ego states more consistently than in the case of shorter-term sufferers.

The potential capacity for internal dialogue using the Adult ego state function as observer, mediator and negotiator is shown in Figure 9.2 below. The diagram indicates the possible internal dialogue when all ego states are functioning. Much of the patient's time is spent in a set of dominant ego states whereby one or more are excluded. Exploration together reveals from which ego states the patient functions most of the time and in particular when in her world of overeating. The healthiest position is to have all ego states available and for the Adult to effectively select appropriate ego states from which to communicate and operate at any given time. With practice this would become spontaneous. In reality each one of us will discount (ignore) some ego states in certain situations. This is human. The task here is to maximize the positive energy available in all ego states and to have the option of using different ego states as far as is possible, rather than excluding those that in the obese patient's life would promote health and well-being.

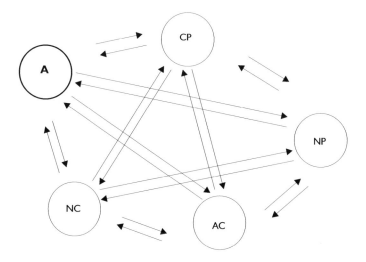

Figure 9.2 Possible communication patterns for internal dialogue and communication when all ego states are functioning

In our social interaction there are 25 communication channels. Each of the five ego state modes can potentially converse with each of the other person's five ego state modes. In reality, patterns are set up between individuals such that some ego states will be constantly excluded. For instance, when Rowena talked about being spoken down to by others, she would want to get out of their way as quickly as possible, a Child response. She was unable to call upon her Adult energy or even find an angry response that would have been self-accounting. When she began to feel a sense of self-worth, she was able to confront the taxi driver, choosing to do so from her previously excluded Adult.

In the following five-chair work, Jill agreed to take an observing Adult role from where she could listen to the internal dialogue, assess and mediate. This is a brief synopsis of the full event. However, it indicates the ego states that were available to Jill at different stages of the process.

Case study: five-chair work, Jill

Jill left therapy when she resolved her relationship with her father, boss and husband and had reduced her eating significantly so that she was losing weight. She felt a renewed sense of self-esteem. Four months later she called to ask if I would see her as she felt a struggle to maintain her recent eating pattern. I agreed. I listened to her account of her struggle. I assessed from her words, tones and gestures that she was seeking help from her Adult and not from her Adapted Child. She had not regained weight but felt that she might revert to binge-eating again if she did not understand her turmoil.

In the course of the brief-term therapy that followed I invited Jill to do some five-chair work. Though we had not met for four months the therapeutic relationship and working alliance were quickly re-established and she trusted me to hold the process. I asked Jill what she wanted from me and she said she needed me to watch and comment when necessary. We agreed that I would make observations to her Adult self if she got stuck or if she asked me to intervene from her Adult chair. I also negotiated with her that I might encourage her to speak from any ego state that was low in energy or silent. I would do this through her Adult.

From her Adult chair Jill made a statement of wanting to know why she felt an internal struggle to keep to what she knew to be a positive way of eating. Moving physically between chairs her dialogue went as follows:

CP: Because you are just stupid. You have no will power.

A: I have not put on weight and I haven't binge-eaten, so you can't say that.

CP: But now you're back here asking for help again. (*This was Jill's mother who would tell her she should get on with her life and not whinge.*)

A: Are you saying it is not appropriate to ask for help? (*Jill had resolved her belief that she needed to get on with life and not ask for help and in doing so now believed that it is OK to have needs, hence her ability to challenge her CP.*)

CP: (*There was no response at this point from her CP. Jill found this amusing. In later analysis she said she felt that her CP was acting 'in accordance with old habits but was like a paper tiger now'.*)

After a pause Jill moved to the Adapted Child chair. From there her tones were sulky and rebellious.

AC/RC: I want to eat like other people do. I want cakes and sweets and chocolate. I don't want to have to think about what I eat. I just want to be able to eat.

A: What do you think other people do then?

AC: They eat what they want. Clare eats whatever she wants. She never puts on weight.

A: We are different. We can't eat what we want. That's our truth. You know that. And you do have nice things to eat. I also think that the majority of people can't just eat what they want if you are suggesting that this means they eat anything and everything.

A: (*Jill then addressed me.*) I am feeling angry from this chair.

Therapist: Does it feel appropriate for you to feel angry there?

A: (*Thinks.*) Well, yes I think so. Actually, I think I feel sad about it. I am not sure, perhaps I feel both angry and sad. It does feel like regret that I can't eat what I want. …and yet…mm…I know lots of people can't eat whatever they want. In fact, it doesn't really make sense to want lots of fatty foods, when I think about it.

A: (*Jill again addressed me from the Adult chair.*) I feel stuck.

Therapist: Do you feel able to move to another chair? One you haven't sat in yet?

NP: (*Jill moved to the NP chair. Silence.*)

A to therapist: She's not saying anything.

Therapist: Ask her why not.

A to NP: Why aren't you saying anything?

NP: I feel pushed out. (*Jill addressed me again.*) This is where the anger is!

A: I am asking you to say what you think. Say what you can do.

NP: When you struggle you only listen to CP. You don't give me a chance. I can help if you tell me how you feel. We can find different ways together. When you get up tight, we get pushed out. (*Points to FC.*) Then it seems to me, things get worse.

FC: (*Jill moves to FC chair.*) I want to play more. I don't have fun at all when you are up tight. I don't want foods that make me fat either. They make me unhappy. I hate the feel of them if I get a lot.

A: You're right. When I get into this sort of struggle, I don't play. I shut off inside myself. I don't have fun and I don't communicate very well.

NP: And you don't ask for help from people either. You struggle alone. (*Jill stopped here. She looked at me and I commented that she seemed to have finished the dialogue but her body language suggested she had more to say. She nodded.*)

A: I think the sadness was from my Free Child self. That's interesting, almost as if I had let her down! It feels now like I need a conclusion, a sort of summing up.

Therapist: Why not draw a conclusion with the other ego states?

A: OK.

A: (*To other chairs.*) I think it is important for us to see that there are lots of people who need to control their eating. In fact the majority of people can't just eat what they want and so it is not helpful to get sulky about it. I think you (FC) are right, if we eat lots of fatty or bulky foods we get very uncomfortable and sluggish. And I recognize what you say about me not having fun, closing down inside myself when I feel that struggle going on. That isn't helpful either. Perhaps some fun is exactly what I need more of. I can also ask Jim for help and he can do things too. Perhaps I could do with a bit more attention when I hit this phase. Or perhaps it's that I am not getting enough attention that sends me into the struggle. Hmm. I will have to think more about that. I think you (*FC*) feel deprived. If I ask for help from Jim (*her husband*)…or attention…cuddles maybe, or just to talk. Yes. I think we will all gain then.

The therapy that followed centred on Jill developing strategies to ensure she asked for help, support and attention; to notice when she was closing down and to find out what she needed for herself in order to prevent decline into a familiar struggle; to have more fun. Jill had kept constant energy in her Adult ego state, which enabled her to understand her psychological process. She was able to see how she discounted her helpful ego states.

A way of plotting the distribution of energy in the ego states is to use the egogram, developed by J. Dusay (1980). Jill was using her Adult ego state as agreed, however, initially her Nurturing Parent and Free Child were low in energy. Her egogram depicting her energy distribution at this stage is shown in Figure 9.3.

As Jill continued, she redistributed energy from her CP and AC to her Nurturing Parent (NP) and Free Child (FC) at the invitation of her Adult ego state. In future, Jill would recognize a repeated pattern of such behaviour that led to this distribution of energy and ensure, whenever possible, that she would check which ego states were operating and which she was excluding. Figure 9.4 shows the redistribution of her energy after the chair work.

Long-term sufferers, the morbidly obese patient and the Adult ego state

For long-term sufferers the distribution of energy tends to centre around the negative Critical Parent and the Adapted Child with visceral fear in the Free Child and an absence of energy in positive Nurturing Parent and low, easily overwhelmed energy in the Adult ego state. It is important to note that this is not necessarily the distribution of energy when patients are functioning in other areas of their lives. I am not suggesting that long-term sufferers do not

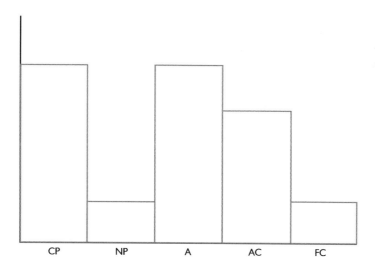

Figure 9.3 Jill's energy distribution at the beginning of her chair work using Dusay's egogram

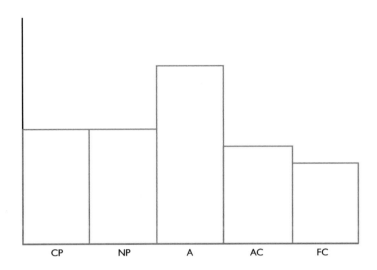

Figure 9.4 Jill's redistributed energy in her ego states after five-chair work

function from Adult at any time. This would certainly not be true. But in terms of their pain and suffering and their struggle to lose weight the influences of the Child and the Parent are far more dominant than the Adult who would make appropriate choices to avoid the pain.

It is this heightened energy, principally in the Child ego state, that implies a different treatment direction from those who have experienced briefer-term obesity. This is particularly so, as was seen in Chapter 8 on the Child ego state, for those whose eating and/or obesity is a defensive survival strategy. Whilst it is essential to build up the Adult ego state this is done primarily in the realm of the therapeutic relationship and work with the Child ego state for as the Child develops into health and leaves behind archaic beliefs, the Adult is strengthened. The process of integration involves accepting and incorporating the painful experiences and the healing of the effects of those experiences. It also requires acceptance and inclusion of the darker side of self. Work with patients towards a goal of heightened self-esteem and self-worth is not about making them all feel good. It is about accepting the shadow side into the self as part of the self and not as a part that cannot be tolerated and needs to be split off. Tolerance of this shadow side is difficult for the obese patient who sees the total self as worthless, which she confirms by her huge size.

I find that morbidly obese patients hold down emotion. They feel they should not cry and yet they are full of pain. Suppressed emotion leads away from Adult energy. Emotion is an organizer rather than a disorganizer or disrupter (Levenson 1999). Emotion shapes and informs cognition. It is important then that the patient is enabled to feel what she feels and act in accordance with those feelings even if she does believe that if she cries she will cry a tidal wave or if she hates she will be uncontainable. Releasing this pent-up emotion lets out the genuine and appropriate responses she has been holding down for years for fear of being too much and being alienated, responses she has held down with food. There is a marked difference in a patient's ability to be in the here and now before release of suppressed emotion and after that release. The Child becomes calmer and energy is released into the Adult ego state.

On the Free Child fun days (see Chapter 8), my patients learn that they can have fun by experiencing doing so in a safe environment. As they test me and experiment with their freedom with each other, they are able to demonstrate emotions of glee, frustration, sadness and fear. In consequence those like Rowena gain inner strength, which I interpret as increased Adult energy in the sense that the Adult is able to integrate the experiences and observe that she can have fun, she can play, feel sadness and fear and not be overwhelmed by these emotions. Rowena learnt this and she also importantly learnt that she did not overwhelm others. This recognition enabled her to face the fear of working at the earlier developmental domain of knowing she is lovable. Attention to and loosening of the visceral nature of that earlier phenomenological experience led her to be able to investigate her need for her large container represented by her extended body self.

Empathic enquiry, attuned responses and demonstrating that the therapist wants to get the patient's story right, provides an environment within which the patient also begins to piece her life story together in a way she will not have done before. The verbal mode enables organization in a way that the internal dialogue does not; hence the releasing nature of multiple-chair work in which the internal dialogue becomes ordered in so far as the patient moves deliberately from one ego space to another and uses verbal skills to 'communicate' between those ego states. Multiple-chair work is *a* method, not *the* method. In chair work, the patient becomes aware of the different modes of self from which she operates and specifically aware of the Adult ego state as different from her other ego states. There will be a recognized stage in the therapeutic treatment when it will be apparent that this would be an appropriate intervention for the patient.

Multiple-chair work for the long-term sufferer is likely to be emotionally charged unless the patient is avoidant or in denial. The therapist's task then is to both remain available at any time to support the patient in any of the ego states and to be part of the process and dialogue where indicated. In this way, the therapist stays in close relationship with the patient, providing a safe and holding environment whilst being ready to meet any part of the patient self that is in need of attention and contact. In my experience it is an intensified mode of relational psychotherapy. The therapist stays available to and aware of the total combined energy of the patient. Although the patient may be displaying significantly imbalanced distribution of energy in her domains of self, no ego state stands alone without the others being affected. Even if an ego state is excluded or devoid of active energy, the whole self is presented within the force and effects of that exclusion.

Assessment of the patient's Adult energy specifically in relation to her overeating and obesity will guide the psychotherapist's choice of interventions. The Child ego state will be active in replaying old coping strategies and displaying adherence to archaic belief systems and entrenchment in past trauma. She will draw the therapist into the relational realms of transference and games. The therapy room is a patient's safe space to be seen and heard, a place to regress and test out the relationship and a place in which to make meaning, understand and find resolution. Patients need to be seen and acknowledged as adults. Obese patients find themselves in an environment that often demeans them. Their ability to think clearly and constructively is often discounted. The patient will be used to discounting it herself as well. As the contract I have with the patient is not for weight loss but to understand the reasons why she eats and stays fat, whatever work she and I decide to do together can be understood at the appropriate time in this context. This way the patient is encouraged to make meaning of her struggle and conflict in wanting to reduce her weight and yet being unable to do so. She makes this meaning in her Adult ego state.

Chapter 10

Psychological Hungers

I have referred to the psychological hungers in other chapters and so far have relied on the fact that the term is indicative of there being hungers other than biological hunger that cause patients to eat excessively and guard themselves with layers of fat. In this chapter I describe those other hungers and how I see the patient feeding them with food or defending against them with a large body size.

Just as we need to feed our biological hunger with food and drink in order to thrive both mentally and organically, so we need to attend to our psychological hungers in order to develop both physically and mentally. Berne (1973) named such hungers as: Stimulus Hunger, Recognition Hunger, Contact Hunger, Structure Hunger, Sexual Hunger and Incident Hunger. He also referred to Leadership Hunger, which I, influenced by such developmental theorists as Daniel Stern, think of as hunger for mastery or Power Hunger. When needs or hungers are not met in infancy and throughout formative years they do not 'go away'. Denied or substituted needs continue to unconsciously influence thoughts, feelings and behaviours.

A baby who is left in a bare room, with little human contact will not thrive physically or mentally. In the early 1940s Spitz (1945) reported on his studies of children in care who had been separated from their mothers before bonding and who lived in a clinical environment with little stimulus. He found that by the end of a year they were both physically and mentally retarded through sensory deprivation. Their growth was stunted and they were mentally impeded. Studies also showed that most children so deprived will catch up in their physical and mental development if given adequate and appropriate caring. This is clearly pertinent to clinicians who will strive to provide a reparative experience for the patient within the therapeutic relationship. The power of the relationship is not to be underestimated. It is significant to bear in mind the hungers that are or can be met within the working alliance and the process of psychotherapy or other clinical or practical intervention.

Stimulus Hunger

Stimulus Hunger 'drives the individual to social action in order to avoid sensory deprivation' (Berne 1973, p.191). Stimulus Hunger in fact can be seen in the light of all the other hungers for human contact: recognition, structured time, sexual activity, the need for incident and exercising power may all be seen as providing some level of engaging stimuli. A dictionary definition of a stimulus is: 'a thing that rouses to activity or energy' (*Oxford English Reference Dictionary*).

In analysis, that activity and energy might be seen as towards growth and thriving as an infant, which would be an involuntary activity, or voluntary activity when the infant has the capacity for this. A stimulus might be a sound, a colour, a texture, movement, in fact anything that is perceived by any of the senses. An infant is intrigued by a colourful mobile, can relate to music and movement of self and others. The infant learns about herself through her mother's touch and holding and through buffeting against her physical environment. A variety of stimuli are needed in order for the infant to thrive. In the same way, as adults we need a variety of stimuli and particularly purposeful stimuli.

Eugene Heimler (Heimler 1975) studying behaviour of prisoners in Buchenwald and Auschwitz noted that when the prisoners were given a repetitive purposeless task of moving sand and rubble over four miles from one end of the camp to another and then back again, some prisoners gave up and died, some threw themselves against the electric fence and committed suicide, some attacked others and some escaped into 'internal immigration' and became insane. A prisoner himself, Heimler describes reverting to extreme detachment, that internal immigration that allowed him to believe that he was somewhere else for at least some time during each day. This in fact was his survival mechanism. The process of internal immigration then, can be either destructive, resulting in insanity, or constructive in the way that Heimler imagined himself to be somewhere else so effectively that he could, at least in his mind, escape the brutality of the camp for some period each day. This process involved a high level of detachment over which Heimler at least had some control. When that control is forfeited, insanity results. When later he worked with the unemployed in London he discovered similar options applied for those who felt they had a meaningless existence: self-destruction, insanity or antisocial behaviour.

The lack of purposeful activity and occupation that provide the stimulus to act and generate energy leads to deficit in all the hungers. The patient becomes unable to accept strokes of recognition from others when she no longer has the wherewithal to make meaning of them within herself. Perhaps this entails another hunger, that of meaning and purpose.

Stimulus Hunger may be met in the infant by touch, sounds, sights, tastes, movement, and smells and in appropriate levels of attention relating to the five senses. The infant has the capacity to 'switch off' or turn her head away in order to avoid overstimulation. The child knows what is enough for her and will close her eyes and sleep when she has been stimulated enough. A baby can be seen to divert her attention away from the stimulus as a means of disengaging. If the carer insists on continuous contact and fussing over the child, she will develop defences to cope with the intrusion. Engulfment is as threatening as abandonment. Using the body as a defence against intrusion, the patient may have decided to withdraw the body self, such as in anorexia or push out the body boundary to keep others at bay, as in obesity. It is also true that these defences may be used in opposition to this structuring, that is, that the obese patient who is understimulated will push out the body boundary to meet the world that is not meeting her, whilst the anorexic learns to withdraw within the self.

It is clearly pertinent to investigate the patient's ability to respond to stimuli, whether she can find ways of stimulating herself towards a feeling of at least temporary well-being or contentment in ways other than reaching for food; whether she feels overstimulated, as some do in their bid to please others and 'buy' friendship and love through doing. When the patient is ready to move into providing strategies for herself to maintain behavioural change then the broad spectrum of stimuli available to her in addition to those that relate to the other major hungers would be usefully examined. If a patient eats when alone it would be apposite to look at ways in which she can use other stimuli to 'feed' her. This could mean finding pleasure and satisfaction in art, colour, sounds, sights and so on that combine sensory stimulation with activity (time structuring).

To acknowledge the significance of food it could also include ways of preparing healthy foods to stimulate sight and texture as well as taste and smell. This is largely a cognitive behavioural approach that is only accessible when the patient is either psychologically well self-supported or is supported by the therapy significantly enough to experiment with finding behavioural alternatives. I use the word experimentation as the patient can discuss the reactions she has in response to her discovery of possible options for stimulus provision without feeling she is plunging prematurely into definitive new ways of being. In the context of experimentation, the patient can explore, try out and stop as necessary or desired.

For some patients the stimulus that tells them they exist is food and the sensation of fullness, or nausea when having eaten too much. There is a sense in which the food-dependent patient will enter into a transitory state of detachment similar to that described by Heimler (1975) in his study of prisoners of war. When eating, the patient may withdraw into herself, stare into space and in a detached euphoric state will consume. The detachment is a stratagem in which the Child engages to prevent Parent and Adult involvement. She does not hear, or wins the fight against hearing, the Parent that tells her she should not be doing this. When she returns from the dream state she feels anxious, resentful, angry with herself and disgusted. Her Parent rushes in to chastise her. This is also however, a part of the construct that tells her she exists. In her unmet world she reverts to one of the defensive behaviours described by Heimler and turns her anger in upon herself. Overeating is physically self-destructive and the ensuing self-beating, psychologically so. This is discussed further in Chapter 12 in terms of early development and the need to dissociate and withdraw into the self. This dissociated state can occur in patients when eating is the only means of self-soothing or as one patient described it 'all you have left is your body'.

Let's return to my patient who displayed extreme excitement in thinking about what she was going to prepare for her dinner. As she described it, her face lit up, her eyes became animated. It was something like watching a well-acted sensual scene in *Moll Flanders*. She would think about what she wanted for dinner early in the day and then savour the thought of preparing it, cooking it and finally eating it. By the time she got to eat it she was highly stimulated, excited and alive. This excitement was a time in which she really felt she existed. When first in therapy, talking about her desired foods was the only time she displayed emotion. She reported never feeling any emotion about anything else until she came into therapy. She seemed essentially unmoved by any other stimulus.

Recognition Hunger

In TA, a unit of recognition is called a stroke by analogy to physical caressing in infancy. Berne referred to an infant's understanding of her developing self through mother's touch or strokes and the later transformation of these physical strokes into other forms of recognition and self-defining found in communication and interaction other than physical touch (Berne 1961). As we grow older we necessarily leave behind the high levels of holding and physical contact that are part of the infant world. However, just as we needed to be touched and held, mirrored and met in infancy so we need a correspond-ingly adequate supply of 'touch substitutes', that is, strokes, throughout life in order to thrive. A stroke as this unit of recognition of our existence and per-ceived worth can be anything from a nodding acknowledgement, and a smile, to a close or intimate relationship.

Strokes may be positive or negative, conditional or unconditional. Bec-ause throughout life we need recognition, if there are no positive strokes to be had, negative strokes will suffice to indicate that recognition. Conditional strokes are about what we do, unconditional strokes are about who we are. In simple terms a positive unconditional stroke might be 'I like you', uncondi-tional negative stroking might be 'I don't like you'; positive conditional stroking, 'I like the way you do that' and negative conditional stroking, 'I don't like the way you do that'. There are also counterfeit strokes beautifully exemplified by the theatrical 'Darling, what a performance!', being unspecific about whether the performance was good or bad or implying it was good whilst actually knowing it was awful. The obese patient will have a height-ened awareness to counterfeit strokes, which is why it is essential to be aware of and to have worked with one's own prejudices as a therapist or practitioner.

The obese patient tends to be deprived or feel deprived of positive strokes. Some obese patients are rarely told they are beautiful, look lovely, do things well. They are often ignored or stereotypically thought to be slovenly, lazy and unintelligent without there being evidence for any of these negative qualities being attributed. Given the cultural attitude towards obesity, obese and specifically morbidly obese patients, feel they receive far more negative than positive strokes. Since they are often the recipients of name calling and undisguised rejection from strangers and there also tend to be negative strokes from within the family or with friends, if not directly, then indirectly, with comments such as 'You should go on a diet' or 'Should you be eating that?' the stroke imbalance of negative over positive is a reality. Nonetheless, if a patient believes she is not worthy, the negative strokes will be the ones she will relate to most. Patients often find great difficulty in hearing and internalizing positive strokes.

Stroke hunger is a visceral sensation that can be easily confused with biological hunger. The patient knows in her body self that she is not getting the recognition she desires though she is unlikely to be able to name her deficit. She will describe it in other ways within the narrative that tells her script story.

The patient uses food in order to feel stroked. The sensation of eating, chewing, swallowing and the subsequent extension of the gut when it is overfull, gives the patient a sense of existing. She rewards herself with food; she eats when she is sad or angry when a germane behaviour is to share her sadness and appropriately receive strokes in the form of gestures and murmurs of understanding and empathic response. When she cannot give herself positive strokes she gives herself plenty of opportunity for negative strokes from others and herself through the amounts she eats and the weight she gains. She is adept at self-castigation and even self-hatred. She desperately wants attention from others and this she will get in doses of negativity. She needs to find ways of getting strokes and feeling stroked other than by food. Slimming clubs provide a supply of strokes. The strokes are of course dependent on her size and her food intake and reduction of both. Her membership is food- and size-related.

Some obese patients will set up a strategy for getting strokes by being interminably available to help and do for others. The patient usually feels dissatisfied with this stroke-seeking behaviour because she tends to feel unappreciated and put upon. However, she will continue to give herself in this way as long as she believes that she will be rejected, and thereby completely unstroked, if she doesn't.

If the obese patient holds Don't Belong and Don't Be Close injunctions, she is axiomatically going to be stroke-deprived. She will not expect positive strokes from others and keeping herself out of close and genuinely intimate relationships, she will discount at the level of existence and or significance any strokes that people may extend to her. That is to say she will deny that she receives any strokes throughout her day because she does not have the ability to hear them until she is 'taught' to do so in the therapeutic process. If she hears them she will discount them by telling herself things like 'She was just being kind, she doesn't really mean it' or 'She had to say that'.

Feeling that one belongs in a community is a human need. The interaction that belonging provides, in whatever capacity that might be, is an essential source of stroking. The patient who withdraws more and more deprives herself of the opportunity for either positive or negative strokes. An extension of this physical withdrawal might be that the patient withdraws inside herself, keeping the body self as a protective shell against those others who are not safe to be with. This patient will clearly not be available to hear or feel positive strokes though she is likely to absorb negative strokes that confirm that withdrawal is the right option. This way she avoids the abyss of a fantasized strokeless existence.

The patient who speaks of fears of disappearing or being nothing, or not being noticed or shrivelling, or becoming invisible or fearing emptiness if she loses weight is talking about this abyss. At least whilst she is fat she is getting strokes that tell her that her existence has some meaning to others.

The obese patient does not usually present as having a history of perceivable positive stroking. Rowena (see Chapter 8) was deprived of the fundamental source of early infant stroking when her mother died. Her father did not talk about her mother; he worked hard as a miner and was not a good communicator. He did not know how to stroke her. He did not resort to overt negative stroking except when angry with her. What seemed to her like his withdrawal left her unstroked by him and confused. Throughout her life the pattern of non-recognition was repeated. At school and in subsequent training she felt her successes were overlooked and at work she was bypassed for promotion. She did not expect others to acknowledge her and it took a very long time before she accepted my genuineness and began to trust me. In the meantime she ate in order to stroke herself, maintained a large body size to keep others at a distance and to hide her hurt, 'unlovable' and vulnerable self. She could not recognize positive strokes, though there were clearly people in her life who did interact with her in a positive way. For a long time she did not know how to let these strokes in. Accepting strokes meant giving herself to trust a relationship and this she could not do. She had a mother who had left her (died) when she was an infant, a father who withdrew, and a husband whom she expected would leave her some day. Since she believed her mother had left her because she was unlovable, it made more sense that she would survive on negative strokes.

Sal (see Chapter 7) had received endless negative strokes because of her size. Her father negatively stroked her by his obdurate preoccupation with her weight. In adult life she continued to get recognition because of her imposing body self and the happy fat clown she created as a persona. Her husband was indifferent. Eventually her two sons adopted the intrusive behaviour reminiscent of father's such that their negative attention was also associated with her size. Without her weight, she felt she or another would shrivel and die, just as an infant would who was stroke-deprived. She did not believe in her own self-worth and therefore could not comprehend how she would get strokes if she did not attract them by being fat.

Until trust has been well and reliably established within the therapeutic relationship, patients such as Sal and Rowena will not recognize the empathic attention, aspiration for attunement and genuine self-presentation offered by the clinician as stroking. There may be a pseudo-psychotherapeutic alliance that could be mistaken for congruence and this will need to suffice until the real multifaceted and phase-appropriate relationship can be entered into by the patient.

Recognition Hunger is also about love. As was seen from the extract of Rowena's journey toward knowing she is lovable, she had assumed she was not lovable because of a Child fantasy that her mother died because she did not love her. Because of her father's subsequent veto on discussing mother, the belief was compounded. This sense of not being loved engenders a notion of scarcity in the infant, which then becomes a belief in the Child ego state. It becomes more generalized as 'There is not enough'. Hence the patient hoards food, needs to have food in the car 'just in case', must eat impulsively 'before it is taken away' or 'in case there is no more to come'. She feels a strong sense of deprivation when she diets. This sense of deprivation is frightening and may be experienced as life-threatening and so provokes the patient into eating again. It is also the force of that deprivation that compels her to increase her weight next time. This sense of deprivation must be a primary target of therapy before the patient can work at more cognitive levels of managing her lifestyle.

For the patient who plays the fat happy clown strokes are readily available. She gets attention and is good to have around as long as she remains in role. They are conditional on her maintaining the joker persona. Since the role she has taken up is a defence against being rejected she is reluctant to give it up. If she does her position in the group will change or she may not be able to stay in the group. As she plays the role she is discounting her ability to be in relationship without this front. Her fear is that she will be abandoned, which means she will be stroke-deprived.

The obese patient who is always available to do for others and rarely says 'no' similarly sets up a structure for gaining strokes by discounting herself. She gets some pleasure out of attending to the needs of others whilst ignoring her own. At the same time she does feel that people are not available for her in the same way and feels the pain of this. It is better for her to continue to operate in this one-way dynamic rather than risking being rejected and losing her source of strokes. The strokes are role-dependent. When she recognizes that others do not respond to her in the same way, she is likely to blame herself and believe that she is not good enough to have an adequate supply of gratitude or reciprocal attention from those she helps. She is also likely to carry the Don't Have Needs injunction, which will support her behavioural decision to be there for others. When she feels she gives so much, she needs something for herself and this something will tend to be food. It is a tangible and highly sensate way of self-stroking.

Some obese patients present as if no amount of strokes will be enough to meet their sense of deprivation and as long as they do not perceive themselves as receiving strokes this belief will hold true. The fact that they feel they need so much supports their belief that they themselves *are* too much and is an indication of the extent of their internal void.

When the patient is ready she can be offered the tools for understanding her stroking profile. This will include how she might discount strokes that are available to her; how she might give herself strokes; how she does not have to accept negative strokes; how giving others strokes can be satisfying and how it is possible to ask for strokes. Accepting positive strokes whether given by others or oneself, whether asked for or freely proffered, feeds into the Child ego state. The Child self can no longer believe there are no strokes for her if she does experience positive stroking.

It is important to enable the patient to see how she is using food and her body size to gain negative strokes and how she discounts positive strokes thus leaving herself depleted. When Rowena was ready to accept that she did get strokes from many sources and had reached a stage where she no longer needed to diminish them as worthless she was able to believe that she was lovable.

The obese patient then, uses food as a substitute to meet stroke hunger. Physiologically she may sense pangs of emptiness (stroke deficit) that she interprets as hunger and she eats. Psychologically she senses a need and meets it with food.

Contact Hunger

In the first few months of life a baby understands her environment in two ways: through touch and sensation when with another, usually the mother as primary carer, and through sensation and impact when in contact with her surroundings in mother's absence. The infant develops an internal world both in relationship when the mother or caregiver holds her, feeds her, changes her and so forth and when lying in the cot alone and awake, or lying on the floor to kick. Impact with her surroundings such as the sides of her cot or the hardness of the floor, the softness of her mattress or the motion of the bouncy chair will all be experiences that will shape her internal world. The child will learn about being out of physical contact as well as being in it. The seeds of self-agency lie in this combination of contact and non-contact.

The infant's sense of her own body boundaries eventually resulting in knowing that she is separate from the mother relies upon both the defining of the body boundaries by mother's touch and stroking and her impacts with the physical world around her. The quality of the caregiver's attention and touch is paramount in the development of the child's cohesive sense of self and the establishment of the psychological self alongside the body self (see Chapter 12). As we grow, auditory and visual stimulation take the place of touch. However, touch remains important and is a hunger that is often not met adequately in cultures where there are taboos around physical contact.

It is significant then that many obese patients feel they are too big or too repulsive to be touched or held. They present with tactile deprivation. This has implications for their relationships and significantly their sexual activity, or absence of it. The emptiness experienced once again leads the patient to eat, which in turn exacerbates her sense of repulsiveness.

Many patients dissociate from their body selves. They do not look at themselves in the mirror and neither do they self-soothe by stroking or touching or holding themselves. Reconnecting the patient with her body self is a significant stage in the therapeutic journey. This too is addressed in Chapter 12. Physical therapies may be appropriate for the overweight patient provided touch of this nature does not retraumatize. Patients who have been sexually abused may find touch threatening. Reflexology may in such cases be more appropriate at first than body massage. Dissociation from the body self is exacerbated by the absence of touch and holding, though the primary reason for not connecting with the body may be the patient's own repulsion.

Each therapist has his or her own opinion of the efficacy of holding and touch and whether holding is seen as a viable therapeutic operation. It is essential that the patient does not interpret the therapist's refusal to touch as repulsion. The patient may not put herself forward for physical contact but if the therapist hugs others in the group he or she needs to be aware of the effect this has on those who are not hugged and particularly on the obese patient who will interpret non-contact with her as emanating from repulsion, as was seen in Yalom's account of Betty in Chapter 1.

Obese patients yearn for physical touch and are instrumental in ensuring they are not held by their belief that they are too big, too heavy and too repulsive to touch. In my reflection on my work with patients who crave for touch I consider the following points:

- What was this patient's experience of touch and being held as an infant?

- Is her body size a way of ensuring she does not get close enough to be touched and, if so, what is threatening to her about physical contact?

- What part does she play in not being touched and held other than using her size?

- What are her fantasies about being touched?

- What does she imagine will happen?

- What is her interconnecting system of beliefs, thoughts and behaviours that ensure she does not get this hunger met?

Food is a way of filling the void that is created from the yearning for physical contact.

Structure Hunger

One of the major tasks of human beings is to structure time satisfactorily. We structure time in order to get needs met and make meaning of our lives. At the very base of structuring time is the need for enough strokes and stimuli to feel alive. Ideally the overall structure we create will include time with others in work or activity and recreation and adequate time to relax and experience calm or to be alone.

The use of time each day may be planned and literally structured, it may be a haphazard ad hoc process of moving from one happening to another or it may be filled with inactivity and loneliness. Whichever it is, eating meals and set meal times are likely to be part of the structuring of the day. In western cultures the day tends to be divided around breakfast, lunch and dinner. Between-meal snacks are so called because they represent food that is not eaten at the culturally prescribed times and by implication, they are not instead of, but in addition to, a meal. Other breaks structured into a day might be morning coffee, afternoon tea in addition to the snack in front of the television in the evening. People often say that they eat because they are bored. Eating means something to do. If a patient feels lonely, unstroked, unstimulated and uninvolved, mealtimes become a significant landmark in the day and the between-meal snacks offer a sensory stimulating activity.

Berne (1964) described six ways of thinking about how we consciously or unconsciously use time. Each of these has significance in thinking about how the overweight patient uses food. The six options are: withdrawal, rituals, pastiming, games, activity and intimacy.

Withdrawal

It is well known that humans have a limited attention span such that even in the presence of a most scintillating speaker our minds will wander to internal dialogue or musings or we may become aware of a ticking clock that we did not notice before and will not notice again for another span of time. This conttitutes a basic withdrawal.

We can withdraw into ourselves but remain bodily present or we can absent ourselves physically. Both have extremes on a continuum from brief and temporary to persistent and encompassing withdrawal and absence. Withdrawing into oneself may be necessary to regulate stimuli. It may be protective. We may withdraw because we are bored and our minds then focus on some issues that might be more interesting or to some considerations that are more important than what is going on around us. Withdrawal can also be experienced as safer than being in the prevailing environment at any time. For Eugene Heimler (1975) in the prisoner of war camps, his withdrawal to a dream world was a form of detachment from his surroundings and his life saver.

Withdrawal can be healthy or unhealthy. The unhealthy withdrawal caused by the fear of contact with others deprives the patient of strokes and opportunities to meet the other hungers so far described. Sal would shut herself in her lounge, with the curtains closed, the television on and no lights, and would eat. She would do this for a few days at a time. She would collect food and keep it beside her. She used withdrawal to 'keep sane', although at times felt that it was an insane thing to do. She escaped from the turmoil of her life and the pressures she felt by becoming a recluse during the day. By withdrawing into a cocoon of safety.

The patient may withdraw physically to eat and/or may withdraw into herself whilst eating. Many patients eat their extra food secretively, and alone. They feel they need to withdraw in order to feed their psychological hunger. If they do not withdraw they fear being criticized for eating. They would also need to face the wrath of the internal Parent that they would project onto others. In other words, whether others comment or not, they would believe that whoever is around would be criticizing their behaviour and thinking negative and rejecting thoughts about them. These negative attributes that they transfer on to others are their own self-rejecting processes. When eating alone patients describe themselves as 'shutting off'. These patients do not concentrate on the food or their eating so much as withdrawing into a temporary dissociative state whilst compulsively consuming. They do not normally taste the food so much as feel the texture of it and eventually they experience the bloated or distended body that tells them they have eaten enough. The chastising internal Parent has no power whilst the patient dissociates but takes up her rejecting, angry stance immediately the patient re-associates with her surroundings. Both long- and short-term sufferers may withdraw with food to varying degrees in this way. However, long-term sufferers are more likely to dissociate and the extent of their withdrawal is more profound.

Rituals

Rituals are governed by cultural norms. They are recognizable sequences of behaviour with some predictability. One recognizable ritual is saying hello when meeting others. This may be accompanied by a handshake. In some cultures, women are not free to engage in this culture with men. Other types of rituals are birth ceremonies, weddings, funerals and other rights of passage.

In western cultures there are no ceremonies for passage into adulthood. It is a stormy time and parents and children tend to survive rather than manage the rocky journey. Adolescence has been proven to be a significant phase for the onset of eating disorders, more specifically anorexia. However, there is also some evidence to suggest that adolescents will indulge in overeating at this time as a way of coping with the uncertainty.

The landmarks of three meals a day may be seen as ritualistic. So too, the morning coffee and afternoon tea. Associated with the ritualistic nature of celebrations, social invitations and family occasions is the provision of food and the necessity to please the hosts by eating what is provided. Though this may not be readily seen in a negative light, it is often these rituals that the patient will see as her 'downfall' when dieting. She sees it as fact that she cannot eat what others eat if she is on a prescribed regime and perceives that this makes her 'stand out'. The discomfort she feels at not being able to eat what others do propels her into relinquishing her diet and once this happens she feels she has lost. It is difficult for her to say 'no' confidently until she has resolved her lack of self-worth. It is as if she needs permission, or 'moral support', to say 'no' and be OK. Patients need to see that they can encompass lapses in their regimes when their social situation requires it rather than allowing themselves to feel that all is lost.

The patient may have developed her own type of ritualistic eating such as snacking at certain times, and such as eating certain foods on certain days, as if there is no space for deviating from the norm she has created. Attention to how and when the patient eats, the ritualistic nature of her eating patterns and the way she allows cultural rituals to impinge on her can be a revealing system of enquiry. This would be specifically so with patients whose cultural origins, and therefore rituals, differ from the prevailing culture and indeed the culture of the therapist. In Chapter 2 are examples of cultural demands on patients who were either from a different ethnic origin or who had married into a dissimilar cultural family. Reconciling the differences in the eating patterns of diverse cultures can be problematic.

Pastimes

Pastiming involves the exchange of inconsequential chatter and community. The content of the discussion is unpredictable. There is little real engagement. We can pastime with complete strangers and never meet them again. However, pastiming does provide strokes. It can be pleasurable and satisfying.

Pastiming seems to be a way of structuring time that is available to many of my obese patients even though they may use withdrawal as well. There are many contradictions in the psyche of the obese patient such as wanting to hide within herself and yet being very much seen because of her size, needing to be big in the world whilst desperately wanting to lose weight, and wanting to lose weight and yet fearing that this will lead to disappearing. Though many patients indicate wanting to hide and disappear they seem to have an ability to exchange greetings and pleasantries with complete strangers and to be the jovial carefree entertainer in their group. Some certainly attract people to them: people who find the fat person to be someone who has time for them and who is a good listener and undemanding. Pastiming is a comparatively benign means of communicating and sharing and structuring time. It avoids intimacy and therefore is safer for the obese patient who may more easily pastime with strangers.

When thinking about a patient's stroking profile as a way of attending to her psychological hungers, it is easy to discount the significance of this way of gaining strokes. The therapist should be curious about the patient's stroking profile and in particular how she will discount the strokes she receives. Highlighting the significance of rituals and pastimes as stroke-providing encounters will be pertinent in the patient's journey towards self-esteem and self-worth.

Games

I have dedicated a separate chapter to the theory of games (Chapter 11).

Activity

Activity is goal-orientated. The main ego state associated with activity is the Adult. When patients are engaging in activity they are less likely to eat. The key is the focus on the outcome or goal as energy is channelled in a specific task towards a specific end. Activity does indeed 'take the mind off other things'. However, as has been demonstrated, though the obese patient may engage successfully in activity it alone will not provide the healing necessary for her to achieve her goal of weight loss. Eventually, she may be able to embark on the activity of weight loss from her Adult ego state rather than yo-yo dieting in response to her internal Parent and scared Child.

To work towards the patient arranging meaningful activity for herself when her eating is related to lack of stimulus might be an appropriate cognitive behavioural approach for the short-term or moderately overweight patient. It would only be a counter-script and thereby an unreliable cure, for the long-term or morbidly obese patient. Counter-script cure means that the underlying issues are not resolved but a different and perhaps more comfortable method of complying with the script is found. This is clearly not likely to be successful for those whose size protects the self and whose eating feeds intensively unmet psychological hungers.

Intimacy

This is a mode of communication in which authentic feelings are expressed. There is no secret agenda. Feelings do not have to be held in and can be conveyed to others without fear of recrimination. Each person accepts their own responsibility for what they say and how they hear what is said. Things are said in a straight way so that there is little room for misinterpretation and there is agreement to check out possible misunderstandings and responses with each other. We gain the most powerful positive strokes from intimacy and yet it is the mode of time structuring we engage in least. Intimacy does in fact involve all ego states but is chosen and negotiated verbally or implicitly by the Adult. There is a sense of integration of the ego states such that even when intimacy is experienced within a Child to Child dynamic, it feels safe and contained. This level of congruence becomes less available the more dominant the limiting energy in Child and Parent ego states.

Intimacy is usually thought to be emotional closeness and warmth and may involve a sexual relationship. Intimacy actually means the freedom to express any emotion, whether it be anger or fear, sadness or joy and to speak or be heard with respect and acceptance. If a patient has little respect for herself, believes she is not good enough and that she is worthless and deems herself to be 'persona non grata' in the eyes of others, as is so often the presentation of overweight patients, there is little room for true intimacy.

The therapeutic alliance aims towards a level of authenticity that is managed by both patient and therapist. This alliance, when achieved, will allow for the expression of anger and disappointment without loss of, or fear of the loss of, relationship. The practitioner needs to model congruence. She needs to be able to share her thoughts and feelings with the patient when appropriate, for by doing this she models what the patient may also achieve. Such self-disclosure is only indicated when it has therapeutic value. The therapeutic relationship is paramount in the process of resolution of the patient's issues. Part of that relationship is a level of availability that allows the therapist to divulge personal responses to what the patient is saying and to what she experiences in the unconscious processes, provided such disclosure is delivered from the Adult ego state and provided it keeps within the therapeutic boundaries.

The absence of intimacy leaves feelings unexpressed and a sense of emptiness that the overeating and overweight patient will endeavour to rectify with food. The patient who holds down her feelings with food for fear of abandonment or rejection if she expresses them, needs to be able to find safe ways of expressing those feelings. She can learn to express them within the safety of the therapy room and with the security of a trust-based therapeutic alliance.

The patient who is confined by injunctions of Don't Be Close, Don't Be Needy, Don't Belong, will be compelled to avoid intimacy. She will not be allowed to be close enough to anyone to risk such congruence. She will not be able to express her own needs and she will fear abandonment if she expresses her feelings or is thought to be needy.

Patients who believe their physical size keeps others at bay may be considered to be avoiding intimacy. For patients like Rowena (see Chapter 8), their belief is that intimacy leads to loss because this has been their experience in the past. Intimacy can only be achieved in an atmosphere of trust but, if the patient cannot trust that significant others in her life with whom she might be close, will stay, she will avoid intimacy in order to avoid the pain of that possible abandonment. Being overweight keeps people physically at a distance from the inner self purely because of the extended body boundary. In addition the patient believes that others would not want to be close to what she believes to be her repulsive body self. While she can hold on to this belief system, she protects herself from facing a deeper and more painful sense of her 'bad' self and believes she hides the bad self from others.

For both the clinical and non-clinical practitioner attention to the patient's lifestyle, which may be considered in the framework of how she structures her time, will provide an overall contextual picture of the patient's day-to-day existence. This is important in understanding the patient as a whole person and significantly how she uses food or her body size in her daily structure. For the psychotherapist it is a way of thinking about the patient's organization and her stroking profile and, if working within a cognitive behavioural methodology, provides a way of thinking with the patient about how she might understand her eating patterns in response to her ways of using time. At a more analytical level, the therapist and patient can search for meaning with regard to the patient's script decisions and fears within her choice of, or commitment to, certain methods of structuring time rather than others.

Sexual Hunger

In normal circumstances we have a natural desire for sexual contact. The transition into a sexual being starts in childhood and becomes particularly pertinent in adolescence. How we are met in our presentation of our developing sexual selves will determine how easily we become appropriately sexual adults. Sexual abuse and inappropriate attention to a child or adolescent's developing sexuality will skew her healthy claiming of her rightful place as an actively sexual being.

A high percentage of my obese patients have demonstrated a Don't Be Sexual injunction brought about by child and pubertal confusion with regard to their erotic feelings through physical or mental intrusion, or absence of acknowledgement of, their developing sexual identity by a parent or parents. Their subconscious belief is that a larger body boundary defends against possible intrusion. Interestingly, they allow themselves to be intruded upon by people who feel it is their right to comment on their size or their eating behaviour. One patient who had been sexually abused described this as follows:

There are always people around who want to tell me what to do; how to eat and what to eat. They tell me about diets or tell me I am OK as I am and encourage me to eat more. They seem to be well-meaning but each time they do that I feel as if I have no skin around my body. I feel exposed and defence-less. I feel as if they can see inside me, into this mass of confusion and empti-ness. It is like they poke inside, right inside the core of me. I hate it but I am defenceless. At times it feels as raw as the sexual abuse. I feel exposed and powerless.

This was a very moving description of this patient's sense of being penetrated by well-meaning others. She feared losing weight because she was able to maintain a sense of this verbal invasion being less threatening than sexual abuse. She felt that her layers of protective fat went some way in preventing the 'poking' going too deep into her flesh.

I have previously noted that many obese patients fear that they will indulge in excessive sexual behaviour or believe that men will line up at their doors if they lose weight. Some of these patients are those who have been sexually abused. If the sexual abuse occurred within the guise of a loving rela-tionship they will have experienced painful confusion in the love and warmth, specialness and sexual stimulation they encountered whilst understanding that there was something at least inappropriate, if not totally wrong, in the relationship. They feel they played an active part in acquiescing to the sexual advances of the abuser and are therefore equally 'to blame' for the sexual activity taking place. These patients do not feel able to trust themselves in the sexual arena. Since they have learnt that to be fat is unattractive and to be slim is sexy, they believe that as long as they stay overweight they will keep some control over the sexual content of their lives even if this means they have no sexual relationship.

If they lose weight, they lose their protection against sexual intrusion and their fantasy is that men will be lining up to have sex with them and they will have no power to prevent it. Or they believe that they will become sexually promiscuous as they have believed themselves to be in succumbing to sexual abuse. Even when the patient, in the course of the sexual abuse dissociated herself from the perpetrator's actions because she was powerless to do other-wise she will still later believe that she could have done something about it but didn't. Hence it is easy for her to fear her own sexuality and to find ways of protecting herself against herself. One way is to be big enough to keep men away so that she is not tempted.

It is not only the survivors of sexual abuse who have this fantasy. The smooth passage into healthy sexual identity is not only disturbed by sexual abuse. The child needs to be met with sufficiently attuned understanding of her development and with appropriate containment and freedom for her to find her sexual self. Many obese patients fear sexuality because of the lack of attunement by parents who have themselves demonstrated sexual neurosis and have therefore been unable to meet their developing adolescent with fitting and meaningful engagement. These patients will also find protection against their seemingly unmanageable sexuality by maintaining a large body size.

Sexual hunger is central to our existence. Without sexual activity we do not reproduce our species. The drive that has maintained the existence of the human race for so many years continues to be an existential force. Sexual maturation is an observable process and although we do not normally talk about needing to develop sexually for the purpose of procreation per se, as we grow we become more and more aware of a sexual role to be played. We can assume that the level of importance of sexuality will give rise to sexual hunger and that sexual hunger develops in response to an innate species-related survival mechanism. Because of taboos in modern society that have changed and changed again throughout history sexual development becomes a hunger that is met with cultural limitations and complexities. Since the development of the body goes hand in hand with sexual maturity it is not surprising that the body can be used both to beguile and to repel depending on the integration of the sexual self of each individual. Both anorexic and overweight patients use their bodies to deal with unresolved issues relating to sexual development.

Sexual hunger, if not gratified, leads to both a physical and emotional deficit. It is experienced within the body self as well as in the psychological self and manifests itself in dissatisfactions in unrelated areas of life. That deficit compels people to attempt to find alternatives and once again eating food is an endeavour to fill the void.

Incident Hunger

Incident Hunger is a need for excitement and impact. Incidences may be positive or negative experiences and are created in order to counteract a monotonic lifestyle. It may be fact that a patient's life is restricted and boring or it may be that she is unable to be impacted by events because of her closed affect. Some overweight patients restrict their activities either by their size preventing them from being involved in some pursuits, recreation and interests or because they do not believe they have the right to engage in such activity. It is not uncommon to hear people say things like 'Fat people shouldn't expose themselves like that' on a beach for instance, or if seen dancing: 'How can she display herself like that?'. These sayings and many like them form the internal dialogue of many overweight patients who sense themselves as having no entitlement to fun or exciting activity that puts them in any way in the discriminating public eye. Other patients seem to be immune to sensing excitement or emotional involvement except in extreme circumstances. They are unable to feel, at times almost blocked from physical and emotional sensation.

Because of these observations I feel it is important to know whether my patients have a deficit of meaningful and impactful incidences to satisfy this hunger and how they might create negative episodes in order to feed it. Higher degrees of game playing (described in the next chapter) may be one way of ensuring impactful incidents. I was fascinated with my patient's excitement about deciding what she would eat for dinner. Her exhilaration grew throughout the day culminating in virtual orgasmic excitement on finally eating her chosen food. In every other circumstance she reported having no feeling at all. Other patients dissociate from the body self and thereby from body sensation. Since excitement is experienced physically as well as mentally it would take some extreme experience for such dissociating patients to feel this level of stimulation.

I consider with these patients whether being large and receiving negative attention produce the sense that something is happening, and whether starting yet another diet gives any sense of stimulation that might be experienced as having some impact. Even the failure of the diet might be seen as eventful as it is accompanied by such severe self-rejection and reprimand. These experiences stir something in the patient. She may also meet this need by becoming ill or incapacitated as these behaviours are impactful. I think surgery is perhaps an extreme method for obese patients to satisfy incident hunger.

I have concentrated here on the behaviours that relate specifically to eating and overweight. As with any self-harming patient I would want to be curious about whether the behaviour exhibited is fulfilling a need for some impactful activity or experience. Addictions, particularly alcohol and drug dependency, provide recognizable exciting or impactful events from the secrecy in buying, hiding and using the substances through to the apprehension of being found out, to the exposure and consequential repercussions. The same is true of an eating addiction where the patient is secretive in her eating and yet eventually leaves evidence of her eating around in order to be found out. If she does not do it this way, her very size will display her habit and, as can be seen in the following chapter on game playing, result in possible alternatives such as incapacitation, abandonment and death, the ultimate impactful incident.

Power Hunger

Power may be seen and experienced in different ways. My attention here is not on the power of wealth and possessions or position at work, it is about a sense of my patients' personal ability to control and direct events in their lives. The sense of self-agency begins early in life as the infant meets her physical and emotional environment. Disruption in this development will mean that the child is unsure of her own power to be effective. The associated injunctions might be Don't Be You or Don't Be Important, and the types of injunctions that directly prevent an individual from exercising mastery. The child needs to feel that she impacts on the world and can provoke responses from those around her. This need continues throughout life. It is a psychological hunger that may be less obvious in the analysis with the patient and yet plays an important part if the patient is to shift to an adequate sense of self-esteem and self-worth.

The experience of effectiveness in directing events in one's life or lack of it will determine an individual's sense of satisfaction and corresponding behaviour patterns. It will determine the ego states from which someone transacts in order to bid for effectiveness or to give way to others' power. In game analysis this may be taking up the position of the Persecutor or Rescuer in order to gain some power over others or the Victim in order to succumb to others' power. This sense of effectiveness will also have persuasion on the internal dialogue. If the overweight patient is always striving to be slim and feels powerless to achieve that, she will be persistently in a state of dissatisfaction and self-deprecation. Weight becomes the central issue regardless of other life achievements. Overweight patients will describe feeling powerless in a number of ways and particularly with regard to their weight. Patients with a large amount of weight to lose feel powerless in even beginning the task. They feel the undertaking is too great and feel overpowered by their weight.

Psychologically power is about having meaning in the world. Being important enough to be seen and heard and have the right to be here and to take up a place equal to any other. Some patients talk about needing to 'be big in the world' in order to cope with the burdens of their childhood as if there is power in their large presentation. A common ego image is that of an elephant, which is a powerful and forceful animal that has the appearance of being docile and gentle.

Patients will also talk about their sense of power or powerlessness when they eat. At times their powerlessness enables them to dissociate from their eating. Patients describe this dissociated state of eating as succumbing to a need to blot out the internal Parent dialogue that criticizes them for eating again. The internal Parent uses deprecating vocabulary such as 'disgusting', 'worthless', 'weak-willed', 'useless' and 'stupid'. The internal dialogue involves a struggle for power between the Parent who would restrict the eating and the Child who wants to eat. Their sense of effectiveness is in the ability to switch off the internal dialogue even though that entails dissociation from other stimuli and affect. The negative Critical Parent resumes after the food is eaten when the Child has been indulged. This dissociated eating behaviour may last a few minutes or less or may be a longer period of bingeing.

It may be that the patient eats as a form of rebellion. This may be rebellion against the internal dialogue or the demands of others around her or her social context. Rebellion feels powerful and comes into play in the diet–binge cycle as was seen in Chapter 8 on the Child ego state.

A treatment direction towards self-esteem and self-worth will attend to the patient's psychological hunger for power and self-agency. Perhaps the true sense of potency for anyone is rooted in the ability to love and be loved and to feel contentment in the very core of the self, the soul. The peacefulness and self-understanding that can be learnt through meditation is a viable way of feeding the soul as are relaxation techniques and body therapies. Psychologically releasing the Child from unnecessary limiting and often persecutory introjects will allow the patient to continue her development of self-mastery and effectiveness that was curtailed in infancy.

Summary

When eating is compulsive or impulsive rather than planned and when food is eaten to excess, in secrecy, with urgency or just persistently, then it is being used to meet a psychological need. Each of the psychological hungers, if starved, can lead to the patient using food or her body size in an attempt to satisfy them. Any of the hungers can be experienced physiologically and those physical sensations can be misinterpreted as biological hunger. Few obese patients have a true sense of when they are actually in need of food. Neither do they know when they are full until they have eaten too much and feel distended or nauseous. Food cannot feed psychological hungers so there can never be a moment when the patient can feel that she has had enough. She can only rely on the point at which her physical sensation tells her she cannot take in any more.

We are social beings and find our sense of self in interaction with others. Each of the hungers is dealt with in contact with or withdrawal from others. In the therapeutic journey therapist and patient have choices of where to focus in order to maximize psychological and social change. The choice will depend on the patient's needs, the aetiology (causes) of her decision to eat and be big and the amount of time available to work. Considering psychological hungers allows discrete domains of working that may be towards 'cure' in terms of social control or in terms of shifts in the psychological self.

Chapter 11

Games

A game entails a repetitive pattern of behaviour that is played outside awareness. Once this unconscious interplay is brought into awareness we can gradually learn to recognize when we are playing games or have played a game and
indeed when we are being drawn into a game or embarking on one ourselves.
When we understand why we play games we can meet the needs behind the
game playing in more appropriate here and now ways. This sounds simple, but
game playing involves a complex formula both in terms of the stages of the
game and the script beliefs that compel the player to use games as a defensive
mode of communication and a source of strokes (see Chapter 10).

Psychological game playing is a powerful way of getting strokes. We all
play games and it is important for all practitioners to be aware of the games
they play and their response to game invitations as well as how they might
entice someone into their own games. There are three stages to a game – the
beginning, middle and the end phases:

1. The beginning phase is when there is an invitation into the game
    and the invitation is accepted. This phase in itself is a source of
    strokes.

2. The middle phase is all the interaction that follows. This is the
    'response' phase and can last anything from moments to years, to a
    lifetime. This phase is, of course, an ongoing source of recognition
    strokes.

3. Each game then ends in what is called 'the pay-off', the final
    phase, which is always negative and reinforces the player's
    unhelpful beliefs about herself, others and the quality of life. At

the same time the co-conspirator in the game aids the player to experience the script supporting negative pay-off at the same time as achieving his or her own familiar negative feelings.

Game playing avoids real intimacy even though in the process of the game the players might feel as though they are being intimate. When in a game the player replays outdated strategies for managing the world. These are strategies she will have learnt as a basis of interaction or inter-relatedness that she will perceive subconsciously as having worked for her in the past. She may be looking for the comfort and support that she had as a child or that love and caring she wishes she had had but that was missing in infancy and beyond. She may be replaying strategies that gained her negative or positive strokes so that she may invite anger, rejection, aggression and abandonment, or nurturing, caring or even engulfment.

Patients play games both outside and inside the therapy room. Since games are used to reinforce script beliefs that will keep the patient in her uncomfortable and familiar negative life position, analysis of game playing is a powerful intervention in the patient's psychotherapeutic journey towards freedom from the obese script. Although everyone plays a variety of games there are some that I perceive as strategies chosen repeatedly by obese patients and it is these I will describe specifically.

When games are played in the therapy room there exists the luxury of an active here and now mutual experience to investigate with the patient. Games involve a display of unresolved archaic issues that will be evidenced in the psychotherapeutic process and throughout the relationship that develops between patient and therapist or patient and other practitioner. Any of us can 'find ourselves' in a game with someone else at their or our own instigation. For a game to run, the people involved will be psychologically committed to the position they take up and to playing the game to its negative conclusion.

How the game works

There needs to be a 'con' or invitation into a game. There is both a social and a psychological level of communication. The social and overt transaction appears perfectly normal but it is the psychological content that induces the players into the game. For the con or invitation to work, the second player's beliefs about him or herself will fit in some way with the belief system of the first player otherwise he or she will not join in.

Let's take an example of a familiar game played by overweight patients: I will call it 'Do I look OK in this?' The con or invitation into the game is those words: 'Do I look OK in this?' The player is actually looking for a negative pay-off in which she reinforces her sense of self as being unattractive and, maybe, worthless and unlovable. The other player, let's say her husband, is actually in a dilemma, for whatever he says is likely to be twisted to fit the patient's need to maintain her poor self-image. If he responds in the affirmative he is perceived as lying and if he should dare to say 'no' she will dissolve into tears saying she never looks good in anything, or accuse him of being unable to be nice to her. His commitment to the game will reside in his own sense of being unable to get it right. He will have a recurring experience in his life of feeling impotent. Because he cannot win with this game, and being ineffectual fits his script, he will play it again and again. It is almost failsafe for the two players to get their negative feelings, and their beliefs confirmed.

The source of the wife's game is her beliefs about herself and her inability to see herself as OK. She is not just asking about how she looks, she is asking whether she *is* OK; she is asking if she is lovable and worthwhile. With the responses described above she is bound to get her game pay-off, which is the feeling of being unloved and maybe unlovable or of not being good enough. In order to maintain these script beliefs she needs to keep finding situations that prove to her that she is right about her perception of the world and her place in it. The source of her husband's willingness to keep playing is his feeling of powerlessness, which undoubtedly lies in messages he internalized in his early years, perhaps of being unimportant and useless. It is a feature of games that they form a repeated pattern of behaviour resulting in the same reinforcement of negative feelings and beliefs about self.

The game then, begins with the con 'Do I look OK in this?' The husband will answer her, so he is already hooked into the game. He responds. The game is on. This particular game is fast moving, though with some games the 're-sponse' period can go on for a long time, or even last a lifetime. In this game he tries to say the right thing but soon finds whatever he says, his wife will find a way to feel criticized and Not OK at which point there is a moment of confu-sion and a switch in the tenor of the interaction. The pay-off then comes and they both feel wretched. This progression from invitation to pay-off is a feature of all game playing.

Games are played again and again, in similar circumstances and always with the same script-maintaining outcome. It is because of this repeated pattern that the patient can be enabled to recognize when they are in a game. Enquiring of the patient what she experiences as a persistently recurring negative feeling, or what patterns of behaviour she recognizes she is repeating, and which could provoke the words 'there we go again', opens the opportunity to begin to unpack the progression of a game. In the same way, in the patient's narrative the practitioner will perceive repeated patterns of behaviour that constitute a game and that the therapist can reflect back to her and use for analysis when appropriate.

I will now describe another way of analysing a game that entails the use of the Drama Triangle (Karpman 1968). It is an easy and user-friendly way of understanding this set of overt and covert transactions and a tool that can be easily understood by the patient.

The Drama Triangle

Stephen Karpman (1968) devised the Drama Triangle as a means of analysing games. He observed that there are three existentially related positions we can adopt. These are: Rescuer, Persecutor and Victim. He puts one of these roles Persecutor (P), Rescuer (R) and Victim (V) at each point of the triangle as shown in Figure 11.1 below. Each of these roles relates to another on the triangle, which clarifies why I said earlier that the person giving the game invitation (con) and the respondent must have scripts that lock into playing the inviter's game otherwise the game would not progress. The two players will start on different corners of the triangle. They interlock in that a Victim will need a Persecutor or a Rescuer and both the Persecutor and the Rescuer need a Victim to persecute or to save. When a game is played out, the players move around the triangle. There is always a shift in position, otherwise it is not considered a game, or it has not yet come to its conclusion. The switch around the triangle to a different position is how we know that a game has been played although with insight we can know when we are in a game, before it reaches its final pay-off stage. We can also learn to recognize when we are being invited into a game and refuse to play. However, the more subtle the game, the more difficult it is to spot it.

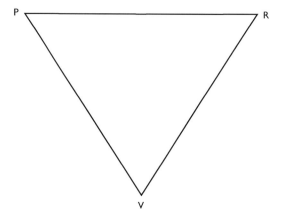

Figure 11.1 The Drama Triangle

Let us now trace the game of 'Do I look OK in this?' on the Drama Triangle and consider both the overt and covert, or social and psychological transactions. The patient starts in the Victim role. She is discounting (ignoring) her ability to decide for herself whether she looks OK in what she is wearing. She does not use her own judgment. If she looks in the mirror she will know for herself how she feels in what she has chosen to wear. Her psychological message, unspoken, is 'Am I OK as a person?' and perhaps 'Tell me I am lovable' but this is out of her awareness. At the social level she is looking for a Rescuer, her husband, who will tell her she is fine. However, at the psychological level she is aiming to reinforce her beliefs about herself and she will do this whatever her husband replies. As noted above, whatever he answers she will turn it to match her script beliefs. Likewise her husband plays the game to reinforce his beliefs and so he readily takes up the role of Rescuer.

The psychological messages at the heart of this game for her are: 'I am worthless and you cannot say anything right' and for him 'I am useless and I cannot get it right'. It makes a good fit for repeated game playing. Now the pair move round the game triangle as she becomes angry and accuses him of not finding her attractive, never supporting her or not loving her and so she moves to Persecutor. He is suddenly catapulted into the Victim of her angry outburst. She feels bad, no good and angry, all of which are familiar to her. He feels defeated, caught, and helpless and this is also familiar to him. Whatever happens next, whether he comforts her (he Rescues, she goes back to Victim) or walks away, which would be perceived as heartless (she moves back to Victim and he would be perceived as Persecutor) it is certain that the game will be played again with the same outcome unless it is confronted and options for interacting differently are found. The game moves are shown on the Drama Triangle in Figure 11.2 below.

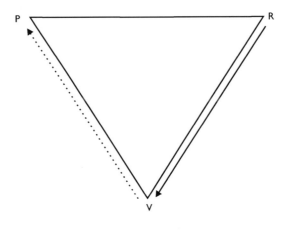

Key
..➤ Patient's shift from Victim to Persecutor
—➤ Husband shifts from Rescuer to Victim

Figure 11.2 Moves round the Drama Triangle in the game of 'Do I look OK in this?'

Why play games?

We play games to support script beliefs about self, others and the world. In his book *Games People Play* (1964) Berne suggested that game playing has 'advantages' relating to the psychological, social, existential and biological needs of the patient. I will summarize these first:

The psychological advantages

Psychological advantages maintain the internal script beliefs in order to sustain a level of psychic stability. This will be uncomfortable because of its origin in archaic and irrational early decisions. The pay-off tells the story. Games also aim to avoid the disclosure of the patient's perceived or unconsciously held 'deficiencies', so this psychological advantage has the potential to state the fear that the patient wants to avoid. In the example of 'Do I look OK in this' described above, we can see that when analysed at the psychological level the game exposes the beliefs about the self of the initiator, for example, 'I am not OK' or 'I am not good enough' or 'I am not lovable' and for her husband: 'I am useless'. The feelings and associated beliefs perceived in the pay-off will reveal the domain of negative self-belief. The response phase will expose the relational need. When analysis of the feelings and respective verbal descriptions of the patient's experience in the pay-off is carried out with the patient, the therapist can progress towards uncovering and working with her script system. When analysis is made of the response phase the therapist can begin to understand what the patient is looking for from the other person. This reveals the relational need of the patient and will form the basis of the transference explained later in this chapter.

The social advantages

Games structure time and provide a pseudo-intimate form of communication. They can shift responsibility, which is very much a feature of overweight games. Let's take the example of the game of 'NIGYSOB (Now I've got you, son of a bitch'). This is quite a subtle game played by patients to test out the possible prejudice the therapist might be holding against fat people, if not against the patient herself. A patient will check out in cunning ways within the dialogue whether the therapist is really accepting of her size and thereby, herself. The aim is to catch the therapist out and to prove that she or he, like others, is not truly accepting of fat people. When this was played with Betty and Yalom as described in Chapter 1 the game went on until the final therapy session with Betty. Yalom had ignored his prejudiced feelings and she waited until the end to reveal her observation of his prejudiced behaviour. The pay-off for her was that she was unacceptable, which was one of her script beliefs. He felt wretched at the fact that he had not confronted his own discomfort regarding Betty in the therapeutic process. She waited until the end to catch him out.

I was 'caught out' by a patient in the early days of my psychotherapeutic work when she announced she had lost weight and I rejoiced with her and congratulated her. The transferential paradigm was the expectation of me as a monitoring and judgmental authority who would see her as 'not good enough' as she was. She was therefore able to interpret my rejoicing with her in her weight loss as me only really accepting her if she was thinner. She felt self-righteous in having 'got' me. I felt the confusion that is common in game playing. I felt surprised and caught out. I had played the game from Rescuer by colluding with celebration of her weight loss. She had then moved to the Persecutor position and I shifted and became the Victim of her attack.

When the patient moves to the Persecutor position: 'Now I've got you' she has an internal sense of satisfaction. My patient set the game up by gleefully telling me about her weight loss. At that point she invited me to be pleased with her. I joined the game and the switch inevitably followed. I now ensure that I ask a patient who has lost weight how she feels about her weight loss and mirror or respond to those feelings if it is right therapeutically to do so.

A social advantage then, is in the title of the game: 'Now I have got you' (I knew you weren't what you said you were). When this is taken further to represent the patient's belief system it is likely to become 'No one can really be trusted' and specifically for the overweight patient 'No one really is OK with me being fat, they just pretend to be'.

The function of the game was exactly the catching out that the patient was waiting for. This proved her right in her expectation of others and therefore in her expectation of me. She had not wholly entered into the psychotherapeutic process and once the game had been played I realized that she had been waiting to see if she could trust me at the same time as looking for an opportunity to find evidence that she would be right not to do so. She was structuring some time in the group by watching and waiting. In playing this game she could validate her perception that others are disgusted by and rejecting of obese people. It might then provide a good topic for pastiming (see Chapter 10) or playing another game called 'Ain't it awful' where the focus is on how difficult it is to be in this world and how everything works against the overweight person. In this case it might have the focus of 'Everyone dislikes a fat person, even the therapist!'

The biological advantage

The biological advantage concerns the stroke quotient that the players receive. The need for strokes was the attention of Chapter 10 and therefore needs little further explanation here. The game of 'Do I look OK in this?', as we have seen, is a fast-moving game that is experienced physiologically as well as psy-

chologically because of the intensity of the strokes that are destined to be negatively received whatever words are used.

The existential advantage

The existential advantage is the position from which the game is played. The
existential positions are 'I am OK and you are OK' abbreviated to I+ U+; 'I
am OK and you are not OK' (I+ U-); 'I am not OK and you are OK' (I- U+)
and 'I am not OK and you are not OK' (I- U-). Persecutory games may be seen
as being played from I+ U-, although there is often a difference between the
social action of the game and the internal psychological belief. Hence, when
Rowena played a persecutory game she played it socially at an I+ U- position
in order to defend her deeply held psychological belief that she was Not OK.
The I+ U- was a defensive position in an attempt to hide from her I- belief.
When patients play Victim games they are playing from an I- U+ existential
position. Rescuer games are played from an I+ position. The OK and Not OK
positions imply a one-up or one-down stance with regard to other people in
the game. Whenever the patient puts herself in a one-down position she is
playing from a Not OK existential position; if she is in a one-up position, that
is, either Rescuer or Persecutor she is likely to be playing, at least at the social
level, from an I am OK and You are not OK existential belief. Games are not
played from the I+ U+ position. There is no one in a one-up or one-down
position that would give them places on the Drama Triangle.

The advantages described above are clearly centred on a script-reinforce-
ment process. Below is a diagram (Figure 11.3) that summarizes some specific
social and psychological reasons for game playing.

Explanation of the social/psychological reasons for game playing

1. *To uphold the existential position*, that is, wherever the patient's sense
of self lies within the three inter-relational stances with regard
OK-ness: I'm OK – You're not OK; I'm not OK – You're OK or
I'm not OK and You're not OK. Games are not played from the
I'm OK – You're OK relational position. Obese patients tend to
play games from the existential position of 'I am not OK'. In a
further defensive strategy they may play games from the 'I am OK
– you are not OK' position but this would normally cover an I-
belief.

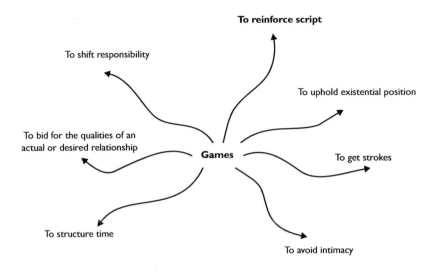

Figure 11.3 A diagrammatical summary of script reinforcing reasons for playing games

2. *To get strokes*, both negative and positive in the response phase and negative in the pay-off. As was seen in the previous chapter on psychological hungers, overweight patients will find strategies to get negative and positive strokes using their weight and eating practices. They choose games that support these strategies.

3. *To avoid intimacy*: games are characterized by pseudo-intimacy. The relationship between the players avoids true expression of needs and genuine communication of thoughts and feelings. Backed by the patients' archaic beliefs about self in the world, the players could not risk true intimacy. Obese patients commonly feel worthless, unlovable and even 'bad' inside. They would believe that true intimacy risks being found for what they really are.

4. *To structure time*: games are one of the major choices for structuring time alongside pastiming. They are a major source of social intercourse. Since games keep others at a psychological distance and provide a means to avoid real closeness and being seen, they are necessarily a prevalent choice of time structuring for the obese patient who fears intimacy.

5.   *To bid for the qualities of an actual or desired relationship*: games are played in response to relational needs. They will be played in order to re-establish qualities of an actual relationship that may have been negative or positive, or to aim at establishing a caring response from an idealized other. In the Victim game that Jill played (see the case study in Chapter 5) she saw her boss and her husband as the father that she had experienced as rejecting her at an earlier period in her life. She transferred the attributes she had assigned to her father on to them, thus she was able to recreate the familiar negative experience of the relationship with her father in the game pay-off.

6.   *To shift responsibility*. From the analysis of games so far described it is clear that there is the potential for the player to try to shift responsibility for her behaviour on to the other person. From the Victim position there is always a Rescuer or a Persecutor. The Rescuer is invited to take responsibility and rescue and the Persecutor to punish or bully so that they can feel put down by another. Game playing does not allow for the patient to recognize her own responsibility in finding ways to get her needs met authentically.

Degrees of games

Games are played at three degrees of intensity:

First degree games

These games seem very akin to pastiming (see explanation in Chapter 10) though there is the switch where there is some comeback or element of surprise that makes it a game rather than just the social discourse that is the property of pastiming. The game of 'Ain't it awful' 'that losing weight is such hard work', 'that no one can really help', 'that I've put on 5lbs in one evening' is often played at this very benign level. This game is familiar to anyone who has a weight issue whether they are overweight or just very weight-conscious. The conversation repeatedly centres on what it is like to be fat, or not to be able to lose weight. It might be played around the availability of luscious foods and the problem of resisting them. There is nothing very serious happening in the game in this first degree. It has a lot of mileage for strokes. It fills a deal of time, it is good to feel that lots of people are 'in the same boat' and think the same way and so it feels very supportive. It has the pseudo-intimacy of understanding how the other person feels. The positions of Victim and Rescuer are well divided up. The Victim who starts the game gets supportive information and sympathy from the Rescuer, or Rescuers. Then the Rescuer moves to Victim to tell her own story and gets the support from the other Rescuer(s). At the end of each session of playing this game, no one feels particularly disturbed by it. The switch may not be enacted for years but it will still cause some confusion and surprise when it comes. It will not be particularly disturbing to the players and the pay-off is tolerable.

'Help me lose weight' may also be played in the first degree. It might be, for instance, two people going on a diet together, it might be keeping a log of each other's weight. It will be light-hearted and there would be minimum shame felt when the arrangements don't work out, they don't lose weight or the idea never even got put into action. There would be a familiar mild disturbance in the pay-off.

This game would be unlikely to be played in first degree by long-term sufferers or morbidly obese patients. They would be likely to play it at the higher levels. It is more likely to be played in the first degree by people with little weight to lose, by those who do not have deep-seated fears of losing weight and those who do not have punishing and self-rejecting internal dialogue. Berne (1964, p.57) described first degree games as 'socially acceptable in the agent's circle'. (By 'agent' Berne meant the person playing the game and his circle would be the company he keeps.)

Second degree games

Second degree games are more consequential. They are characterized by embarrassment and the patient not wanting other people to know she has played them. These are not light-hearted games and when the switch comes the patient will have noticeable physiological sensations accompanying the psychological and social discomfort.

'Help me lose weight' at this level has a very different feel about it. When the players enter into the game they both believe that one can help the other and that one can be helped by the other. This is, of course, the con described above. At some stage the switch will come where the patient leaves the contract, does not lose weight, or loses weight and then puts it all and more back on. The patient feels shameful at least, if not mortified at having 'failed'. The other party has two options: she may feel she has failed the patient in some way in which case she takes the Victim position. Or she becomes the Persecutor, blaming the patient, saying she has no willpower and other familiar negative attributes. The patient may move to Rescuer or Persecutor momentarily in the switch. She may blame the 'helper' for her inability to really help or she may rescue the helper by saying she was good and that it was her own fault that she did not lose weight. She may bounce between the two, but eventually the patient will move back to the Victim position. Admission of her 'failure' may well seem to indicate an acceptance of it, but there is no doubt that each time an obese patient goes on a diet or submits to a regime and is unsuccessful she feels deep shame.

The long-term behaviour of weight gain – weight loss can be seen as a game in itself. It would be played at least at second degree level. The patient will constantly be in switches around the Drama Triangle as she involves others in her game in the roles she assigns to them. She constantly receives negative strokes that are both conditional and unconditional and when she loses weight she receives conditional positive strokes that are related to her weight loss. This upholds her belief of not being OK 'unless she conforms to what others want her to be'. All the negative cultural attitudes come into play to support her negative sense of self in the game.

Berne (1964) described this level of games as ones 'which the players would rather conceal from the public' (p.57). There is of course no conceal-ment of the patient's body size, which is the evidence of her weight game. She will defend by playing other games such as 'fat and happy clown' (see below) because she cannot conceal her overweight self from public view. This is a very different experience of game playing than that described as first degree. Most overweight patients will play games to this second degree level.

Third degree games

Berne described third degree games as 'for keeps and which end in the surgery, the courtroom or the morgue' (1964, p.57). In other words third degree games are hamartic (from hamartia, a fatal flaw leading to the downfall of the tragic hero or heroine!). They are played at a level with extremely serious consequences. Being morbidly obese can be seen to be the weight game in the third degree. The behaviour is self-harming because of the effect of carrying so much extra weight on the health of the patient. Harmful diets, yo-yo dieting, which itself has organic implications, invasive surgery and the ultimate risk of death, are all indications of the third degree game.

Games and transference

Games involve transference phenomena. Transference is the process by which patients transfer attitudes, beliefs and feelings that belong to either someone else, usually from the past but sometimes from current relationships, or that they themselves believe, onto another person in the present. Patients will also transfer situations from the past onto situations in the present. They will expect to re-experience the same thoughts and feelings as they did in the past situation or with the person from the past. There is clearly much to say about transference and there are many books and articles that give attention to this complex unconscious process. Therefore, I will discuss some examples of transference that will illustrate the process and complexity and leave the reader to explore the concept in more detail elsewhere.

Transference of another nameable person or group of people

If one can say anything is simple about transference this is perhaps the most obvious and easily recognizable form of transference. The patient transfers a person or set of people on to the other person. For example, the set of people may be 'authority figures', so that each time the patient meets someone whom she sees as an authority figure she will transfer the qualities of other authority figures on to him or her. An example of this is when patients generalize about all doctors being impatient with obese patients when actually they have met one, or heard of some, that are. More specifically, the patient may come into therapy expecting that the therapist will control and direct her towards weight loss, which has been her experience with other practitioners in the field who give diets, count points and monitor her weight.

One patient saw aspects of me that were like a teacher who had seemed to dislike her and in the transference with me she expected, and indeed said she experienced me as not liking her. As she had been overweight as a child, she had concluded that this was the reason why her teacher did not like her and so surmised that it was the same for me. When we looked at the transferential process, her ability to see me as her teacher seemed to rest on three aspects: one was my diction, another was the colour of my hair and eyes and the third was the way I sat. She avoided discussion about her weight as much as she could and seemed to be trying consistently to please me.

Patients will of course, persistently exercise this sort of transference in their everyday lives. Given the sense of the culture being intolerant of fat people, it is easy to see that the patient will expect a large number of people she meets to be rejecting of her size. Since she is unable to see her true self as separate from her body self, she will conclude that they reject her whole self. She will play games around this expectation either trying to please or perhaps games aimed at rejecting before being rejected.

A way to begin to dissolve this transference, once it has been identified, is to account for the differences and the similarities between the person being transferred and the recipient of the transference in the present. The differences will distinguish one person from the other and the similarities will highlight the triggers that make the transference possible. Modelling a different and respectful relationship is the most powerful means to dissolve a negative transference.

Transference does not of course necessarily imply negative attributes. The patient will also transfer positive attributes of other people. For instance, the patient may see the therapist as a mother figure who was warm and caring and looked after the patient lovingly as a child. She will use constructs to try to get the therapist to mother her in this way and will therefore play Victim to Rescuer games.

Jill's transference with her boss and husband

An example of transference can be seen in the story of Jill (Chapter 5) who had unresolved issues with her father whom she still believed, in her Child ego state, to be angry and rejecting. She transferred these attributes on to her husband and her boss, so that she perceived them as acting in ways she perceived her father as behaving. Distinguishing differences between the parties involved did not seem to be an appropriate method of working with her transference since her relationship with her father was held in a paradigm established in and continuing from early childhood. Naming differences is an Adult to Adult approach with the Child as witness and I suspected that Jill's Child would not be convinced by this method. Resolution of the perceived rejection from her father through the Parent work described in Chapter 7, held the opportunity to both see her father as having moved on from the angry phases of his life and as loving her and wanting her to be herself, and by association to see her boss and husband as themselves in the here and now.

Here Jill played a Victim game, experiencing herself as being persecuted. She turned her anger in upon herself and tried to self-soothe with food. She moved to the Persecutor position but turned her inexpressible anger upon herself. Her decision was to behave in a manner that had been available for her in the past, that is, she binged. Jill played a Victim game with her boss and husband and a persecutory game with her food through bingeing. The common property of these people was that they expressed anger that Jill related wholly to the angry outbursts of her father. She could not hear any anger without cathecting her Child ego state defence. It seemed that this would happen, no matter how mild their anger was.

She resolved the transference by the two-chair work described in Chapter 7 when she realized that the behaviour she attributed to her father was not the reality. When she did that she was no longer able to transfer his negative attributes on to her boss and her husband. Realizing that her father was not the angry person she held him to be but someone who cared about her gave her the space to see her boss and her husband as being something other than angry people.

The authority figure

Patients regularly see the therapist as an authority figure and so the relationship is ripe for transference and related games. If she sees the therapist as an authority figure on whom she transfers negative attributes she may expect the therapist to chastise her. She will play Victim to Persecutor games. If she believes that no one can help her because this has been her perception throughout life, she will expect that the therapist will be ineffectual as well and may play games from a Victim stance or a Persecutor position.

As was seen with Pat, she expected that I would lead each session with my suggestions of 'where we go next'. She was typical in this stance of many obese patients. The aim of therapy is to render the patient potent and autonomous and so it is important that they take some control of the process. However, it is also fair to say that practitioners trained in this area clearly have more overall knowledge than the patient and therefore it is not surprising that the patient will ask for guidance and expect some direction. Indeed, part of the focus of this book is to suggest methods of working with patients. There is a very different feel from the dependence on the therapist for direction when in a game to that which present if a patient is asking for guidance from Adult. A patient who holds on to the idea that she does not know what to do and cannot think at all for herself is in transference with the therapist and will play games either from the Victim or Persecutor position.

Transference of the self-rejecting Parent in the Child ego state

This type of transference is when the patient transfers her own negative sense of self on to another person and not only expects the other to respond to her as if she holds these views of the patient but will experience her as doing so, filtering the other's communication with her through a frame of reference that will select information to support her script beliefs. It is a transference of P1, the Parent in the Child ego state. Rowena's initial behaviour on the Free Child fun day previously described in Chapter 8 is an interesting example of this transference.

ROWENA'S USE OF THE DOG DIRT IN THE TRANSFERENCE OF HER SELF-LOATHING

One of the activities on the Free Child fun day (Chapter 8) was to play the small child collecting treasure. Rowena brought back some dog mess along-side other dirty objects. Clearly she was testing me out to see if I was really accepting of her. Rowena believed she was not lovable and she also believed that her mother died because she was unlovable. She transferred on to me that part of herself that believed she was unlovable, expecting me to prove this was true by my own rejection of her and that maybe I would abandon her in some way in response to her bringing foul objects into the room.

The foul-smelling and repulsive dog mess represented Rowena's sense of herself as being so bad that her mother had to die. She was presenting to me and the rest of the group a clear metaphor for her belief about herself and a clear test of our acceptance of her. In addition it felt to me as if Rowena was unconsciously intending to disarm me and with no arms I could not love her.

Dog mess would be cleared out of the way as quickly as possible and may even induce retching if the smell is foul. It would certainly be accompanied by expressions of disgust and strong rebuke of the dog that defecated. It was important for me to avoid expressing the disgust Rowena wanted from me in order to support her beliefs. I refused the transference and accepted her 'treasures' with interest. It was a major transactional interchange in the shifting of

Rowena's Free Child energy such that later in the day she was able to be held without feeling that the holder would be repulsed by her. Rowena felt empowered and eventually moved on to resolve her belief that her mother died because she was unlovable as illustrated in Chapter 8.

A patient described her internal dialogue when buying food. She transferred her self-admonishing Parent in her Child ego state on to the sales person such that she was working out in her head how best to avoid the vendor's imagined painful, unspoken, critical judgement. She worked out that if she asked for portions for two people the vendor could believe that she was buying food for someone else rather than for herself.

The idealizing transference

The third type of transference is the idealizing transference where the patient transfers on to another the characteristics of the ideal parent she yearns for. This gives rise to Victim games when the patient expects the therapist to fulfil the role of an idealized persona who is all loving and caring and can do nothing wrong. Clearly such a relationship is doomed to fail as at some stage the therapist will fall off the pedestal. Managing this transference is complex and therapists have the choice to work within the transference or outside of it. In other words the therapist may take on the role of some of the aspects of the idealized Parent, in awareness and with a specific therapeutic goal in mind or he or she may decide to refuse such transference. Accepting the idealized transference may result in the patient leaving psychotherapy with an internalization of the therapist, which she then uses to guide her actions in future. This might be typified by her internal dialogue asking the question: 'What would my therapist do or say now?' This can be useful. However, the patient may also stay in the idealization in an unhealthy way, such that she feels unable to function without the continued presence of the therapist. It is always advisable to work towards the patient's psychological integration that results in her being autonomous.

Games played by the patient will be from a Rescuer and Victim positions when all is well. She will see the therapist as being the Rescuer to her Child, always being loving and doing the right thing and she will look after this idealized mother by adapting. She will grieve when the therapist is sick or on leave and may feel unable to survive without her. She will hate the idea that the therapist sees any other patients and will find ways to avoid encountering this reality. She will feel angry when the therapist is going away on holiday but may not be able to express this until the relationship allows for the dissolving of the transference.

Sal was a patient with whom I decided to work within the transference, taking on the role of the Parent figure she so yearned. There were times when I felt that she was too much and too demanding and almost as if she was under my skin. She wanted to be like me. She at times came in items of clothing that matched mine, wanted to have her hair styled like mine. She wanted to know about my family and my interests so that she could emanate these. At times she hated me if I did not meet her idealization. Sal needed to experience the positive warmth of a caring other and the frustrations arising from disappointments that would have been available to her had she experienced an attuned and appropriately mirroring mother. The process for us was one of bonding through to individuation and separation and it was only in the final phases of this therapeutic journey that Sal began to accept herself as existentially OK whatever her size.

Every relationship involves transference

The patient will be in transference with people around her in her everyday life. Transference is likely to be present to a greater or lesser extent in all relationships. We learn how to be in relationship as we develop and so each new relationship will have some qualities that remind us of past relationships. There will be similarities and the rest we supply from past experience until we discover the differences.

The transference in the therapy room therefore is not one way. The therapist will also transfer attributes on to the patient. If the patient reminds her of her own daughter she may be drawn into games where she plays the Rescuer. If the patient presents in ways that remind the therapist of a negative other from the past, she may be lured into persecuting the patient or into becoming the Victim of the patient's actual or perceived persecution. If the therapist holds some prejudices about overweight people they will surely come through in the transference. A patient who is highly defended is often also highly perceptive and will pick up the prejudice in the unconscious process. This will invite her into Persecutor or Victim.

Analysis of the transference and the games played will reveal the patient's script beliefs and will provide fertile ground for deconstructing limiting strategies in favour of more autonomous behaviour. Recognizing the transference will lead the therapist and patient to identifying a game and likewise, identifying a game will enable recognition of transference phenomena.

How to recognize game playing

There are a number of ways in which game playing can be exposed:

1. by the familiar behaviour patterns and sense of a repeated scenario which ends with a recognition epitomized by the words: 'here we go again'

2. by investigation of the familiar negative feeling that accompanies the pay-off

3. by investigation of the transference relationship

4. by analysis of the physiological experience.

Familiar behaviour patterns

Games are repeated patterns of behaviour. Obese patients play a complex series of weight games that support the underlying unresolved issues. Some of the games patients play are described later in this chapter and for each game played there will be a recognizable set of behaviours that concur with the stages of the game. When the therapist looks at the game of 'Do I look OK in this' she will see that there is a recognizable pattern of behaviour and the patient will be able to report this sequence of behaviours once they are brought into her awareness. She will know that each time she goes through this sequence she will feel wretched in a familiar way. She will also have a sense of what happens next. In the game of Fat Clown, the patient will be able to recount how she amuses people, how she laughs at herself and then how she gets disappointed and confused when she is not taken seriously or feels rejected when she changes her behaviour and wants to be serious.

When a patient describes things that she recognizes happen to her repeatedly, it is likely she is unawarely revealing the moves in a game. The obese patient will pay games with others around her weight and eating but may also play games with the food in so far as her eating brings about an intermittent soothing followed by guilt and self-reprimanding or self-hate. Asking the patient about her eating behaviour and her related feelings before and after eating as in the questionnaire in Chapter 5 will begin the process of finding the games the patient plays in relation to her eating and food.

Investigation of the familiar negative feeling

To begin an investigation into game playing the therapist may ask the patient what familiar negative feeling she experiences repeatedly. Generally the patient is able to answer this question easily. Often this feeling is what will drive the patient to eat as well as being what she feels after eating.

When Jill felt dismissed by what she perceived to be an angry response from her boss she resorted to binge-eating. She was able to trace this feeling to other times when she also resorted to food. She was in a game with the boss and in a game with the food she ate, which reconfirmed her poor sense of self as an OK person.

The patient who plays Fat Clown may feel sad and rejected, missed and alone, not good enough or similar familiar feelings. When the therapist enquires about these recurring negative feelings he or she is likely to be picking up the game at the point of the negative pay-off.

Investigation of the transference

Every game played with another person involves a transferential relationship. The patient psychologically confers a role onto the other player, which, for the game to run, the other person accepts and plays accordingly. In terms of the Drama Triangle the roles taken up by each player will be one of Victim, Rescuer or Persecutor and when the game is played to its negative conclusion, these roles will have changed for each of the players.

The clinician can know when he or she is being invited into a game and then have the choice of whether to play along or whether to stay out of the game, depending on the therapeutic value of doing either. In more general terms, the therapist may be able to recognize when a patient is subconsciously wanting the therapist to nurture her or indeed compelling the therapist to punish her. If her issues relate to early deficit in the infant-carer relationship she may be looking for a magical mother to make things right so she does not have to be big to cope in the world or to eat to meet her psychological hungers. She may also be looking for the relationship that confirms the validity of her experience of a withholding or rejecting parent figure. The therapist can sense the pull from the patient for him or her to take up a certain role ascribed by the patient by analysis of the counter-transferential feelings and sensations. I use the term 'counter-transference' in this sense to describe the response the therapist has to the patient's presentation of herself and her story. For instance, does the therapist have an urge to punish, reject or dismiss the patient or maybe, a strong pull towards nurturing her? If the therapist unwittingly acts upon these counter-tranferences, she will be playing the game. If she detects the game and may decide to play along for therapeutic reasons, she has already stepped out of the game.

Investigation of the physiological experience

A game can be identified by the body sensation that accompanies the pay-off. When games are played at second and third degree level there is commonly a physiological response at the moment of the switch. The patient may be able to describe a recurring body sensation before she is able to give words to the social dynamic of the game. If the patient is out of touch with the body self she would need to be re-connected to her body self before she can recognize these recurring sensations. However, as has been noted, the patient may more easily be in touch with the body sensation before reaching for food and exploration of this sensation will provide a forum for identifying the games played that entail bingeing in the pay-off.

Staying in and moving out of the game

Games are played out of awareness so until they are brought into the patient's awareness they will continue to be played. Once in awareness there is the opportunity to understand their meaning and why the patient plays them and it is then that the practitioner can work with the patient to find ways in which she can get her needs met authentically and without the uncomfortable negative script-confirming feelings that are part of the inauthentic communication when game playing.

The patient can learn to recognize the sensation that accompanies the pay-off in order to first understand that she has just played a game. She can identify regular patterns of behaviour and can work through the sequence with the therapist or practitioner. For instance in the game of 'Do I look OK in this?' she can trace the stages of the game.

The transactions that followed this line of enquiry with a patient were interesting. She gave this clear résumé of her way of playing the game:

> When I say 'Do I look OK in this' I can now detect in myself the sense that I do not like myself as I am. When I ask the question, he says, 'Yes you look fine', then I get angry because I don't believe him. I shout at him, feel

wretched, sometimes I throw myself on the bed and react like a small child. He will then either walk out or try to comfort me. Or, he might say he doesn't really like me in something and then that is even worse. Then I feel ashamed and humiliated. I see that he cannot win and each time this happens I feel dreadful, whatever he says. I suppose I know I do not really blame him at all. At the end I feel the hate I hold for myself. I don't know what he could say that would make it any different.

With this clarity of recognition of her game, we were able to investigate what she really wanted for herself. Of course in the first instance she said she wanted to lose weight, then she would feel OK. This in itself was an interesting transaction, since it was a stopper accompanied by a sense of defeat, which I felt instantaneously. I was picking up this sense of defeat in the counter-transference and momentarily felt deskilled. It felt like another game invitation that involved the belief that 'no one can help and I cannot do it myself'. The patient in that moment was able to project her experience of feeling defeated on to me. I crossed her transaction by returning to the focus of our enquiry, which was the analysis of her game. I reflected to her what I had experienced, demonstrating congruence and inferring my own experiential understanding of something of how she felt herself. This broke the spell of the game she had played with me and modelled a way of being genuine and straight. If I had responded to her statement that she would feel OK if she lost weight we would almost certainly have played the game out.

What the patient came to realize was that she needed her husband to tell her he loves her and reassure her that she is lovable in his eyes. She also needed to accept herself regardless of her weight and to know she is essentially the same person with or without her large body size. Communicating from her Adult ego state with congruence and clarity would help her to recognize her potency and develop her self-mastery. She became able to discern for herself whether she was satisfied with what she was wearing and to ask her husband for strokes from her Adult rather than her Child ego state.

Games with the therapist

Inevitably games are played in the therapy room. It is important to understand that games are defensive strategies and therefore confronting a game with a patient needs to be guided by a clear understanding of the therapeutic value of doing so. The patient's story is told within the transference and the counter-transferential experience and the game that is played as a result of it.

When the therapist experiences being drawn into the role ascribed to her by the patient she will learn about the patient's struggle in a way that is not available to her in the process of attention to the overt verbal exchange. Provided the therapist recognizes the game she has a choice to play along, to confront the game or not to play it but not expose it. If she chooses to stay in it, she is playing along with the game in awareness, rather than playing it with the patient out of her awareness.

Once a clear therapeutic relationship has been established it is more likely that exposing a game, by attention to the relationship and explanation of the observed process that is alive and available to both or all parties in the room, will be a viable therapeutic intervention. However, even if the clinician teaches the patient game theory so that she has the tools to look for her own game patterns in her everyday life, it is not necessarily going to follow that she will be ready to be challenged in therapy. Since the patient will be playing many games, it is expedient to use 'dosage' in exposing the games. This means that some games will go unchallenged in favour of emphasis on other games. The therapist needs to be circumspect in choosing when and how to expose a game and, as ever, the guiding force will be the therapeutic value of the intervention at any given time in the therapeutic journey.

Some games are more obvious than others and it is these games that are easier to name and describe than the more subtle games that can become part of the psychotherapeutic process. For instance if a patient and therapist get into a game of 'Why don't you… Yes but…' the pattern quickly becomes evident to the alert and self-observing practitioner. She or he makes a suggestion and the patient responds with a reason why this would not be appropriate for her. This might be followed by another idea that the patient has another reason for dismissing. It soon becomes apparent that both are in the game. The therapist then has a choice of naming the game, and discussing what has happened with the patient or simply withdrawing from the game without exposing it, and choosing other interventions based on her understanding of why the game was likely to have been played at this time.

I do not think there is any value in continuing to play a game of 'Why don't you… Yes but…' whereas there would be therapeutic value in playing along with a game that demands a particular relationship that would be healing for the patient. For instance, Sal was looking for a much-needed reparative relationship. She needed to bond with me before she could move to healthy separation. She transferred on to me the idealized other she had not experienced as an infant and at times she needed me to be the strong, caring and holding other with whom she could find expression for her fears and later her hatred. It was within the bonded therapeutic alliance that she was able to test me out, to love me and hate me and know that I would still be around. If I had confronted this dynamic there would not have been the therapeutic space for her to expand her skills of both authentic and inauthentic communication of her emotions, or to resolve the relationship with her father or separate from her mother in whom she still looked for the mirroring relationship she had never had in the frame of reference that contained her fear of her ability to destroy. Sal's container for these fears and repressed emotions was her large body size.

Common games played by obese patients

I will now discuss some of the games I have come to associate with overweight patients. I describe their presentation and refer to some of the psychological and social advantages of playing them. Games are played by the patient in her everyday life, with practitioners whom she has asked for help and psychotherapists. I deal with the playing of these games both outside and inside the therapy room where I see this differentiation to be helpful. The games described here are those that are specifically observable by their repeated patterns and can be named accordingly.

I sometimes think the label of game playing sounds unsympathetic and somewhat derisory. When described in this clinical fashion it can seem to suggest that it is shameful to play games and particularly for the psychotherapist to be drawn into or play her own games. It is worth repeating, therefore, that game playing is part of the richness of our communication with each other. We all play games and it is doubtful that anyone, even the most enlightened person would ever be 'game-free'.

I have given the games I describe here identifying names, some of which are commonly known as categories of games in TA and others that are types of games significantly played by obese patients. The names, though somewhat popularistic, are meant to portray the content and are in no way meant to diminish their significance as essential strategies for maintaining the patient's frame of reference or their power as defensive tactics.

'Help me lose weight'

I will take the analysis of this game a little further and look at it from a second degree perspective. In this game the patient is the starter. She needs to find someone who will be willing to play the game with her. This is usually her partner, whom she has chosen because of the way their scripts complement each other, or it could be a friend. It might also be the slimming club, doctor or other authority. The other player will be someone who likes to help or take control or feels he or she has something to offer. The remit is usually expected to be someone to watch over the patient, to advise, direct, take interest, maybe even magically to 'do it for her'. If the patient is in the game the person who is hooked into it will be doomed to fail the task of helping her lose weight. The patient does not really want to lose weight if she unconsciously uses it as a survival mechanism or to stop eating extra food if her psychological hungers are perceived as being met through eating. She may want to lose it when she is thinking from her Adult, but if her Child ego state does not concur she will play games that maintain the status quo.

Depending on who the patient is playing the game with, there will be different response periods both in terms of length and content. Let us take the scenario that gets played out at home with say the patient's male partner.

If we look at the transactions that set up the game (see Figure 11.4 below) we see that the social message is 'Help me lose weight' (S1). This is usually plotted as Adult to Adult as the request sounds as though it warrants Adult agreement. The psychological message (P1) is 'You won't be able to help me, no one can'. Her partner accepts the role (S2) but his psychological message (P2) is 'I know I can't help you, I have no power over your eating and I feel useless'. I have shown these transactions from Child to Child. I have done this because the belief systems from which the messages spring are in the Child ego state. The social transactions are shown with solid lines and the psychological ones with dotted lines.

The game is now set up with the patient on the Victim corner of the Drama Triangle and her partner on the Rescuer corner in Figure 11.5 below.

Now the patient diets and loses some weight. This is the response period described earlier. All seems well but then the patient eats something she shouldn't and her partner reminds her of her diet. She sees this as criticism. She then becomes angry and accuses him of criticizing her and tells him he does not understand what it is like to have to diet. Her partner is surprised at

Patient/Game con   Partner/2nd player

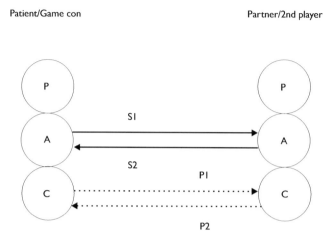

Figure 11.4 Transactional diagram of the game of 'Help me lose weight'

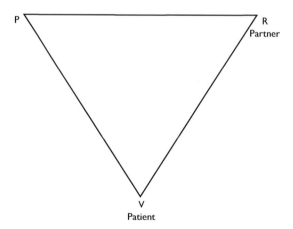

Figure 11.5 The starting position in the game of 'Help me lose weight' between patient and her partner

214 / *The Overweight Patient*

the attack and feels helpless and hopeless. There is a hiatus in the relationship for a while.

The Transactional Analysis indicates the change. The primary change is in the patient's behaviour in that she has blown the diet (S3). S4 is her partner's reminder that she should be dieting, which she experiences as a criticism. She therefore sees him as transacting from his Critical Parent to her Child. She retaliates from her Critical Parent in defence (S5) and this is the switch that forces him into Victim role and her into Persecutor. This is demonstrated in the transactional diagram in Figure 11.6.

The players move round the Drama Triangle so that the patient becomes the Persecutor and her partner the Victim as in Figure 11.7

In the scenario of the slimming club a similar dynamic may arise though in a more subtle way as the patient is likely to transfer her expectation of a negative response on to the leader of the club even though the leader is unlikely to feel angry with the patient. She may be disappointed but any leader needs to be pragmatic about those who are not able to keep to the rules of the regime.

If the patient is looking for this help from a desperate Child need or adaptation, the game starts when she joins the club expecting that the leader will provide a solution to her weight problem and direct her towards weight loss. Whilst she is losing weight all is well and she gets strokes from the leader and other members of the group who applaud her each week. She then has 'a bad week' and puts weight on. She may be able to tolerate one or two such weight gains but there will come a time when she feels hopeless and she will not attend the group. Her psychological rationale for leaving will be that the leader will be angry with her and think she is useless, thus transferring her own negative feelings onto the leader. It is clearly the patient who feels useless. She may then continue the game process by blemishing the slimming club (playing Persecutor), or perhaps shift to another game that returns her to a familiar Victim position and fits with this one such as: 'Look how hard I am trying' or 'If it weren't for you I would be able to diet' or perhaps 'Kick me'.

The game of 'Help me lose weight' may be played for ever if the patient remains in the slimming group as a lifelong member or as she continuously searches for new clubs, groups or alternative practitioners who might help her lose weight. She has not learnt to do it by herself and so chooses to stay in the Parent–Child dynamic.

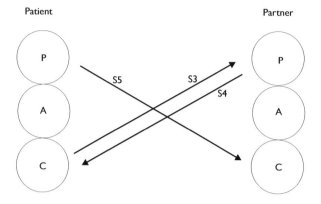

Figure 11.6 Transactional diagram of the switch in the game of 'Help me lose weight'

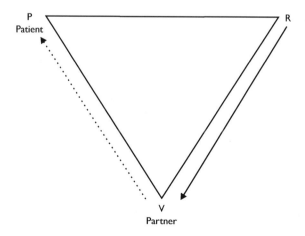

Figure 11.7 The switched position in the game of 'Help me lose weight' between patient and her partner

Whilst the patient's psychological hungers are not being met and she is not resolving the issues that compel her to eat she will undoubtedly stay in these obesity-related games. They all discount her own ability to resolve her issues for herself. In the therapy context she can discover why she is playing the games and why she is eating amounts of food that keep her fat. Nonetheless, she may still fight against taking responsibility for herself as long as her fears and fantasies remain dominant. She is able to change her eating behaviour when she understands what is behind it, however, when her body size and food are part of her survival strategy she is bound to resist change even knowing what compels her to stay fat until her Child self feels safe enough to do so. Playing games will be part of her defensive strategy both within and outside the therapy room.

This is a game that needs to stay in awareness throughout work with overweight patients. Even though I do not contract with the patient for a goal of weight loss as a therapeutic outcome, it is still possible to be drawn into the game of 'Help me lose weight' since the patient's need, desire or at least her presenting issue is ultimately to lose weight. The pull to play this game will be strong.

'If it weren't for you' (IWFY)

This is an interesting game and it is one that I see played in two ways. The first way is when the patient believes that someone makes her eat. We saw this with Jill who felt her father and her boss's behaviour made her eat. What happens here is that the true reason for the eating is discounted in favour of what appears to be happening at the social level. In that situation, there were clearly psychological reasons for Jill's eating based on her misconception that she was not good enough in her father's eyes. It was the internal sensation of agitation that compelled Jill to eat and the agitation was because of her sense of not being good enough if she thought she had done something wrong in her boss's eyes. Others however, play the game by saying that they cannot refuse food in various circumstances such as when their mother provides it for them; or when they go out to dinner because they feel compelled to eat so as not to spoil others' enjoyment; or when they are persuaded by others to eat because they have been so kind to provide the food, or they feel the pull to join in and enjoy 'naughty foods' with someone who might say 'Just one won't hurt', when there is a sense of camaraderie in sharing forbidden fruits; or 'Please have something, I don't want to eat alone'.

In this latter case the patient is the Victim of the control of the others who want her to eat. They could be seen to be in Persecutor mode. Their need is accompanied by the ulterior message of 'You have to make me feel good by complying with my wishes' and perhaps: 'If you don't comply, I won't like you'. The patient complies from her Victim corner putting the needs of the others before her own. At the same time she is providing herself with a situation in which she feels she does not have a choice so that she can justify her eating. She also needs to be liked. It feels as though it takes a lot of willpower to resist in the face of the powerful invitations into the games of others who want her to eat for their own needs not hers. However, willpower needs a positive sense of self. It needs a level of confidence and self-esteem that eludes many obese patients. Their fears of rejection will keep them available for these games.

In all these situations the patient perceives other people making her eat. She discounts that she has a choice, that she can do this differently and that if she does so she will survive. In fact she discounts herself in favour of adapting to others. She discounts options for behaving differently. And at these times she will discount the significance of her need to lose weight and the consequences of succumbing to other people's needs and demands. Learning about game theory so that the patient can understand these processes may be helpful to the patient depending on her Adult availability to process and use the theoretical construct to her advantage.

The second way I see patients playing 'If it weren't for you' is with regard to their size. This is not the way game playing is normally perceived but I take the liberty of seeing this behaviour in terms of a game. Though the body is clearly not another player in the game, the patient can both objectify and subjectify her body self. She will see the body as having a life and existence of its own.

Her dialogue will entail thoughts such as 'If it weren't for my size I would...get a good job...travel...find a really nice mate...meet more people...have this operation...have a baby'. In fact her inner fears are that she would never be able to do these things. This is the psychological component of the game and her unconscious fear would be that if she loses the weight she will be put to the test and be found wanting. There are deeper psychological beliefs underpinning these fears and these relate to her lack of self-worth, of importance, trust and survival.

A patient who had always said she couldn't have a baby because she was fat, in the process of her therapy discovered that she was fearful of having a child because of her belief that she could not look after a baby and that she had nothing to offer a child. It was not her weight that prevented her from conceiving but her psychological scare and beliefs about herself. Released from these beliefs she conceived, gave birth and recognized that she quickly became a very competent and knowledgeable mother.

A patient who believed she would never get a good job came to acknowledge that she had never tried to get what she considered to be a good job. When working through her game she revealed her underlying belief that she was not good enough and that she was stupid. She realized she had taken on board 'Don't Make It' and 'Don't Think' injunctions. Getting a good job would be going against this injunction and her sanction for doing so would be to be abandoned. Once these psychological advantages of her game were discovered we were able to work with them to release their spell. She became a PA to a senior manager of a large computer company where she was given a rewarding degree of responsibility and an excellent salary she never thought she would receive. She could not have done this without the script release that came from analysing the game with her.

A patient who believed she would travel if she were not fat discovered that her fear of travelling was that she would be forgotten whilst away as she was not important enough for people to bother to remember her. She would then have no friends to come home to and her fantasy image was having to travel in a void forever.

One of my patients lost weight quickly. She transferred on to me the watchdog she was craving, imagining that I was expecting her to lose weight even though I had explained that this was not a contract I would enter into. She was so pleased with herself and reported feeling so much better that it was difficult to confront her shift in behaviour even in terms of the transference she was clearly imposing on me. I felt caught in a game and found myself compelled to rescue by not challenging the game. She began to wear different and very feminine clothes and to feel sexual. She became flirtatious, enjoying playing first degree games around her new-found sexuality. In response she was criticized by some of the friends she had spent time with over a number of years. They found her new presentation uncomfortable. They had clearly depended on her staying in her fat and essentially Victim, one-down role. She felt the abandonment that she had feared. Her beliefs about herself as being too much, unlovable and bad all surfaced in the pay-off of the game. It was very painful for her and needless to say she regained weight.

This patient was still conforming to her script beliefs and played a second degree game around her weight such that she achieved the negative pay-off of perceived abandonment in that some of the group members seemed to reject her. She used her sexuality in the very way she feared she would and this provided the additional component of the game that would ensure she would get the snubbing she expected when operating from her script beliefs. She could therefore believe that if it weren't for her weight she would become inappropriately sexual. And if it weren't for her weight she would be abandoned.

When this patient resolved her underlying issues in psychotherapy, she lost weight gradually. She did not need to flaunt her resulting sense of sexuality but integrated it so that it became part of her right as a feminine adult rather than the objectified persona she had made it out to be in her first flush of weight loss. Some friends drifted away from her circle in response to her new presentation of herself but she was robust enough to see that they had needed her to be fat for their own reasons. She made new friends. In her previous period of weight loss she had still been in her script, though playing it out in a different way. In the latter phase she had changed enough of her script beliefs to make changes that did not have negative outcomes and that she could sustain and appreciate from her Adult self.

'Fat clown'

'Fat clown' is played with any number of players who will laugh at the patient as she is the target of her own derisive humour. In this game she belittles herself but gets a huge amount of strokes from the attention she gets from being the life and soul of the party. She will quite possibly play the game within the work setting with her team colleagues. Whilst she is seen to be an all-round good egg, her opinion is rarely sought. She is in fact not taken seriously and her switch comes when she realizes this is the case and gets fed up with always being overlooked for promotion or serious discussion. She gets angry and changes from the happy clown, which is received with some surprise by her colleagues. The period of discomfort will last until she resumes her preferred and assigned role, which she will surely do.

In her social setting, her membership of the group is dependent on her being the fat happy clown. If she wants to be serious, listened to and taken seriously she will experience a strong pull from other players for her to remain in the ascribed role. When she realizes she is not taken seriously she gets angry and resentful. She shifts to the Persecutor role. The others who want her to remain in the clown role are keeping her in the Victim position and are themselves in Persecutor. Because of the high stakes of not belonging, the patient can be swiftly drawn back into her familiar role.

This patient needs to have resolved essential issues of self-worth and self-esteem before she can withstand the group pressure. When she does this she can actually find a place in the group that does not depend on her being fat and playing the clown. In the analysis of the game, the clinician can ascertain with the patient why she plays this position when it causes her to be both sad and angry, feel rejected and not taken seriously, which are essentially the components of the game pay-off.

In the therapy room the patient will play the game with gallows laughter. This is when she is describing something that is painful and yet smiling or laughing at the same time. It is not unusual for the patient to make light of many events and to use derisive laughter, turned against herself. I would normally confront gallows laughter but, when it happens repeatedly, it is inappropriate to continuously expose the behaviour. There are other ways of reflecting to the patient that her words are being taken seriously even though she is laughing, without naming the gamey behaviour.

Overweight patients often express their fears of being 'too much'. It is sometimes related to expression of emotion when they feel that if they allow themselves to release their feelings they will 'go too far'. Most significantly they often believe that if they cry they will never stop and they present as afraid of their own anger. Playing the game of 'fat clown' guards against expression of emotions they imagine will be too much for others to contend with.

Not all patients play this 'entertainer' game. For some it would be impossible as a defence structure because of the intensity of interpersonal communication and self-exposure it requires.

'Look how hard I'm trying'

This game is usually played out over a lengthy period of time. By the time patients come into psychotherapy or counselling, they have usually tried numerous diets both from magazines and self-help books and in attendance at one or more slimming clubs. They may also have tried alternative therapies like hypnosis, kinesiology, acupuncture and endless pills and diet biscuits etc. They really have tried hard to lose weight but there is something magical in their thinking that someone or something else will do the work for them. This is by no means a criticism. Patients who play this game need to do so in order to sustain their beliefs about self and others and the world. This is part of their elaborate protective strategy. This game supports another called 'Ain't it awful' in which patients talk about how dreadful things are such as how difficult it is to lose weight and how many things they have tried that have not been successful. The social benefit of both these games is that they provide a continuous and repeated focus for pastiming (Chapter 10) conversation about the trials of trying to lose weight, the pressures around that make it difficult, the fact that nothing works and 'So what can I do, I've tried everything. There must be some other reason why I am fat'. The patient will find someone to play these games with who will support the fact that they have tried everything. They will get lots of strokes from the interactions both in terms of the attention and the sympathy they get.

If the patient is anxious about losing weight, or the weight is a survival issue, then she will continue to try new diets, attend slimming clubs or engage in other treatments and feel a sense of righteousness in her continued attempts.

It is important to be aware that counselling, psychotherapy or other treatments may be another way of the patient playing this game. Her statement might be 'Look how hard I am trying to lose weight, I have even tried therapy. That's how hard I am trying'. If a patient is playing this game by attending for therapy or in association with any other practitioner it would need to be exposed early in the process otherwise the patient will play it to its conclusion and leave the therapy or group having ensured her psychological and social game advantages.

'Do you love me even though I am fat?'

This game is usually played outside the therapy room between partners and inside the therapy room with the therapist. The question at the social level is a request for reassurance that the patient is loved whilst at the psychological level the patient is looking for verification that she is not loved if that is her script belief. If her partner says 'yes' then she will discount his answer in some way. For example she might say 'But you'd love me more if I were thinner'. What does her partner now say? If he says 'No I wouldn't' she will hear a note in his voice that belies his words. She might turn it to 'There's no point me losing weight then' or 'Why do you make comments about what I eat or about my weight if it makes no difference?' She has engineered her familiar negative pay-off and reinforced the sense of her own inability to be loved that she sub-consciously maintains by remaining fat and with her necessary accompanying belief that no one loves a fat person. Her partner feels he cannot win. If he avoids or ignores the question, he is merely continuing to play the game. He feels tricked and she feels she has caught him out. She moves from Victim to Persecutor. He moves from Rescuer to Victim.

In the therapy room the patient will test out the therapist and may be ready to play 'Now I've got you...' as soon as she tricks the therapist into saying something that supports her belief that she is not good enough as she is. She will test the therapist's love for her by such manoeuvres as pushing against the boundaries, seeing if she is too much for the therapist, being late, cancelling or changing appointments. 'Do you love me even though I am fat?' and NIGY may be played by the patient who needs to believe that the practitioner is as rejecting of her size as anyone else. It is played specifically when trust in the therapist is still an issue.

'Why don't you... Yes but...'

As the name suggests this game entails someone making suggestions as to what the patient can do in order to lose weight. She will provide names and addresses, phone numbers, book titles, clubs, evidence of what has worked for others and so on. The game usually starts with the patient wanting help, or at least giving the impression that she does (Victim). The other is a helper (Rescuer). Say this is a female friend. She wants to find the solution but at an unconscious level she knows she can't. The patient will play the game but she too knows that nothing the other person says is going to impact on her. She cannot afford to let anything the other person says be useful to her unless of course she plays an intricacy that allows her to go and try whatever the suggestion is in order to prove that 'it' will fail. The switch occurs when the helper runs out of suggestions and the patient thanks her for trying to help, indicating in her manner a resignation that she knew no one could help. Both feel deflated, the patient because once again her beliefs have been proven right and the Rescuer because she has once again been defeated. She moves to the Victim position whilst the patient feels irritated and persecutory.

'Kick me'

Another game that may be played over a period of time, being set up stage by stage is 'Kick me'. Given all that has been said about the overweight patient's script beliefs and her negative experience in a less than tolerant culture, it is not surprising that a game that would support her beliefs would be this game of 'Kick me'. By being obese she expects to be, and regularly experiences being kicked.

The patient may also attempt to play the game of 'Kick me' with her friends, partner, practitioner or therapist by not losing weight. She will feel kicked simply by being overweight. At the social level, the patient's weight will justify her need to be kicked. Psychologically she will feel the need to be kicked because of her sense of harbouring a bad, worthless, or unlovable self inside.

'At your service'

The obese patient's need to please others was described in other chapters. She rarely says no to others for fear of being disliked if she does not cooperate. She buys love with her endless availability but eventually feels resentful that others don't do for her or discount what she has done for them. She moves from the Rescuer to the Victim and then persecutes. Her persecution, however, is likely to be confined to grumbles in the safety of her own home rather than with those for whom she has become the tireless helper. She would not dare risk being angry with them. When she stops doing for a while, those who have received her help feel that she has deserted them and that 'she has changed', the implication being 'for the worse'. They become angry and persecutory, usually expressed in passive aggressive withdrawal for a while rather than verbal condemnation to her face. They too are likely to complain about her to other people. When the pain becomes too much she will revert to the helping behaviour again.

Some patients will be prepared to risk saying 'no' a few times to some people if their analysis of the relationship suggests they can trust the other person or persons to keep a connection with them. This enables a patient to feel something of her self-agency. However, she can only do this in small doses until underlying issues are resolved. The game is a defensive strategy, which, if stopped, will leave her exposed to her injunctions and the perceived reality of her fantasies. As with other games if friendships or any relationships are founded on the patient taking an assigned role, in this case 'At their service', change in her role will rock the foundation of the relationship and her fears of abandonment, rejection, not being good enough etc. will seem to be confirmed. The fact that the relationships are based on such dynamics is central to the games.

'You're the expert'

This is also commonly played in the therapy room. It tends to imply the game of 'Do me something'. In this game, the patient clearly wants the therapist to tell her what to do. The con is strong, for indeed, the therapist or qualified practitioner working in this field would be assumed to have more expertise than the patient. The pull in the therapy room is to take charge of the process and for the patient to be the passive receiver of the practitioner's wisdom. The patient who has tried numerous diets, attended slimming clubs, had medical help and advice will be used to being the recipient of directives from others and will expect, to some extent, that a therapist will conduct a treatment programme in much the same way.

The patient needs to be enabled to feel her own potency so that she can eventually take charge of the process and focus of the therapy. This may take some time and the therapist or practitioner will need to accept the role whilst working towards this end. However, this is not to say that the therapist is playing the game. Firstly she is aware of the patient's unconscious process and therefore can stay out of the game. Secondly she decides on a course of action from her Adult judgment that leads her to choose certain therapeutic interventions over others. She is therefore not in a game since games are played out of awareness and roles taken up through consideration and choice cannot be out of, but are very much in, awareness.

In summary

Games are played outside of Adult awareness. The Adult ego state is not used in the playing of a game. If the practitioner chooses to play along with the game as a therapeutic intervention she or he is making that decision in awareness and from the Adult ego state and therefore is not playing the game in the sense of being unaware that it is happening until experiencing the pay-off.

Games are repetitive, which enables the therapist to discover the games patients play by asking 'What is it that happens over and over again?' Despite this repetitive nature of games, the patient will not be aware that she has been game playing until the fact has been brought into her awareness in the therapy room. She will, however, be aware that something happens again and again and that she gets a recurring negative feeling that she can identify. The familiar 'happening' will be characterized by a sense of 'Here we go again' and an element of surprise when the switch occurs.

The negative feeling that a patient experiences at the conclusion of the game, or the pay-off, is central to the analysis. It is possible to identify her most essential script beliefs from unpacking this discomforting sensation. The roles she plays within the games will be identified, which will lead to an understanding of her existential position. The therapist is then able to trace the patient's fears of losing weight by working through the social, psychological and biological needs she fulfils by playing these games and will identify with her the psychological hungers she is trying to meet through her weight-related games.

With the analysis of the relational component of the games played out with the therapist, there arises the hands-on, here and now material with which to work. That is to say, the games the patient plays will reveal the relationship she desires, whether this is the idealized sought-after relationship, the need for the good parent that has been lost, or the need to recreate the familiar experience of the rejecting parent or any of the intricate combinations that exist within these recognizable bands of intersubjectivity.

There is always a psychological or ulterior message that differs from the social communication. It is this psychological message that draws the other player into the game. A person whose script beliefs do not fit with that of the instigator of the game will not be available to play it.

When the therapist 'finds' herself in a game with a patient, it is an indication that something in her own script has led to this position. The something, a need or a belief, has rendered her ready for game playing and necessitates investigation because it is most certainly a component of the therapeutic relationship and in what I call the 'betweenness' or psychotherapeutic space. It will be central in the clarification of the nature of the intersubjectivity and to the transference and counter-transference phenomena.

Games may need to be confronted in small doses, remembering they are defensive strategies learnt early in childhood. The clinician can offer the tools of TA game theory to the patient so that she is active and involved in her own behavioural analysis and the practitioner can work totally within the transferential relationship, which will include the gaming relationship, in order to effect cure.

As I have said before, the choice of method in working with games is the responsibility of the practitioner until such time as the patient is ready to negotiate for a mutually agreed dynamic. Clearly the depth of actual and psychological trauma, the extent of the fears of the patient and the extremity of her defence strategies that govern her inability to lose weight will determine the choice of intervention at any given time in the treatment process. Games involve a mode of survival, the foundations of which are usually created in childhood and built on in later years. Behind the game playing is the patient's story, her reasons for playing them. For this reason the concept of games is a potent tool for psychotherapy and other clinical attention. To teach the patient at the most appropriate juncture about games is offering her a powerful self-help tool. Games are in fact intriguing and it is this description I offer the patient.

Games are part of the foundation stones that support the patient's script. They have been carefully built from a defensive structure that the patient unconsciously perceives as being safe. It is only possible to remove or change small parts of the structure at any time or it will surely collapse.

The therapist can very effectively 'teach' the patient about game theory so that she has the tools to identify her games in her everyday life. The choice of when to move into this more cognitive approach will of course depend on the patient's needs, the stage of her therapy and the practitioner's preferred style of working. The clinician may not choose in her style of therapy to give the patient these tools. Understanding the games patients play is important in linking their psychological script system with their behavioural patterns.

Patients who have a briefer experience of obesity and who are not morbidly obese will more easily respond to confrontation of games and to learning and using game theory in their everyday lives than the long-term and morbidly obese patient. This is because the underlying issues are not likely to be as entrenched or traumatic as those underpinning the long-term sufferer's games.

Chapter 12

The Creation of the Body
and Eating Functions
as Defence Structures

The purpose of this chapter is to explore and raise awareness of some specific developmental theory that might be considered in working with obese patients. My aim is to invite ongoing thinking about the early developmental experience of the patient and how this might have contributed to her decision to use the body and/or the function of eating, as a defence. There are three specific areas of interest:

1.   the development of the internal and external body boundaries and the corresponding development of the psychological self; how this might lead to the patient's confusion with regard to the body self

2.   the early stages of the infant's sensory-dominated world and the bid to create or recreate those sensations through eating

3.   the ability of the patient to withdraw into her self and to dissociate when eating or bingeing.

When discussing developmental theory it is difficult to get away from terminology that might imply complete and discrete stages of development. It is important to consider that the infant develops a sense of self in overlapping and fluid phases. However, there is a commonality in conclusions of studies of infant development that suggest that, by a certain age, specific developmental components will be present in normal physical and psychological growth together with relational maturation that allows for healthy initial differentiation, and later separation, from the mother.

Daniel Stern (1985) writes about domains of relatedness, all of which 'remain active during development'. And 'Once formed, the domains remain forever as distinct forms of experiencing social life and self. None are lost to adult experience' (p.32). This is why the therapist can be with and learn from the 'clinical infant' and how she or he can know, understand and relate to the different ego states or regressive 'psychic chunks of experience' (Clarkson 1992) of patients. It explains how what is thought of as past experience is here in the present and therefore allows for the healing and reparative nature of a positive and empathic relationship since any domain of relatedness, established in the past and brought with the patient into adulthood, can be re-met in the present. It also explains how the past can remain functional in the here and now. Obese patients carry their infant experience into the present in two ways, in their body size and in their need to overeat.

Although attention to all 'phases' of development will have something to offer in explanation of a patient's script decisions, I confine myself to those phases that seem to me to be particularly instrumental in the patient's choice to use her body defensively. These are the early infant experience, early development of self-mastery and the sense of effectiveness, the drive towards separation in all its phases, the development of identity and the passage through to adulthood via adolescence.

Alongside this, it needs to be borne in mind that the choice to use food to feed psychological hungers could have its onset at any period in the patient's life when she feels starved of strokes, sexual activity, power, stimuli, physical contact or structure in her life. If this starvation is continuous then compensation with food will be continuous and the patient will suffer long-term obesity. If however, it is episodic, the patient is more likely to use food for the duration of the episode until she satisfies the psychological hunger in congruent ways. This would be the difference between the long-term and short term or reactive obesity. Nonetheless, I consider the choice to use food to feed psychological hungers as deriving from the infant's early experience of feeding and related body sensations and activity whether the problem is short or long-term.

The early experience of self through touch and sensation

The infant develops its early sense of self primarily through touch and sensation and secondly through sound and then sight. Through a process of mirroring and attuned response from the caregiver she will eventually know that she is and has a right to be both physically and mentally separate from any other. She needs to develop the sense of her own body boundary in order to know that she is an entity that will survive independently of mother. The certainty in the body self development translates into a certainty of the psychological self, the body and psyche being inseparable. It follows then, that disturbance in the process of developing a cohesive sense of the body self will result in disturbance in the psychological self and an incomplete sense of a coherent self.

David Krueger (1989) refers specifically to this process. He states that the self develops around the early experiences and sensations relating to the external surface and the internal functioning of the body. He says: 'As the kinaesthetic body boundaries are being determined, an important parallel process occurs with the psychic boundary formation and functioning' (p.4). As the infant develops the sense of her external body surface area through touch and contact with the world, she begins to understand she has body boundaries that contain her as separate from her caregiver. In the process of demarcation of body boundaries she begins to distinguish between her internal sensation and her external body surface area. Krueger maintains that it is essentially this establishment of the inner body self and outer boundaried container that informs the child psychologically of what is self and what is not and leads to an awareness of self as an entity and the creation of a self-image. The self-image develops in relation to others and throughout life. The quality of the self-image spans both the physical and the psychological self. Obese patients have a poor self-image in both these realms.

The knowledge of self as separate from another is dependent on the ability to subjectify and objectify both the self and the other. That is to say, the infant can experience herself and the other as both object and subject. This in turn is dependent on the permission from the caregiver to separate and on the coherence of the self-image that renders such separation safe. The awareness of self is further delineated in the observation, through subjectivity and objectivity, that oneself is different from another. I have observed that many obese patients have issues that relate to the inability to hold a clear sense of self, which impeded their healthy passage through stages of separation. The extension of the body is a way of both separating from another and containing the self in the best way available to the patient given the unsafe world around her in infancy, which has perpetuated into adulthood.

If we take Stern's notion of the infant's predesigned awareness of self-organizing processes it follows that the baby is driven towards the natural development of separation and individuation rather than this being an acquired predisposition. The task of the caregiver then is to meet this need, not to engender it in the child (Stern 1985). The mother's ability to perform this task will determine whether the infant develops a clear sense of the body self alongside the psychological self and thereby a cohesive sense of self. The infant has the desire and need at times to seek a sense of mergence with, and emergence from, the mother who was the container during gestation when the infant was truly merged with her. The mother needs to be attuned enough to respond appropriately to the infant's need both to be merged and to have space.

Body boundary definition

There is agreement throughout theories of infant development that touch and physical contact with the world are paramount in determining the child's sense of self and that mother or primary caregiver's ability to be adequately attuned to her infant is essential to ensure balanced physical and psychological growth. (I describe the primary caregiver as mother because this is more usually the position, however the primary caregiver may be father or another carer and so each time I write 'mother' I imply any caregiver–infant relationship.)

In the earliest psychic experience of the body, the quality of the mother's touch and the message received by the infant from her ability to stroke, caress, hold and contain the infant will determine the infant's sense of her body self. The mother defines the infant's body boundaries with her hands and 'awakens' the first sense of self invested in the body (Krueger 1985). Mother's defining of the body boundary then is not separate from the attention she may give to what appear to be the psychological and emotional aspects of her infant but actually arouse the energy of psychological selfhood in the body.

The infant's earliest sense of external reality is represented most significantly by the mother's unconscious for it is the mother's own introjects and belief systems arrived at through her own infant and adolescent developmental experiences that will determine her manner of relating to her baby. A mother who has unresolved issues from her own difficult past may find that they are such that she is unable to fully see her infant as separate from herself or to differentiate between her own feelings and those of the child. She sees the child only in her own terms rather than the infant herself. When this happens she is unable to mirror the child accurately, which will in turn mean that the infant's attempts at effectiveness will feel thwarted and confusing.

The infant has heightened intuition and sensitivity towards her environment in her sensory-dominated world and so, in a way, she is ripe for receiving messages that tell her she exists as a being in her own right but will also internalize messages that speak to the contrary. Though she is programmed to seek separation she is also reliant on being released from her total dependency on the caregiver through the caregiver's permission to her to be released manifested in her ability to see her child as separate from herself.

Hargaden and Sills (2002) see the earliest child, the emergent self in Stern's terminology, as C0 (the earliest Child ego state). C0 'is experienced as bodily-affective states' (p.18). The environment, which includes mother but also the physical surroundings against which the infant is buffeted, would be represented by P0. The environment shapes the infant, in the process of which she forms both a physical and a mental sense of her self on some scale from organized and integrated to disorganized and disintegrated.

This early psychic experience of the body is a starting point from which the infant develops a sense of herself as not only separate from mother but as having substance in herself as a being. Therefore, if the caregiving is not adequately carried out, body self distortions will arise such that the child is not clear about her own body boundaries as distinct from another. If the body boundary is not well defined through the infant's tactile experience, the patient may seek to define her boundary in later life. This may result in behaviours that define the body boundary through pain, such as cutting or excessive exercise that delineates the body with firm musculature.

The obese patient is continuously searching to establish her outer limit, though that limit is always ill-defined. She does not have the ability to demarcate a muscular boundary because she does not have a clear enough sense of integration to allow her to self-focus in this obsessive way. There is not the ego strength to support the differentiation of self and other without the enforcement of space through extended body boundaries.

She does, however, have a visual sense of an outer boundary in her unconcealable large body size. She also promotes the uncomfortable physical sensation that arises from overeating and from being large. In addition, being large means at times being buffeted against both hard and soft surfaces that can recreate that early experience of contact with objects that, when encountered, help create the sense of a containing shell.

Obesity as a psychosomatic representation

Obese patients are telling their story in their body presentation. The long-term obese patient somatizes (converts psychological distress into bodily symptoms) by producing a large body with its concomitant aches, pains, eruptions, cardiovascular disturbances and other illnesses. McDougall (1989) in investigating psychosomatic representation concludes that when the infant 'feels impelled to struggle against the primordial division that gives rise to an "individual"' this may result in a variety of psychic solutions' (p.43). One of these psychic solutions McDougall says might be towards addiction (in this case food) and another is the non-verbal expression found in somatic presentation, in this case the layers of fat she produces around herself.

The patient's fat body becomes an important defensive structure. McDougall notes that patients invested in this non-verbal representation will 'fight with a determination of which they are unaware, to *protect* their somatic creations' (p.43). At times it certainly seems as though the obese patient is unwilling to engage in the therapeutic process or plays games around it. If, however, the patient's body is a defence against disintegration, it can be seen that she is very likely to want, subconsciously, to resist change that she unconsciously fears would annihilate her.

Boundaries between outer and inner body self

Krueger (1989) describes the second stage of development as aiming for 'the definition of body surface boundaries and the distinction of the baby's internal state' (p.9). This stage concerns the distinction between the internal and surface body sensations necessary to enhance the development of the sense of a physical and psychic self independent of and separate from mother. As the awareness of an inner body self arises the infant has a greater sense of self. There is, in effect, more information now to support the notion of being separate. With the growing awareness of internal sensations and the continued process of definition of the external body boundary comes the capacity for increased recognition of self as an entity. The infant is not just a body but a body with an outer and inner capacity for different and distinguishable sensations. 'By distinguishing inner and outer, a demarcation is drawn between body boundaries, while a parallel coherent reality of internal body functions and needs, independent of the self object, is developed' (Krueger 1989, p.9).

The infant has the skills of primitive communication with which she wants to let the carer(s) know her needs, such as when she is tired, angry, scared, sad, cold, hot, hungry, thirsty, wet, or otherwise physically uncomfortable. The attuned parent will attempt to get it right for the child and respond accordingly. Each time the child communicates her physiological sensations and gets appropriate caring responses her internal sensation is validated. Thus she begins to understand that there is an internal physical self that is different from her external boundary with the world. If the parents, for by now father and others have a role to play in the development of the infant, are unavailable to respond accurately enough, or are unavailable to the child, the boundary between internal and external, may be blurred and result in an inability to distinguish internal states.

As the infant moves into the domain of a subjective sense of self, she has the capacity to begin to see others as subjective, rather than just objective. Seeing the other as both objective and subjective gives rise to another sort of anxiety: the anxiety that the infant might be potent enough to drive away or even harm, her carer(s). The way through this anxiety is in the continuing development of a coherent sense of self enabled by attuned and responsive parents.

Disturbance in this stage gives rise to:

1. the inability to distinguish internal sensations that are interpreted as food hunger as was described in the chapter on psychological hungers

2. the patient's fear of her powers of destruction

3. distortions in self-image that leave the patient feeling ill-defined, physically and psychologically shapeless

4. patients' bids in later life to recreate the sensations that promote awareness of internal states.

The inability to distinguish internal sensations

As previously described, obese patients dissociate from some body sensations and misinterpret others. Anxiety, sadness, anger and fear, all of which are accompanied by physical sensation, are repeatedly either mistaken as hunger pangs or are emotions met and swallowed down with food. The infant that is always silenced with a feed will develop a poor relationship with food. In such feeding there is both the comfort of the familiar transitional object and the anger or passive acceptance of being missed. The obese and overeating patient recreates an illusion of the comfort and either the passivity, transposed into powerlessness, or the anger that she turns in upon herself in the form of chastising for eating and for being fat.

She continues the process of being missed as an infant by discounting her needs as an adult and thereby feeds her psychological hungers with food rather than having to face those needs. She fears encounter with herself whom she sees as worthless, unlovable, bad, unwanted, unlikeable and so forth.

Fear of powers of destruction

As the infant moves towards a level of subjectivity she senses a power within herself. Accurate mirroring within containment is important at this infant stage. With the potency comes a fear that she may be able to destroy the caregiver whom she will now experience as being, at least notionally, separate. If good enough attunement, mirroring and containment are not available for the infant these fears prevail and remain in the Child ego state. They form an unconscious barrier to separation from the mother and against intimacy. Becoming too close provides opportunity to use destructive powers. If the infant interprets the emotional absence or engulfment of mother as being mother's desire to be rid of her, for engulfment is suffocating, the infant may decide that she needs to find a way of neither killing nor being killed.

Case study: Sal

Sal had the sense that she could destroy another person, starting with mother, then father, other authority figures and me. Sal kept her weight, which she magically believed would prevent her becoming the executioner for if she could bury her 'bad' self deep enough she could not use this destructive power.

Sal's mother was unprepared for her pregnancy and the child became an inconvenience to her. This was transmitted to Sal in her mother's touch and erratic caring and lack of effective mirroring. Sal sensed the danger that mother might want to be rid of her and therefore struggled with the fear of the danger of needing to kill or be killed. This gave rise to Sal's terror of separation that she carried through her adult life. After some years in therapy, Sal was able to contact these fears and to recognize that she had channelled them into a more simple dynamic that meant that, provided she was not as attractive as mother, that is, as long as she stayed fat, both she and mother could survive.

Distortions in self-image

The infant develops the capacity for imaging and, with this, the primitive understanding of the distinction between her own body and the body of others. She now develops the potential to initiate action and to know that this ability comes from within herself. She forms a self-image that represents both a body and a psyche.

Long-term obese patients struggle with both their physical and psychological self-image. Many describe themselves as being insubstantial and shapeless. Their weight gives the protection against disintegration and their body size gives them a physical image that becomes their identity: a fat person. Losing weight means they lose this protection and this self-image.

It is common for morbidly obese patients to avoid looking in the mirror at their bodies and some do not look at their faces either. They avoid facing their true image. For some this means distortion resulting in believing themselves to be fatter than they are and for others, though more unusually, thinner than they are.

I use work with a mirror that encourages the patient to meet and integrate her physical self. If she looks into her eyes she connects with her internal self. This work can feel very scary for the patient and therefore once the therapeutic relationship and trust are well established, timing, preparation and contracting in respect of safety and the patient's right and ability to stop when she needs to, are essential.

Case study: Rowena

Rowena experienced the death of her mother in infancy and the inability of her mother to care for her during her illness before her death. She was cared for by two other parent figures, both of whom were empathically unavailable, one who overstimulated and overfed, the other who understimulated and erratically fed. Rowena yearned for the mother that she had never known and could not know whilst her father maintained the stance of protecting her from hurt by not talking about her mother.

Rowena's use of her body as a defence was complex. Though she was clearly overweight, with hindsight, I had little recollection of her body shape or body boundaries. This is unusual as generally I will have a clear picture of the physicality of my patients. It was as though I was seeing the unestablished body boundary and an emergence with the environment that might epitomize the early infant experience before her body boundaries are defined by mother. This gave me further insight into how Rowena could have been overlooked at school and at work; how she could ensure she carried out the injunction of not belonging and how vulnerable she was without a firm outer container. She had a small husky voice and a fear of expressing the rage she held within her. It was as if, should she become rageful, she would burst the thin outer layer of her body surface boundary.

When Rowena risked knowing that her mother loved her, she needed to be held and surrounded with cushions that provided her with a womb-like container that would not give way, and which was secured by another member of the group who held her. It was interesting that she chose a member of the group to hold her. Was she the surrogate mother with whom Rowena had spent her early years? Did she see me at that moment as the mother who might not be strong enough to stay? Did she need me as the strong container of the whole experience of the group and her within it? She talked retrospectively of wanting me to be there in control of the process and the rest of the group but I also had a sense that, since she was on the brink of deciding that her mother did love her and had not yet internalized that truth she might have felt that she could 'destroy' me in the same way that she believed she was instrumental in her mother dying.

Recreating the sensations that promote awareness of internal states

Krueger (1989) suggests that if the boundary between the internal and external body self is not established the patient will be unable to distinguish internal states. In later life symptoms may emerge that will 'promote awareness' of these internal states. These would entail eating, distension, fullness, induced defecation through laxatives and urination with diuretics and self-induced vomiting.

Morbidly obese patients do not normally use elimination tactics as do bulimics or anorexics. However, it is clear that the body distension caused by overeating is reminiscent of the fullness that the infant feels after feeding and that defines an internal boundary. The patient will eat until overfull as the familiar experience of body distension becomes the marker for repleteness. These induced sensations attempt to define the inner as separate from the outer self. Self-induced elimination with the aid of diuretics and laxatives, and fingers down the throat are more likely to be a feature of lower range obesity.

Again, because of the incomplete sense of the boundary between the inner and outer body functioning, true sensations of hunger elude the obese and overeating patient such that pangs related to psychological hungers, agitation, stress and psychological disturbance are misinterpreted as, or transposed into hunger for food.

Krueger puts this second developmental stage as beginning at a few months and extending into the toddler phase. When the child becomes mobile she moves into a new stage of separateness and by developing verbal symbolism she adds another medium in which to practice assertiveness. This challenges the caregiver in a different way for now the child needs to be allowed to explore, to be close and, maybe, feel merged, at the same time as enjoying the freedom to be apart. She needs freedom to move within a psychologically and physically contained environment.

For mothers who enjoy or at least relate to the highly dependent infant, this can be a trying and difficult stage when empathy wears thin (or even thinner). It seemed that Hazel's (see the case study in Chapter 7) mother was less tolerant of this and all subsequent separation stages of Hazel's development. It seemed to me that in the primal stages of her life Hazel was fighting for space from mother who needed the infant to mirror and respond to her rather than being available to see her baby as separate and having emotional and psychological, as well as physical, needs. Hazel would not have developed a sense of her body boundary independent of that of mother. The body surface would have been indistinct. In this second stage when Hazel needed confirmation of her body limit and a safe base from which to wander and explore, there was confused containment. The limits were set more by aggression than love. In neither of these two stages was Hazel able to reach out and be met.

She developed a system whereby she used her body to protect her from mother's needs, trying different body sizes and always remaining fat. She used her body as protection from the world in which she had had to explore with confusion and in that sense it became the symbolism of the mother-protector. This became particularly apparent during adolescence, when her mother again resented her bid for independence and attacked Hazel's sexuality. Hazel gained weight rapidly and continued to do so, having spells of weight loss followed by significantly higher weight gain.

When I used mirror work as a therapeutic intervention, Hazel could not relate to certain body parts, most specifically her arms. She did not know how to reach out, either physically or verbally. She also disassociated from her pelvic area, stomach, hips and buttocks. Her contact and recognition hungers were starved. She feared becoming inappropriately sexual if she lost weight. Her indistinct boundaries made it impossible for her to see that she would have mastery over her body if she lost weight. Hazel was one of many patients who believed she would disappear completely if she lost weight. There was no cohesive sense of self.

It is worth noting that inability to relate to the arms is not unusual with obese patients. I interpret this as the patient having experienced rejection when reaching out as an infant and representative of their inability to self-soothe. In a sense, their arms have become redundant in the context of their use to gain strokes through physical contact. Patients often dissociate from the area of their body from their abdomen to their thighs. This discounts the focus of their sensations that tell them when they have had enough to eat, their sexual organs and is the part where they sense both the void and their 'bad' selves.

Krueger's third developmental stage

The third developmental stage described by Krueger (1989) entails the foundation of self-awareness based on the integration of the differentiated internal states and outer body surface as a cohesive whole and the growing experience of the self as constant regardless of external changes.

At this stage the perception of what is real is dependent on the experience of being this cohesive entity that is constant. Obese patients, psychologically, do not have the robustness this implies. Their need for robustness is channelled into a large body size. It gives them a sense of being big enough to 'cope', 'carry the burden', 'face critical others' and indeed, their Critical Parent selves.

For those overweight people who accept themselves as they are, this physical robustness works positively. As one person said to me 'I enjoy being big, it gives me presence and stature'. She did identify herself as a big woman and her psychological self paralleled her body image. She was outgoing, forceful and successful in her own business venture. At times she would show the extreme vulnerability and pain of her unmet self, but her potent body and psychological construct was always there for her to return to.

This is not the case for the obese patient who suffers and seeks help from psychotherapists and other practitioners. The robustness she tries to produce in her body is a fantasy because her body's internal and external boundaries are not defined clearly enough and cannot provide the container she needs. Psychologically, however she continues to attempt to use her body to contain her impaired sense of self and to buffer against the scary world. As we have seen, this is illusionary as being obese attracts negativity and prejudice. However, the patient experiences this defensive mode as the lesser of the evils.

Progression into a healthy level of self-awareness entails movement away from a reflex action to a stimulus, to a thinking and feeling assessment before action. If the patient's early experiences do not provide for a cohesive sense of self the ability to put this distance between impulse and action fails. This lack of ability to use the evaluating space is typical of the overeating patient. She is at times compelled to eat without consideration of the consequences, reverting to an encapsulation of self for the duration of the eating spasm. The patient stuffs food into her mouth as if there is scarcity. She hardly chews or tastes it.

At other times the lack of use of the evaluative space takes on a more subtle form with the patient psychologically diverting her (and indeed others') attention from her eating whilst internally she reacts to the impulse by eating second helpings, or larger amounts of food whilst discounting the significance of doing so. The methods are subtle, such as talking about something engaging, making jokes about eating, making excuses for eating, in fact any behaviour that ensures that she does not evaluate whether she needs more food. In ego state terms, her Child finds useful strategies to exclude her Critical Parent and her Adult ego states that might stop her from eating.

A significant shift for this patient is to be able to put distance between her impulse to eat and the action of eating. She needs to interpose her Adult ego state whilst reassuring her Child self that she can still have the food and may not have to wait longer than a few seconds for a decision. This pacifies the Child self who fears starvation or disintegration. At first the patient will undoubtedly decide to eat the food as planned. However, provided she had left some evaluative space, something different has happened and it can be built upon. Gradually she can decide that she will have the food in five minutes, ten minutes' time, later that day or even tomorrow. This develops the Adult energy she needs to consider her behaviour and make a decision.

Ogden's sensation-dominated existence in the autistic-contiguous position

I now turn to Thomas Ogden's description of the early sensation-dominated existence of the infant and have extracted key components that add to the understanding specifically of the patient's use of her body and the extremes of disassociation of which some patients are capable.

Ogden names the sensation-dominated experience of early infancy as the autistic-contiguous position (1989). In this position 'the most primitive form of meaning is generated on the basis of the organisation of sensory impressions, particularly at the skin surface' (p.4). He emphasizes that the infant does not at first have a sense of the actual shape of the object with which it comes into contact but describes them as 'felt shapes'. Thus the feel of the object is a subjective experience complete in itself without meaning as to what the object represents to the outside organized world. He maintains that these felt shapes include 'the soft parts of his own body and the body of the mother as well as soft bodily substances' (p.55). Like Krueger (1989), he associates such tactile sensations, even before they have descriptive meaning such as soothing, comforting, safe or connected, with the development of a cohesive self.

Ogden refers to Tustin (1980) when describing the infant's experience of autistic objects. These he says are the hard surfaces with which the infant will come into contact. 'An autistic object is a safety-generating sensory impression of edgedness that defines, delineates, and protects one's otherwise exposed and vulnerable surface' (p.56). Ogden maintains that in the autistic-contiguous mode there is no sense of the 'objectness' of the thing that is being felt but purely the sensation of it. Through contact with such objects the infant experiences his or her own body surface as a hard and protective armour. It is not therefore, only the mother's touch with the presence or absence of softness and specificity that Krueger (1989) describes that defines the infant's world from which she can develop her sense of self but her body contact with other surfaces, particularly hard surfaces that provide knowledge of the presence of an encompassing shell.

The obese patient can be aided to use these different body sensations for the purpose of re-contacting the body self. Given the dissociation with the body that the patient maintains, this re-contacting is essential if the patient is to achieve the cohesive sense of the body and psychological self that she needs in order to lose weight.

The therapist can aid the patient by using a three-part repetitive programme:

1. The patient is guided through awareness of body sensations in contact with objects such as her clothes against her skin, the feel of her buttocks on the chair, her back against soft cushions, in fact any contact she might be able to experience with contrasting soft and hard surfaces.

2. The patient is encouraged to awareness of internal sensations starting from the head and slowly moving through each body area down to the feet.

3. The patient is then guided to feel the external objects against her body alongside her internal sensation.

This technique is both soothing and liberating if carried out in a calm and gentle way within an atmosphere of safety. It encompasses the three stages of developing a coherent sense of self that Krueger (1989) describes.

Fear of loss of the body boundary

Ogden goes on to say that in this early stage 'a unique form of anxiety arises in this psychological realm: terror over the prospect that the boundedness of one's sensory surface might be dissolved, with the result of falling, leaking, dropping, into an endless and shapeless space' (p.68). If the quality of caregiving does not provide and enable adequate containment for the whole experience of the infant then the infant will find a defensive mode in which she can operate. One such mode is what Ogden sees as isolating the self within the body and from body sensation.

There are two implications of Ogden's observations in considering the obese patient. One is that the patient fears that if she loses weight she will lose herself. The other is that the autistic mode of coping can be seen in the patient's total withdrawal at times when eating becomes vital.

Some patients fear losing themselves completely if they lose weight. They talk about their fear of being in a void, being empty and disappearing. Losing their weight means losing their container, without which they feel unbound and unboundaried. For some it would mean not just exposing a raw and vulnerable self but a loss of self completely. This makes sense when acknowledging the unity of the development of the body and psychological selves.

Patients who enter into the procedure of imagining dialoguing with their weight on a chair, as described in Chapter 7, almost without exception experience fear. Most fear disappearing or disintegrating or floating away or being unable to exist in some other way. When Rowena realized she had made a statement that would logically challenge her long-held belief system, she became extremely scared. I believe that she was about to test out whether she would survive should she accept that she was lovable. She needed to be cushioned. It was an artificial womb that would contain her if her ill-defined body boundary should give way.

The ability to withdraw into the eating experience

Obese patients describe total detachment in a type of autistic mode as if nothing else exists around them. They will report being completely unaware of their surroundings when compulsively eating, the force or need being so great that there is no space for other awareness. It is, as one patient put it, as if 'all there is is my body and my survival in it'. I need to make it clear that I am not suggesting that obese patients are autistic. Indeed Ogden distinguishes the autistic mode as a style of being and the autistic-contiguous position as a mode of generating experience.

The implications of premature loss of weight

The obese patient experiences her body as a mass of containment for the uncompleted coherent sense of self. It is not a good barrier against her frightening environment but it suffices. It is all that she feels she has. A common pattern emerges with obese patients who attempt to lose weight before they are psychologically robust enough to do so, in that each time they lose they regain even more weight thereafter. It is as if they find the body boundary inadequate and are attempting to create a yet thicker layer of protection. They are trying to find the level of the solid outer layer that is not available to them and never will be, because it is tied up with the early development of the body self and the psychological integration that should have accompanied getting to know the world and the self within it through mirroring and attuned response. This clearly has implications for the therapeutic relationship and the types of intervention chosen to work at this early level of experience.

Eating as a defensive and palliative behaviour

Some patients self-soothe with food but can never get the satisfaction from it that they seek. Patients either attempt to recreate early feeding that was a positive experience, like those whose mothers related to them when dependent but not when they started to explore the world. Or they try to create a soothing experience that was either non-existent or inconsistent in infancy. To experience the idealized sensation becomes a compulsion. The frustration that arises from the unsatisfying process further compels the patient to eat.

Case study: Pat

Pat was one such patient who experienced warm and safe contentment when presenting her clinical infant in therapy. She would move her mouth as if suckling and would indicate comfort and soothing by her physical, non-verbal communication. However, when she aged a little, she became fearful. She saw the 'big people' as being unavailable to her and she felt lost and alone.

Pat was aware that she wanted the food she ate to re-connect with this early sense of safety. She found that if she ate certain foods that were, interestingly, those with a soft texture and ate when sitting down away from the table, she would feel something of the warmth and safety she sought. However, as we saw in the chapter on the Parent ego state, when Pat had a plate of food in front of her at the table, she saw the need to eat it as her father's control over her. The contrast in these two eating experiences was stark. Pat could not sit in a comfy chair away from the table to eat normal meals and so she always felt compelled to eat everything on her plate, losing any sense of choice or self-mastery. She was able to relate this to the sexual abuse she experienced at the hands of her father as it was he who 'spoke' from the food. She described dissociating from the activity of eating in the same way she needed to withdraw herself psychologically from the experience of the abuse. She excluded thinking, hence eating all the food on her plate, and at times the rest in the serving dishes, became an automatic behaviour.

Case study: the double-edged sword of feeding

One patient who always overate at times of stress or loss of self-worth and who said she hated food and what it did to her agreed to psychotherapeutic body work. In the process she was able to express a reasonable but still tentative level of anger. She continued to make noises that were wordless and then indicated she needed to be held. She became more and more energetic until finally discharging rageful tears she pleaded: 'Just hold me, don't feed me, just hold me, don't feed me!'

In the absence of her mother, she had been overfed to the point of convulsions by her grandmother who interpreted every whimper as a need for food. Grandmother did not seem to see the expanding body of the infant as cause for alarm. My patient realized that she had attempted to self-soothe with food because it was a time in infancy when she was held with what seemed like love and warmth. However, she constantly had the sensation of being overfull and bloated, which she realized was reminiscent of her feeding experience with grandmother. Her anger was channelled against her mother who was sick during the first six weeks of her life, not against the grandmother who overfed her. Three times in her life she controlled her weight through self-induced vomiting. She associated the relief she felt in vomiting to the temporary physical relief she gained from vomiting in infancy. She described how she felt in 'precise' (her word) control at these times. However, whenever she discussed her infant experience (which she was able to check out with her mother) she contacted fear of being fed again even after vomiting, as if grandmother 'topped her up' when she brought back some of the excessive food.

This body work was a major turning point in her understanding of her condition and she did change her eating patterns and maintained her desired weight most of the time. When she didn't she was able to tolerate and understand lapses. An important decision she made was never to eat at someone else's demand or request. She realized that when being invited out for meals she would feel extremely anxious about being 'forced' to eat. The option of self-induced vomiting had been a way she could calm herself enough to face social eating.

Treatment considerations with regard to the body self

The primary tool the therapist can offer is the therapeutic relationship. In this relationship the therapist becomes attuned and uses mirroring and empathic interventions. The deficit that has occurred for these patients, occurred in relationship and will be resolved in relationship. For long-term obese and morbidly obese patients attention to the developmentally needed relationship (Clarkson 1992) and work with the transferential phenomena will be central to the treatment direction. Clarkson describes the developmentally needed relationship as 'providing the therapeutic relationship most needed by the individual patients in terms of their developmental stages' (p.299). I believe that the quality and analysis of the practitioner–patient relationship is always the most important consideration for the success of any treatment. I invite the reader to find resources for understanding the complexity of such relationships.

Attention to the patient's eating behaviour, use of food and its meaning have been described in previous chapters. I focus here on the body self of the patient. The patient needs to understand that she is using her body as a defence and then to accept and integrate her body so that it no longer represents the enemy in her battle. In order to do this she needs to reconnect with her body self. This is a two-step process. Firstly she needs to reconnect with her body and then she can reconnect with internal sensations. This brings about the unity of body self and psychological self as well as enabling the patient to read her body sensations accurately and know when she is hungry for food and when she has had enough to eat without overeating. Any interventions that bring the patient's awareness into her body self will be significant. Checking body sensations with the patient, mirroring or enquiring about her physical movements and using the therapist's own physiological sensation to inform and model the process will be effective choices of intervention.

The therapist can enable the patient's body 'to speak' and sensation can be interpreted into images that the patient can describe in terms of shape, size, colour and texture such that the image-object can be used as a focus for understanding. This process encourages the use of the creative part of the Child ego state and eliminates or reduces the power of the Critical Parent.

Referring the patient for body-touch therapies such as head massage, reflexology, body massage or other similar relaxing treatments will aid the patient's reconnection with her body self. The patient needs to be ready to attend for such treatments and to remain in psychotherapy whilst receiving them.

Free expressive movement workshops by experienced practitioners can be very releasing. Jung (1912) explored the psyche and physical as being connected through a mutuality of action and sensation. More recently it has been recognized that actual body movement, from birth onwards is instrumental in giving messages to the infant about the world around her and in relation to her caregivers. This sensorimotor activity determines a quality of connectedness and differentiation that not only defines the relationship between self and other but also the relationship with one's own body and the sense of self that that gives rise to.

Body movement in adulthood, freely entered into, can be a psychologically charged and releasing experience. Obese patients tend to limit the movement of their whole or parts of their body. This manifests itself in restrictions from being unable to join in on and enjoy physical exercise or dance to literally feeling unable to reach out with their arms.

Attention to the body needs caution, since the patient is usually ashamed of her size. Touch and holding are difficult for the patient to experience. Such interventions need to be within a firm contract if the therapist sees a therapeutic value in using such methods.

There is no doubt that the patient arrives in the therapy room with her psychological self and her body self as one. The skilled therapist will attend to both.

Glossary of Clinical and Transactional Analysis Terms

Adapted Child (AC)

The use of the Child ego state to conform and adapt to demands of others. Conforming may be a necessary and appropriate behaviour in order to meet legal and practical needs of our existence. When a grown-up is adapting as if she is still responding in ways she used in childhood, her behaviour is neither autonomous nor age-appropriate. Familiarity of behaviour, thoughts, feelings and beliefs, is indiscrimanately associated with safety and 'how things are done'.

Adult ego state (A)

Behaviours, thoughts and feelings that are direct responses to the here and now.

Archaic

That which belongs to the past.

Attunement

'The sense of being fully aware of the other person's sensations or feelings and the communication of that awareness to the other person' (Erskine 1998).

Autonomy

Autonomy The capacity for awareness, spontaneity and intimacy and to behave in a script-free manner.

Bilateral agreement

An agreement that involves two people with equal responsibility for the outcome and process of achieving it.

Bipolar traits

Traits that indicate that the patient is vacillating between opposing polarities of thoughts, feelings and behaviours.

Cathect
To take uup and experience the energy of a part of self, for example an ego state.

Child ego state (C)
Behaviours, thoughts and feelings replayed from childhood.

Con
An invitation into a game. That which starts the game off or lures someone into playing a game.

Congruence
The agreement or unison of all ego states such that there is no feeling of opposing energies in the internal dialogue. At the social level: authenticity in communication.

Contamination of the Adult ego state
Parts of the belief systems of the Parent or Child ego states that are mistaken for Adult content or truths. Such contaminations effectively reduce the extent of Adult energy available given Dusay's constancy hypothesis (1980), that is, when one ego state increases in intensity, additional energy is diverted to that ego state and must be reduced in another or other ego states if the total amount of energy available remains constant.

Counter-injunctions
'Messages' acquired in later childhood that specify behaviours that the developing child believed would gain the approval (and perhaps love) of parents (Tilney 1998). These form a psychological defence against injunctions.

Counter-transference
The therapist's reaction to the transference from the patient, often experienced organically and exhibited behaviourally.

Critical or Controlling Parent (CP)
The use of the Parent ego state to control, direct or criticize others or self. Used positively to promote well-being and negatively to control, overpower and discount others.

Decisions
Conclusions made in childhood and ensuing years as to how it is best to adapt to the world and its demands. They involve decisions about self, others and the quality of life and are only as sophisticated and realistic as the child has capacity for. Hence many decisions are irrational and even absurd but have somehow been adequate and seemingly purposeful in the child's bid to survive. In later life decisions will become more circumspect and appropriate.

Deconfusion
The process of freeing the Child ego state from unwarranted fearful fantasies and restraints and the identification of unmet needs.

Decontamination
Freeing the Adult ego state from contamination by the Parent and Child ego states. This results in higher energy levels in the Adult to think, assess and make decisions from here and now reality.

Defended
When a patient is using her defence mechanism or defensive armouring (see 'defence mechanism', 'defensive armouring').

Defensive armouring
The use of the body as a protection against fantasized attack, annihilation or psychological overburdening.

Defence mechanism
A psychological process that the patient uses to defend against internal stress, fear and pain and which will give rise to both psychological and physical defensive structures. The physical defence lies within the adverse use of the body self in an attempt to armour the self against perceived attack, intrusion or annihilation.

Deficit
Something missing in the spheres of caring and relationship that is needed for healthy, integrated development.

Discounting
The process of unconsciously ignoring information that would aid resolution of a problem.

Dissociate, dissociation
The ability to separate unconsciously functions of the self, that is, thoughts, feelings and behaviours, for self-protection.

Dissociation of the body self
Unawarely disconnecting from body sensations and the existence and significance of body size and shape.

Domains of relatedness
The differing experiences of the developing sense of self in relationship (see Stern 1985).

Ego state
An ego state is a consistent pattern of feelings and experience related directly to a corresponding pattern of behaviours.

Empathy
'The power of imaginatively entering another's experience by using verbal and non-verbal information and intuition' (Tilney 1998). The therapist reflects this experience back to the patient in order to check her understanding of the patient and to create a safe place as the patient believes she is understood.

Empowerment
The process of enabling the patient to regain mastery through decontamination and deconfusion. Giving power back to the patient.

Engulfment
The psychological need to possess and control another that is felt by the object of the engulfment to be stifling and restrictive and is accompanied by a sense of powerlessness and fear.

Environment
The physical, relational and psychological world into which the infant is born and develops.

Fairy tale script
The fairy story that the patient most relates to, which when analysed, reveals the patient's core beliefs about self, others and the way the world works.

Frame of reference
An overall conceptualization of the patient's world, which is used to define self, other and the world and as a formula for choosing strategies for communication, action and understanding.

Free Child (FC)
The use of the child ego state in expressing her feelings or wants without censoring and without reference to the rules or demands of family or society. Used positively for creativity, intuition, expression of emotion and appropriate physical contact. Used negatively to flout the rules, which may result in harming self or other.

Functional model of ego states
Ego states in action. These terms are used to show *how* the patient uses these parts of the self. They indicate how the patient functions and communicates from her ego

states. Functional ego states are termed: Controlling Parent (CP), Nurturing Parent (NP), Free Child (FC), Adapted Child (AC), Rebellious Child (RC) and Adult (A).

Impasse
The experience of being in a stuck place. It is often used to describe the point at which the internal dialogue between the ego states reaches a stuck point when the conflict is recognized and heightened but resolution seems unavailable.

Injunctions
Psychological self-regulating strategies, formed by the child in response to verbal and non-verbal messages from the Child ego state of the actual parents and parent figures. Injunctions prevent autonomy. The injunctions are: Don't Be You, Don't Be Important, Don't Feel or Show Feelings, Don't Be Sexual, Don't Make It, Don't Belong, Don't Grow Up, Don't Be a Child, Don't Be Close, Don't Exist, Don't Be Well/Sane, Don't Think, Don't Have Needs, Don't Have Fun. A patient may be living within the constraints of these embargos in different degrees of intensity.

Integrated Adult
A stage of having incorporated positive aspects of Child and Parent ego states commensurate with here and now reality and allowing the choice of options for which ego state to appropriately cathect (bring into use) in a given situation.

Internal dialogue
The 'voices' in the head that discuss, argue and make conclusions usually in response to script protocol and demands. The voices can be recognized in terms of ego states and may be played out in multiple-chair-work.

Internalization
The process of making representations in the mind of other people, places and events arising from the experience of each.

Inter-subjectivity
The experience of self in relationship with another whereby there is a mutual awareness of the subjective self of the other together with awareness of that recognition.

Intervention (therapeutic)
Any verbal or non-verbal communication the therapist might decide upon that is valuable to the psychotherapeutic process and agreed goal.

Intrapsychic
Within the mind as distinguished from that which is interpersonal, that is, that which involves transactions with other people.

Introjected Parent

The representation of a parent or parent figure that is internalized and used by the patient to regulate behaviour. Introjection is a process performed outside of awareness.

Mastery

The presence of the power and choice needed to act autonomously.

Mirroring

Indicating, through behavioural choices, an understanding and awareness of another. Ideally, in infancy, the primary caregiver's behaviour towards and responses to the infant, will indicate sufficient understanding of the infant's needs. Mirroring affirms the infant's acceptability and OK-ness. This type of affirmation is a valuable intervention in therapy.

Nurturing Parent (NP)

The use of the Parent ego state to nurture, care or help others as the outwardly behavioural manifestation. Nurturing may also be directed towards the self. Used positively out of genuine thoughtfulness and regard for another and negatively to subvert, discount, overpower and smother.

Overadaptation

A non-problem-solving, passive behaviour whereby the patient complies with what she believes to be the wishes of others without checking and without reference to her own wishes and needs.

Parent ego state (P)

A set of behaviours, thoughts and feelings that have been copied from parents or parent figures.

Pastiming

A form of time structuring that involves spending time talking on topics that are inconsequential and need to action. Tends to be a social activity where no action is required.

Permissions

Positive and freeing messages issued by the parent in contrast to the negative messages of the injunctions.

Presenting issues

Issues that the patient presents in therapy that may or may not represent the actual areas of concern for the patient.

Re-decision

The process of changing a former script decision that usually entails release from negative script influences. A new age- and time-appropriate decision that replaces early self-limiting decisions that were made without the full capacity for rationality and assessment.

Scarcity

A sense of there not being enough, often related to a sense of an inadequate supply of love and manifested in behaviour that suggests neediness in substitute areas. For example, food and eating.

Script

A patient's script is a life plan that she builds from infancy in relation to her experiences with her primary carer, significant others and the quality of the world about her. Because the development of the script is dependent on a system of communication between self and other, the parent figures will reinforce the script that the child is developing. The ensuing events in life will justify the child's beliefs and the patient will have a conscious or subconscious idea of how the plan culminates. The script involves a set of beliefs peculiar to the individual about self, others and the world and a corresponding set of behaviours that will play out the consequences of those beliefs. It may also be understood in terms of a 'transferential replay of unresolved issues, the drama being cast from people currently available who transferentially represent people from the past' (Tilney 1998, p.109).

Self-accounting

When a patient uses her own autonomy to guide her thoughts, feelings and behaviours.

Socialization

The process of preparing and influencing another, to fit in with the norms, rules and expectations of the culture, family and parents.

Somatization

Converting psychological dis-ease into physical dis-ease or disease. Use of the body to express what is perceived to be inexpressible and unresolvable. This involves the Child within the Child ego state, C1 or 'somatic Child'.

Stroke

A unit of recognition that can be anything from a nod or smile to true relational intimacy.

Structural model of ego states
This shows *what* is in each ego state and is used to understand the content that drives the patient to interact with others in certain ways. I have specifically referred to the Parent in the Child (P1), Adult in the Child (A1) and Child in the Child (C1), which I have also labelled as somatic Child.

Supply issues
The patient's issues that relate to an actual, or psychological sense of, unavailability of 'enough'. At the social level the patient may create shortage or abundance in response to an unconsciously felt deficit of strokes and/or love. Overeating represents one such behavioural manifestation of psychologically perceived deficit.

Survival issues
Problems or concerns related to the patient's struggle, or right, to survive.

Symbiotic relationship
A relationship that involves two people sharing three ego states such that neither ever uses all ego states when in relationship with the other. The most common dynamic is dominant Parent to submissive Child. When both parties are happy with this unconscious process there will be no discomfort. However, such a relationship is usually transacted out of Adult awareness and thereby without cognitive choice. It denies autonomy.

Touch-substitutes
Strokes that acknowledge one's existence and which replace the intensity of physical contact allowed in infancy.

Transference
Unconsciously transferring attitudes, beliefs and feelings on to another person that have been the attributes of a significant other in the past or another in the present. Such transference may entail positive or negative attributes. The process occurs when there is some commonality of experience, though this may entail the minutest similarity to the person, place or experience transferred. There is then an expectation that the recipient of the transference will behave in the same manner as the person in the past, or the outcome of the situation will be the same as in the historical experience. The patient may also transfer aspects of her own script beliefs and sense of self onto another.

References

Berne, E. (1961) *Transactional Analysis in Psychotherapy*. New York: Grove Press.

Berne, E. (1963) *Structure and Dynamics of Organisations*. New York: Grove Press.

Berne, E. (1964) *Games People Play*. Harmondsworth: Penguin Books.

Berne, E. (1973) *Sex in Human Loving*. Harmondsworth: Penguin Books.

Berne, E. (1975) *What Do You Say After You Say Hello?* London: Corgi Publishers.

Berne, E. (1994) *Principles of Group Treatment*. Menlo Park, CA: Shea Books.

Bowlby, J. (1969) *Attachment and Loss: Vol. 1. Attachment*. New York: Basic Books.

Clarkson, P. (1992) *Transactional Analysis Psychotherapy*. London and New York: Routledge.

Cozolino, L. (2002) *The Neuroscience of Psychotherapy*. London, New York: W.W. Norton & Company.

Drego, P. (1983) 'The Cultural Parent'. *Transactional Analysis Journal 13*, 4, October, 224–28.

Durkheim, E. (1984) *The Division of Labour In Society*. New York: Free Press.

Durkheim, E. (2002) *Suicide*. Oxford: Taylor & Francis Group.

Dusay, J. (1980) *Egograms: How I see you and you see me*. New York: Bantam Books.

Erskine, R. (1998) 'Attunement and Involvement: Therapeutic Responses to Relational Needs'. *International Journal of Psychotherapy 3*, 235–44.

Goulding, M. and Goulding, R. (1979) *Changing Lives Through Redecision Therapy*. New York: Grove Press.

Hargaden, H. and Sills, C. (2002) *Transactional Analysis – A Relational Perspective*. Hove, UK: Brunner-Routledge.

Heimler, E. (1975) *Survival in Society*. London: Weidenfeld and Nicolson.

Jade, D. (1999) 'The Genetics of Obesity'. National Centre for Eating Disorders Discussion Paper.

Jung, C.G. (1912) 'The Transformation of Libido'. *Collected Works 5*. New Jersey: Princeton University Press.

Karpman, S. (1968) 'Fairy Tales and Script Drama Analysis'. *Transactional Analysis Bulletin VII*, 26, 39–43.

Krueger, D. (1989) *Body Self and Psychological Self*. New York: Brunner/Mazel Inc.

Levenson, R.W. (1999) 'The Intrapersonal Function of Emotions'. *Cognition and Emotion 13*, 481–504.

Levin, P. (1988) *Cycles of Power.* Deerfield Beach, FL: Health Communications Inc.

Lister, M., Rosen, K and Wright, A. (1985) 'An Anti-diet Approach to Weight Loss in a Group Setting'. *Transactional Analysis Journal 15,* 69–72.

McDougall, J. (1989) *Theatres of the Body.* London: Free Association Books.

Maslow, A. H. (1987) *Motivation and Personality.* New York: Longman.

Morris, S. (2004) 'The Impact of Obesity on Employment in England'. *Tanaka Business School Discussion Papers: TBS/DP04/4.*

Ogden, T. H. (1989) *The Primitive Edge of Experience.* London, New York: Karnac.

PersonnelToday.com (2005) 'The Growing Problem of Fattism at Work.' 25 October 2005, www.personneltoday.com/Articles/2005/10/25/32245/The+growing+problem+of+fattism+at+work.htm

Slater, N. (2003) *Toast. The Story of a Boy's Hunger.* London: Fourth Estate (Harper Collins).

Spitz, R. (1945) 'Hospitalism, Genesis of Psychiatric Conditions in Early Childhood'. *Psychoanalytic Study of the Child 1,* 53–74.

Staunton, Tree (2002) *Body Psychotherapy.* Hove, UK: Brunner-Routledge.

Stern, D. (1985) *The Interpersonal World of the Infant.* New York: Basic Books.

Tilney, T. (1998) *Dictionary of Transactional Analysis.* London: Whurr Publishers Ltd.

Tustin, F. (1980) 'Autistic Objects'. *International Review of Psychoanalysis 7,* 27–40.

Woollams, S and Brown, M. (1978) *Transactional Analysis.* Dexter, MI: Huron Valley Institute Press.

Yalom, I. (1989) *Love's Executioner.* London: Penguin Books.

Recommended Reading

Balsa, A.I. and McGuire, T. (2003) 'Prejudice, Clinical Uncertainty and Stereotyping as Sources of Health Disparities'. *Journal of Health Economics 22*, 89–116.

Blackstone, P. (1993) 'The Dynamic Child'. *Transactional Analysis Journal 23*, 4, 216–34.

Bovey, S. (2000) *Sizeable Reflections – Big Women Living Full Lives.* London: The Women's Press Ltd.

Bovey, S. (2002) *What Have You Got to Lose?* London: The Women's Press Ltd.

Bowlby, J. (1990) *Child Care and the Growth of Love.* Harmondsworth: Penguin Books (original work published 1953).

Bradshaw, J. (1993) *Creating Love.* London: Judy Piatkus Ltd.

Bray, G. (2004) *An Atlas of Obesity and Weight Control.* New York: Taylor & Francis.

Brierre, J. N. (1992) *Child Abuse Trauma.* California: Sage Publications Inc., London: Sage Ltd.

Brownell, K. D. (1998) *Eating Disorders and Obesity.* New York: Guilford Press.

Charlton, B. (1985) *Big is Invisible.* London: Robin Clark.

Claude-Pierre, P. (1998) *The Secret Language of Eating Disorders.* Sydney: Bantam.

Cossrow, N.H., Jeffery, R.W. and McGuire, M.T. (2001) 'Understanding Weight Stigmatization: A Focus Group Study'. *Journal of Nutrition Education 33*, 208–14.

Crisp, A. H. (1994) 'Social and Psychopathological Aspects of Obesity'. *St George's Mental Health Library, Conference Series 62–71.*

Damasio, A. (2000) *The Feeling of What Happens: Body Emotion and the Making of Consciousness.* London: Heinemann.

Dryden, W. (1997) *Overcoming Shame.* London: Sheldon Press.

Erskine, R. (1993) 'Inquiry, Attunement and Involvement in the Psychotherapy of Dissociation'. *Transactional Analysis Journal 23*, 4, 184–90.

Everett, M. (1990) 'Let an Overweight Person Call on Your Best Customers? Fat chance'. *Sales and Marketing Management 142*, 66–70.

Gord, M. and Wright. J. (2005) *The Obesity Epidemic.* London: Routledge.

Griffin, S. (1985) 'Eating Issues and Fat Issues'. *Transactional Analysis Journal 15*, 1, 30–6.

Goulding, M. and Goulding, R. (1976) 'Injunctions, Decisions and Re-decisions'. *Transactional Analysis Journal 6*, 1, 41–8.

Holmes, J. (1996) *Attachment, Intimacy and Autonomy.* New Jersey: Jason Aronson Inc.

Illsley-Clarke, J. (1978) *Self Esteem: A Family Affair.* London: Harper Collins.

Jade, D. (1999) 'The Causes of Obesity'. *National Centre for Eating Disorders Discussion Paper.*

James, M. (1998) *Perspectives in Transactional Analysis.* San Francisco: TA Press.

James, M. and Jongewood, D. (1971) *Born to Win.* Reading, MA: Addison-Wesley.

Janov, A. (1995) *The Primal Scream.* London: Abacus.

Jung, C. (1928) *On Psychic Energy – Collected Works.* New Jersey: Princeton University Press.

Kalshed, D. (1996) *The Inner World of Trauma.* Hove, UK: Brunner-Routledge.

Kaufman, G. (1993) *The Psychology of Shame.* London: Routledge (original work published 1989).

Klein, J. (1997) *Our Need for Others and its Root in Infancy.* London. Routledge.

Leach, K. (1998) 'Treatment Considerations for Female Overeating and Obesity'. *Transactional Analysis Journal 28*, 3, 216–33.

Leach, K. (2001) 'Imagery and Mirror Work as Creative Techniques when Working with Overeating and Obesity'. *Institute of Transactional Analysis Conference Papers*, 104–11.

Leach, K. (2002) 'Working with Overeating and Obesity: The Big Picture. Who Makes Up the Client Group?' *Institute of Transactional Analysis Conference Papers*, 60–5.

Leach, K. (2004) 'Overeating and Obesity – where are the Impasses?' *Institute of Transactional Analysis Conference Papers*, 186–200.

Levy, L. (2000) *Understanding Obesity: The Five Medical Causes.* Toronto: Key Porter Books Ltd.

Lewis, T., Amini, F. and Lannon, R. (2001) *A General Theory of Love.* New York: Vintage Books.

Louden, J. (1992) *The Woman's Comfort Book.* San Francisco: Harper Collins.

Maisner, P. with Turner, R. (1993) *Consuming Passions.* Wellingborough: Thorsons (Harper Collins).

Masterson, J. (1983) *Countertransference and Therapeutic Techniques.* New York: Brunner-Mazel.

National Obesity Forum (2002) *All Party Parliamentary Group on Obesity.* London: National Obesity Forum.

Racker, H. (1968) *Transference and Countertransference.* Madison, CT: International Universities Press.

Rossi, E. L. (1993) *The Psychology of Mind-Body Healing.* New York: Norton.

Roth, G. (1982) *Feeding the Hungry Heart: The Experiences of Compulsive Eating.* London: Grafton Books.

Rothschild, B. (2000) *The Body Remembers: The Psychophysiology of Trauma and Trauma Treatment.* London: Norton.

Sills, C. and Hargaden, H. (eds) (2003) *Ego States – Key Concepts in TA*. London: Worth Publishing Ltd.

Simonds, S. L. (1994) *Bridging the Silence*. New York: Norton & Co. Ltd.

Singer, Jerome L. (ed.) (1990) *Repression and Dissociation*. Chicago and London: University of Chicago Press.

Steiner C. M. (1982) *Scripts People Live*. Sydney: Bantam Books.

Stewart, I. and Joines, V. (1987) *TA Today. A New Introduction to Transactional Analysis*. Nottingham and Chapel Hill: Life Space Publishing.

Stoltz, S. G. (1985) 'Beware of Boundary Issues'. *Transactional Analysis Journal 15*, 1, 37–9.

Totton, N. (1998) *The Water in the Glass: Body and Mind in Psychoanalysis*. London: Norton.

Tustin, F. (1986) *The Protective Shell in Children and Adults*. London: Karnac.

Tustin, F. (1986) *Autistic Barriers in Neurotic Patients*. London: Karnac.

Subject Index

Author Index